MOTHER TONGUE

By the same author

THE LOST CONTINENT
THE PENGUIN DICTIONARY OF
TROUBLESOME WORDS

MOTHER TONGUE

THE ENGLISH LANGUAGE

BILL BRYSON

HAMISH HAMILTON · LONDON

HAMISH HAMILTON LTD

Published by the Penguin Group
27 Wrights Lane, London W8 5TZ, England
Viking Penguin Inc., 375 Hudson Street, New York, New York 10014, USA
Penguin Books Australia Ltd, Ringwood, Victoria, Australia
Penguin Books Canada Ltd, 2801 John Street, Markham, Ontario, Canada L3R 1B4
Penguin Books (NZ) Ltd, 182–190 Wairau Road, Auckland 10, New Zealand

Penguin Books Ltd, Registered Offices: Harmondsworth, Middlesex, England

First published in the United States of America by William Morrow 1990
First published in Great Britain by Hamish Hamilton Ltd 1990
1 3 5 7 9 10 8 6 4 2

Copyright © Bill Bryson, 1990

The moral right of the author has been asserted

Filmset in Monophoto Baskerville
Printed in England by Clays Ltd, St Ives plc

A CIP catalogue record for this book is available from the British Library
ISBN 0-241-13048-4

To Cynthia

CONTENTS

ACKNOWLEDGEMENTS

Among the many people to whom I am indebted for help in the preparation of this book, I must single out Jonathan Fenby of the *Guardian*, Tony Sikkema of the *Sunday Times* and Dr Takasuke Matsuo of Osaka for generously assisting with questions regarding, respectively, the French, Dutch, and Japanese languages; Miles Kington of the *Independent* for kindly allowing me to reproduce two holorimes in the chapter on wordplay; my mother, Mary Bryson, for providing a constant stream of cuttings and other material; the staff of the Camden Public Library in London and the Drake University Library in Des Moines for guiding me to sources that I would not otherwise have found; and above all my wife, Cynthia, for her endless help and support.

Certain passages in this book originally appeared in somewhat altered form in *TWA Ambassador* magazine and in the Canadian textbook *Language in Action*, and I wish to thank both those organizations for permission to reproduce that work here. In this regard I must also thank Laurence Urdang for helping me (alas, so far without success) try to track down the person who has passed off one of these articles as her own in at least three publications in Europe and America, including Mr Urdang's own esteemed quarterly, *Verbatim*.

To all these people I send thanks – except, of course, the elusive plagiarist, to whom I address one heartfelt raspberry.

THE WORLD'S LANGUAGE

More than 300 million people in the world speak English and the rest, it sometimes seems, try to. It would be charitable to say that the results are sometimes mixed.

Consider this hearty announcement in a Yugoslavian hotel: 'The flattening of underwear with pleasure is the job of the chambermaid. Turn to her straightaway.' Or this warning to motorists in Tokyo: 'When a passenger of the foot heave in sight, tootle the horn. Trumpet at him melodiously at first, but if he still obstacles your passage, then tootle him with vigour.' Or these instructions gracing a packet of fast food from Italy: 'Besmear a backing pan, previously buttered with a good tomato sauce, and, after, dispose the cannelloni, lightly distanced between them in a only couch.'

Clearly the writer of *that* message was not about to let a little ignorance of English stand in the way of a good meal. In fact, it would appear that one of the beauties of the English language is that with even the most tenuous grasp you can speak volumes if you show enough enthusiasm – a willingness to tootle with vigour, as it were.

To be fair, English is full of booby traps for the unwary foreigner. Any language where the unassuming word *fly* signifies an annoying insect, a means of travel, and a critical part of a gentleman's apparel is clearly asking to be mangled. Imagine being a foreigner and having to learn that in English one tells *a* lie but *the* truth, that an American who says 'I could care less' means the same thing as someone who says 'I couldn't care less', that a sign in a shop saying ALL ITEMS NOT ON SALE doesn't mean literally what it says (that every item is *not* on sale) but rather that only some of the items are on sale, that when a person says to you, 'How do you do?' he will be taken aback if you reply, with impeccable logic, 'How do I do what?'

The complexities of the English language are such that even native speakers cannot always communicate effectively, as almost every Briton learns on his first day in America. Indeed, Robert Burchfield, editor of the *Oxford English Dictionary*, created a stir in linguistic circles on both sides of the Atlantic when he announced his belief that American English and English English are drifting apart so remorselessly that one day the two nations may not be able to understand each other at all.

That may be. But if the Briton and American of the future baffle each other, it seems altogether likely that they won't confuse many others – not, at least, if the rest of the world continues expropriating words and phrases at its present rate. Already Germans talk about *ein Image Problem* and *das Cash-Flow*, Italians program their computers with *il software*, French motorists going away for a *weekend break* pause for *les refuelling stops*, Poles watch *telewizja*, Spaniards have a *flirt*, Austrians eat *Big Mäcs*, and the Japanese go on a *pikunikku*. For better or worse, English has become the most global of languages, the lingua franca of business, science, education, politics, and pop music. For the airlines of 157 nations (out of 168 in the world), it is the agreed international language of discourse. In India, there are more than 3,000 newspapers in English. The six member nations of the European Free Trade Association conduct all their business in English, even though not one of them is an English-speaking country. When companies from four European countries – France, Italy, Germany, and Switzerland – formed a joint truck-making venture called Iveco in 1977, they chose English as their working language because, as one of the founders wryly observed, 'It puts us all at an equal disadvantage.' For the same reasons, when the Swiss company Brown Boveri and the Swedish company ASEA merged in 1988, they decided to make the official company language English, and when Volkswagen set up a factory in Shanghai it found that there were too few Germans who spoke Chinese and too few Chinese who spoke German, so now Volkswagen's German engineers and Chinese managers communicate in a language that is alien to both of them, English. Belgium has two languages, French and Flemish, yet on a recent visit to the country's main airport in Brussels, I counted more than fifty posters and billboards and not one of them was in French or Flemish. They were all in English.

For non-English speakers everywhere, English has become the common tongue. Even in France, the most determinedly non-English-speaking nation in the world, the war against English encroachment has largely been lost. In early 1989, the Pasteur Institute announced that henceforth it would publish its famed international medical review only in English because too few people were reading it in French.

English is, in short, one of the world's great growth industries. 'English is just as much big business as the export of manufactured goods,' Professor Sir Randolph Quirk has written. 'There are problems with what you might call "after-sales service"; and "delivery" can be awkward; but at any rate the production lines are trouble free.'[1] Indeed, such is the demand to learn the language that there are now more students of English in China than there are people in the United States.

It is often said that what most immediately sets English apart from other languages is the richness of its vocabulary. *Webster's Third New International Dictionary* lists 450,000 words, and the revised *Oxford English Dictionary* has 615,000, but that is only part of the total. Technical and scientific terms would add millions more. Altogether, about 200,000 English words are in common use, more than in German (184,000) and far more than in French (a mere 100,000). The richness of the English vocabulary, and the wealth of available synonyms, means that English speakers can often draw shades of distinction unavailable to non-English speakers. The French, for instance, cannot distinguish between house and home, between mind and brain, between man and gentleman, between 'I wrote' and 'I have written'. The Spanish cannot differentiate a chairman from a president, and the Italians have no equivalent of wishful thinking. In Russia there are no native words for efficiency, challenge, engagement ring, have fun, or take care.[2] English, as Charlton Laird has noted, is the only language that has, or needs, books of synonyms like *Roget's Thesaurus*. 'Most speakers of other languages are not aware that such books exist.'[3]

On the other hand, other languages have facilities we lack. Both French and German can distinguish between knowledge that results from recognition (respectively *connaître* and *kennen*) and knowledge that results from understanding (*savoir* and *wissen*). Portuguese has words that differentiate between an interior angle and an exterior one. All the Romance languages can distinguish between something that leaks into and something that leaks out of. The Italians even have a word for the mark left on a table by a moist glass (*culacino*) while the Gaelic speakers of Scotland, not to be outdone, have a word for the itchiness that overcomes the upper lip just before taking a sip of whisky. (Wouldn't they just?) It's *sgriob*. And we have nothing in English to match the Danish *hygge* (meaning 'instantly satisfying and cosy'), the French *sang-froid*, the Russian *glasnost*, or the Spanish *macho*, so we must borrow the term from them or do without the sentiment.

At the same time, some languages have words that we may be pleased to do without. The existence in German of a word like *Schadenfreude* (taking delight in the misfortune of others) perhaps tell us as much about Teutonic sensitivity as it does about their neologistic versatility. Much the same could be said about the curious and monumentally unpronounceable Highland Scottish word *giomlaireachd*, which means 'the habit of dropping in at mealtimes'. That surely conveys a world of information about the hazards of Highland life – not to mention the hazards of Highland orthography.

Of course, every language has areas in which it needs, for practical purposes, to be more expressive than others. The Eskimos, as is well known, have fifty words for types of snow – though curiously no word for just plain snow. To them there is crunchy snow, soft snow, fresh snow, and old snow, but no word that just means snow. The Italians, as we might expect, have over 500 names for different types of macaroni. Some of these, when translated, begin to sound distinctly unappetizing, like strozzapreti, which means 'strangled priests'. Vermicelli means 'little worms' and even spaghetti means 'little strings'. When you learn that muscatel in Italian means 'wine with flies in it', you may conclude that the Italians are gastronomically out to lunch, so to speak, but really their names for foodstuffs are no more disgusting than the American hot dogs or those old English favourites, toad-in-the-hole, spotted dick, and faggots in gravy.

The residents of the Trobriand Islands of Papua New Guinea have 100 words for yams, while the Maoris of New Zealand have thirty-five words for dung (don't ask me why). Meanwhile, the Arabs are said (a little unbelievably, perhaps) to have 6,000 words for camels and camel equipment. The aborigines of Tasmania have a word for every type of tree, but no word that just means 'tree', while the Araucanian Indians of Chile rather more poignantly have an abundance of words to distinguish between different degrees of hunger. Even among speakers of the same language, regional and national differences abound. A Londoner has a less comprehensive view of extremes of weather than someone from the Middle West of America. What a Briton calls a blizzard would, in Illinois or Nebraska, be a flurry, and a British heat wave is often a thing of merriment to much of the rest of the world. (I still treasure a copy of the old *Evening News* with the banner headline: BRITAIN SIZZLES IN THE SEVENTIES!)

A second commonly cited factor setting English apart from other languages is its flexibility. This is particularly true of word ordering, where English speakers can roam with considerable freedom between passive and active senses. Not only can we say, 'I kicked the dog', but also 'The dog was kicked by me' – a construction that would be impossible in many other languages. Similarly, where the Germans can say just 'ich singe' and the French must manage with 'je chante', we can

5

say 'I sing', 'I do sing', or 'I am singing'. English also has a distinctive capacity to extract maximum work from a word by making it do double duty as both noun and verb. The list of such versatile words is practically endless: *drink, fight, fire, sleep, run, fund, look, act, view, ape, silence, worship, copy, blame, comfort, bend, cut, reach, like, dislike,* and so on. Other languages sometimes show inspired flashes of versatility, as with the German *auf,* which can mean 'on', 'in', 'upon', 'at', 'toward', 'for', 'to', and 'upward', but these are relative rarities.

At the same time, the endless versatility of English is what makes our rules of grammar so perplexing. Few English-speaking natives, however well educated, can confidently elucidate the difference between, say, a complement and a predicate or distinguish a full infinitive from a bare one. The reason for this is that the rules of English grammar were originally modelled on those of Latin, which in the seventeenth century was considered the purest and most admirable of tongues. That it may be. But it is also quite clearly another language altogether. Imposing Latin rules on English structure is a little like trying to play baseball in ice skates. The two simply don't match. In the sentence 'I went swimming', swimming is a participle. But in the sentence 'Swimming is good for you' it is a gerund – even though it is precisely the same word describing precisely the same activity.

A third – and more contentious – supposed advantage of English is the relative simplicity of its spelling and pronunciation. For all its idiosyncrasies, English is said to have fewer of the awkward consonant clusters and singsong tonal variations that make other languages so difficult to master. In Cantonese, *hae* means 'yes'. But, with a fractional change of pitch, it also describes the female pudenda. The resulting scope for confusion can be safely left to the imagination. In other languages it is the orthography, or spelling, that leads to bewilderment. In Welsh, the word for beer is *cwrw* – an impossible combination of letters for any English speaker. But Welsh spellings are as nothing compared with Irish Gaelic, a language in which spelling and pronunciation give the impression of having been devised by separate committees, meeting in separate rooms, while implacably divided over some deep semantic issue. Try pronouncing *geimhreadh*, Gaelic for 'winter', and you will probably come up with something like 'gem-reed-uh'. It is in fact 'gyeeryee'. *Beaudhchais* ('thank you') is 'bekkas' and *Ó Séaghda* '(Oh-seeg-da?') is simply 'O'Shea'. Against this, the Welsh pronunciation of *cwrw* – 'koo-roo' – begins to look positively self-evident.

In all languages pronunciation is of course largely a matter of familiarity mingled with prejudice. The average English speaker confronted with agglomerations of letters like *tchst*, *sthm*, and *tchph* would naturally conclude that they were pretty well unpronounceable. Yet we use them every day in the words *matchstick*, *asthma*, and *catchphrase*. Here, as in almost every other area of language, natural bias plays an inescapable part in any attempt at evaluation. No one has ever said, 'Yes, my language is backward and unexpressive, and could really do with some sharpening up.' We tend to regard other people's languages as we regard their cultures – with ill-hidden disdain. In Japanese, the word for foreigner means 'stinking of foreign hair'. To the Czechs a Hungarian is 'a pimple'. Germans call cockroaches 'Frenchmen', while the French call lice 'Spaniards'. We in the English-speaking world take French leave, but Italians and Norwegians talk about departing like an Englishman, and Germans talk of running like a Dutchman. Italians call syphilis 'the French disease', while both French and Italians call con games 'American swindle'. Belgian taxi drivers call a poor tipper 'un Anglais'. To be bored to death in French is 'être de Birmingham', literally 'to be from Birmingham' (which is actually about right). And in English we have 'Dutch courage', 'French letters', 'Spanish fly', 'Mexican carwash' (i.e. leaving your car out in the rain), and many others.

So objective evidence, even among the authorities, is not always easy to come by. Most books on English imply in one way or another that our language is superior to all others. In *The English Language*, Robert Burchfield writes: 'As a source of intellectual power and entertainment the whole range of prose writing in English is probably unequalled anywhere else in the world.' I would like to think he's right, but I can't help wondering if Mr Burchfield would have made the same sweeping assertion had he been born Russian or German or Chinese. There is no reliable way of measuring the quality or efficiency of any language. Yet there are one or two small ways in which English has a demonstrable edge over other languages. For one thing its pronouns are largely, and mercifully, uninflected. In German, if you wish to say *you*, you must choose between seven words: *du, dich, dir, Sie, Ihnen, ihr,* and *euch*. This can cause immense social anxiety. The composer Richard Strauss and his librettist, Hugo von Hofmannsthal, were partners for twenty-five years and apparently adored each other and yet never quite found the nerve to address each other as anything but the stiff *Sie*. In English we avoid these problems by relying on just one form: *you*.

In other languages, questions of familiarity can become even more agonizing. A Korean has to choose between one of six verb suffixes to accord with the status of the person addressed. A speaker of Japanese must equally wend his way through a series of linguistic levels appropriate to the social position of the participants. When he says thank you he must choose between a range of meanings running from the perfunctory *arigato* ('thanks') to the decidedly more humble *makotoni go shinsetsu de gozaimasu*, which means 'what you have done or propose to do is a truly and genuinely kind and honourable deed'. Above all, English is mercifully free of gender. Anyone who spent much of his or her adolescence miserably trying to remember whether it is 'la plume' or 'le plume' will appreciate just what a pointless burden masculine and feminine nouns are to any language. In this regard English is a godsend to students everywhere. Not only have we discarded problems of gender with definite and indefinite articles, we have often discarded the articles themselves. We say in English, 'It's time to go to bed', where in most other European languages they must say, 'It's *the* time to go to *the* bed'. We possess countless examples of pithy phrases – 'life is short', 'between heaven and earth', 'to go to work' – which in other languages require articles.

English also has a commendable tendency towards conciseness, in contrast to many languages. German is full of jaw-crunching words like *Geisteswissenschaffeten* (a social worker), *Bundesbahnangestelltenwitwe* (a widow of a federal railway employee), and *Kriegsgefangenanentschädigungsgesetz* (a law pertaining to war reparations), while in Holland companies commonly have names of forty letters or more, such as Douwe Egberts Koninklijke Tabaksfabriek-Koffiebranderijen-Theehandal Naamloze Vennootschap (literally Douwe Egberts Royal Tobacco Factory-Coffee Roasters-Tea Traders Incorporated; they must use fold-out business cards). English, in happy contrast, favours crisp truncations: IBM, laser, NATO. Against this, however, there is an occasional tendency in English, particularly in academic and political circles, to resort to waffle and jargon. At a conference of sociologists in America in 1977, love was defined as 'the cognitive-affective state characterized by intrusive and obsessive fantasizing concerning reciprocity of amorant feelings by the object of the amorance'. That is jargon – the practice of never calling a spade a spade when you might instead call it a manual earth-restructuring implement – and it is one of the great curses of modern English.

But perhaps the single most notable characteristic of English – for better *and* worse – is its deceptive complexity. Nothing in English is ever quite what it seems. Take the simple word *what*. We use it every day – indeed, every few sentences. But imagine trying to explain to a foreigner what *what* means. It takes the *Oxford English Dictionary* five pages and almost 15,000 words to manage the task. As native speakers, we seldom stop to think just how complicated and illogical English is. Every day we use countless words and expressions without thinking about them – often without having the faintest idea what they really describe or signify. What, for instance, is the *hem* in hem and haw, the *shrift* in short shrift, the *fell* in one fell swoop? When you are overwhelmed, where is the whelm that you are over,

9

and what exactly does it look like? And why, come to that, can we be overwhelmed or underwhelmed, but not semiwhelmed or – if our feelings are less pronounced – just whelmed? Why do we say *colonel* as if it had an *r* in it? Why do we spell *four* with a *u* and *forty* without?

Answering these and other such questions is the main purpose of this book. But we start with perhaps the most enduring and mysterious question of all: where does language come from in the first place?

— 2 —

THE DAWN OF LANGUAGE

We have not the faintest idea whether the first words spoken were uttered 20,000 years ago or 200,000 years ago. What is certain is that mankind did little except procreate and survive for 100,000 generations. (For purposes of comparison, only about eighty generations separate us from Christ.) Then suddenly, about 30,000 years ago, there burst forth an enormous creative and cooperative effort which led to the cave paintings at Lascaux, the development of improved, lightweight tools, the control of fire, and many other cooperative arrangements. It is unlikely that any of this could have been achieved without a fairly sophisticated system of language.

In 1857, an archaeologist examining a cave in the Neander Valley of Germany near Düsseldorf found part of an ancient human skull of a type never before encountered. The skull was from a person belonging to a race of people who ranged across Europe, the Near East, and parts of northern Africa during the long period between 30,000 and 150,000 years ago. Neanderthal man (or *Homo sapiens neanderthalensis*) was very different from modern man. He was short, only about five feet tall, stocky, with a small forehead and heavyset features. Despite his distinctly dim-witted appearance, he possessed a larger brain than modern man (though not necessarily a more efficient one). Neanderthal man was unique. So far as can be told no one like him existed before or since. He wore clothes, shaped tools, engaged in communal activities. He buried his dead and marked the graves with stones, which suggests that he may have dealt in some form of religious ritual, and he looked after

11

infirm members of his tribe or family. He also very probably engaged in small wars. All of this would suggest the power of speech.

About 30,000 years ago Neanderthal man disappeared, displaced by *Homo sapiens sapiens*, a taller, slimmer, altogether more agile and handsome – at least to our eyes – race of people who arose in Africa 100,000 years ago, spread to the Near East, and then were drawn to Europe by the retreating ice sheets of the last great ice age. These are the Cro-Magnon people, who were responsible for the famous cave paintings at Lascaux in France and Altamira in Spain – the earliest signs of civilization in Europe, the work of the world's first artists. Although this was an immensely long time ago – some 20,000 years before the domestication of animals and the rise of farming – these Cro-Magnon people were identical to us: they had the same physique, the same brain, the same looks. And, unlike all previous hominids who roamed the earth, they could choke on food. That may seem a trifling point, but the slight evolutionary change that pushed man's larynx deeper into his throat, and thus made choking a possibility, also brought with it the possibility of sophisticated, well-articulated speech.

Other mammals have no contact between their air passages and oesophagi. They can breathe and swallow at the same time, and there is no possibility of food going down the wrong way. But with *Homo sapiens* food and drink must pass over the larynx on the way to the gullet and thus there is a constant risk that some will be inadvertently inhaled. In modern humans, the lowered larynx isn't in position from birth. It descends sometime between the ages of three and five months – curiously, the precise period when babies are likely to suffer from Sudden Infant Death Syndrome. At all events, the descended larynx explains why you can speak and your dog cannot.

According to studies conducted by Philip Lieberman at Brown University, Neanderthal man was physiologically precluded from uttering certain basic sounds such as the 'ē' sound of *bee* or the 'oo' sound of *boot*. His speech, if it existed at all, would have been nasal-sounding and fairly imprecise – and that would no doubt have greatly impeded his development.

It was long supposed that Neanderthal was absorbed by the more advanced *Homo sapiens*. But recent evidence indicates that *Homo sapiens* and Neanderthals coexisted in the Near East for 30,000 years without interbreeding – strong evidence that the Neanderthals must have been a different species. It is interesting to speculate what would have become of these people had they survived. Would we have used them for slaves? For sport? Who can say?

At all events, Neanderthal man was hopelessly outclassed. Not only did *Homo sapiens* engage in art of an astonishingly high quality, but he evinced other cultural achievements of a comparatively high order. He devised more specialized tools for a wider variety of tasks and hunted in a far more systematic and cooperative way. Whereas the food debris of the Neanderthals shows a wide variety of animal bones, suggesting that they took whatever they could find, archaeological remnants from *Homo sapiens* show that he sought out particular kinds of game and tracked animals seasonally. All of this strongly suggests that he possessed a linguistic system sufficiently sophisticated to deal with concepts such as: 'Today let's kill some red deer. You take some big sticks and drive the deer out of the woods and we'll stand by the riverbank with our spears and kill them as they come towards us.' By comparison Neanderthal speech may have been something more like: 'I'm hungry. Let's hunt.'

It may be no more than intriguing coincidence, but the area of the Cro-Magnon cave paintings is also the area containing Europe's oldest and most mysterious ethnic group, the Basques. Their language, called Euskara by its speakers, may be the last surviving remnant of the Neolithic languages spoken in Stone Age Europe and later displaced by Indo-European tongues. No one can say. What is certain is that Basque was already old by the time the Celts came to the region. Today it is the native tongue of about 600,000 people in Spain and 100,000 in France in an area around the Bay of Biscay stretching roughly from Bilbao to Bayonne and inland over the Pyrenees to Pamplona. Its remoteness from Indo-European is indicated by its words for the numbers one to five: *bat, bi, hirur, laur, bortz*. There is simply no proven connection between Basque and any other known language.

One of the greatest mysteries of prehistory is how people in widely separated places suddenly and spontaneously developed the capacity for language at roughly the same time. It was as if people carried around in their heads a genetic alarm clock that suddenly went off all around the world and led different groups in widely scattered places on every continent to create languages. Even those who were cut off from the twenty or so great language families developed their own quite separate languages, such as the Dravidian languages of southern India and northern Sri Lanka, or the Luorawetlan languages of eastern Siberia, or the even stranger Ainu language spoken on the northern island of Hokkaido in Japan by people who have clear Caucasian racial characteristics and whose language has certain (doubtless coincidental) similarities with European languages. (For instance, their word for eighty is 'four twenties'). How they and their language came to be there is something no one knows. But then Japanese itself is a mystery. Although its system of writing and some of its vocabulary have been taken from Chinese, it is otherwise quite unrelated to any other known language. The same is true of Korean.

Or perhaps not. There is increasing evidence to suggest that languages widely dispersed geographically may be more closely related than once thought. This is most arrestingly demonstrated by the three language families of the New World: Eskimo-Aleut, Amerind, and Na-Dene. It was long supposed that these groups were quite unrelated to any other language families, including each other. But recent studies of cognates – that is, words that have similar spellings and meanings in two or more languages, such as the French *tu*, the English *thou*, and the Hittite *tuk*, all meaning 'you' – have found possible links between some of the most unlikely language partners: for instance, between Basque and Na-Dene, an Indian language spoken mainly in the northwest United States and Canada, and between Finnish and Eskimo-Aleut. No one has come up with a remotely plausible explanation of how a language spoken only in a remote corner of the Pyrenees could have come to influence Indian languages of the New World, but the links between many cognates are too numerous to explain in terms of simple coincidence. Some cognates may even be universal. The word for dog, for instance, is suspiciously similar in Amerind, Uralic, and Proto-Indo-European, while the root form 'tik', signifying a finger or the number one, is found on every continent. As Merrit Ruhlen noted in *Natural History* magazine: 'The significant number of such global cognates leads some linguists to conclude that all the world's languages ultimately belong to a single language family.'[1]

There are any number of theories to account for how language began. The theories have names that seem almost to be begging ridicule – the Bow-Wow theory, the Ding-Dong theory, the Pooh-Pooh theory, the Yo-He-Ho theory – and they are generally based in one way or another on the supposition that languages come ultimately from spontaneous utterances of alarm, joy, pain, and so on, or that they are somehow imitative (onomatopoeic) of sounds in the real world. Thus, for instance, a Welsh term for owl, *gwd-ihŵ*, pronounced 'goody-hoo', may mimic the sound an owl makes.

There is, to be sure, a slight tendency to have words cluster around certain sounds. In English we have a large number of *sp-* words pertaining to wetness: *spray, splash, spit, sprinkle, splatter, spatter, spill, spigot*. And we have a large number of *fl-* words to do with movement: *flail, flap, flicker, flounce, flee*. And quite a number of words ending in *-ash* describe abrupt actions: *flash, dash, crash, bash, thrash, smash, slash*. Onomatopoeia does play a part in language formation, but whether it or any other feature alone can account for how languages are formed is highly doubtful.

It is intriguing to see how other languages hear certain sounds – and how much better their onomatopoeic words often are. Dogs go *ouâ-ouâ* in France, *bu-bu* in Italy, *mung-mung* in Korea, *wan-wan* in Japan: a purring cat goes *ron-ron* in France, *schnurr* in Germany; a bottle being emptied goes *gloup-gloup* in China, *tot-tot-to* in Spain; a heartbeat is *doogan-doogan* in Korea, *doki-doki* in Japan; bells go *bimbam* in Germany, *dindan* in Spain. The Spanish word for whisper is *susurrar*. How could it be anything else?

Much of what we know, or think we know, about the roots of language comes from watching children learn to speak. For a long time it was believed that language was simply learned. Just as we learn, say, the names and locations of the capitals of Europe or our multiplication tables, so we must learn the 'rules' of speech – that we don't say 'house white is the', but rather 'the house is white'. The presumption was that our minds at birth were blank slates on to which the rules and quirks of our native languages were written. But then other authorities, notably Noam Chomsky of the Massachusetts Institute of Technology, began to challenge this view, arguing that some structural facets of language – the *ground rules* of speech, if you like – must be innate. That isn't to suggest that you would have learned English spontaneously had you been brought up among wolves. But perhaps you are born with an instinctive sense of how language works, as a general thing. There are a number of reasons to suppose so. For one thing, we appear to have an innate appreciation of language. By the end of the first month of life infants show a clear preference for speechlike sounds over all others. It doesn't matter what language it is. To a baby no language is easier or more difficult than any other. They are all mastered at about the same pace, however irregular and wildly inflected they may be. In short, children seem to be programmed to learn language, just as they seem to be programmed to learn to walk. The process has been called basic child grammar. Indeed, children in the first five years of life have such a remarkable facility for language that they can effortlessly learn two structurally quite different languages simultaneously – if, for instance, their mother is Chinese and their father American – without evincing the slightest signs of stress or confusion.

Moreover, all children everywhere learn languages in much the same way: starting with simple labels ('Me'), advancing to subject-verb structures ('Me want'), before progressing to subject-verb-emphatics ('Me want now'), and so on. They even babble in the same way. A study at the John F. Kennedy Institute in Baltimore found that children from such diverse backgrounds as Arabic, English, Chinese, Spanish, and Norwegian all began babbling in a systematic way, making the same sounds at about the same time (four to six months before the start of saying their first words).[2]

The semantic and grammatical idiosyncrasies that distinguish one language from another – inflections of tense, the use of gender, and so on – are the things that are generally learned last, after the child already has a functioning command of the language. Some aspects of language acquisition are puzzling: children almost always learn to say *no* before *yes* and *in* before *on*, and all children everywhere go through a phase in which they become oddly fascinated with the idea of 'gone' and 'all gone'.

The traditional explanation is that all of this is learned at your mother's knee. Yet careful examination suggests that that is unlikely. Most adults tend (even when they are not aware of it) to speak to infants in a simplified, gitchy-goo kind of way. This is not a sensible or efficient way to teach a child the difference between, say, present tense and past tense, and yet the child learns it. Indeed, as he increasingly masters his native tongue, he tries to make it conform to more logical rules than the language itself may possess, saying 'buyed', 'eated', and 'goed' because, even though he has never heard such words spoken, they seem more logical to him – as indeed they are, if you stopped and thought about it.

Where vocabulary is concerned, children are very reliant on their mothers (or whoever else has the role of primary carer). If she says a word, then the child generally listens and tries to repeat it. But where grammar is concerned, children go their own way. According to one study two-thirds of utterances made by mothers to their infants are either imperatives or questions, and only one third are statements, yet the utterances

A SADLY MISSED POINT !

of children are overwhelmingly statements.[3] Clearly they don't require the same repetitive teaching because they are already a step ahead where syntax is concerned.

Some of the most interesting theories about language development in recent years have been put forward by Derek Bickerton, an English-born professor at the University of Hawaii, who noticed that creole languages all over the world bear certain remarkable similarities. First, it is important to understand the difference between pidgins and creoles. Pidgins (the word is thought to be a Chinese rendering of the English word *business*) are rudimentary languages formed when people from diverse backgrounds are thrown together by circumstance. Historically, they have tended to arise on isolated plantation-based islands which have been ruled by a dominant Western minority but where the labourers come from a mixed linguistic background. Pidgins are almost always very basic and their structure varies considerably from place to place – and indeed from person to person. They are essentially little more than the language you or I would speak if we found ourselves suddenly deposited in some place like Bulgaria or Azerbaijan. They are makeshift tongues and as a result they seldom last long.

When children are born into a pidgin community, one of two things will happen. Either the children will learn the language of the ruling class, as was almost always the case with African slaves in the American South, or they will develop a creole (from the French *créole*, 'native'). Most of the languages that people think of as pidgins are in fact creoles. To the uninitiated they can seem primitive, even comical. In Neo-Melanesian, an English-based creole of Papua New Guinea, the word for beard is *gras bilong fes* (literally 'grass that belongs to the face') and the word for a vein or artery is *rop bilong blut* ('rope that belongs to the blood'). In African creoles you can find such arresting expressions as *bak sit drayva* ('back seat driver'), *wesmata* ('what's the matter?'), and *bottom-bottom wata wata* ('submarine'). In Krio, spoken in Sierra Leone, stomach gas is *bad briz*, while to pass gas is to *pul bad briz*. Feel free to smile. But it would be a mistake to consider these languages substandard because of their curious vocabularies. They are as formalized, efficient, and expressive as any other languages – and often more so. As Bickerton notes, most creoles can express subtleties of action not available in English. For instance, in English we are not very good at distinguishing desire from accomplishment in the past tense. In the sentence 'I went to the store to buy a shirt' we cannot tell whether the shirt was bought or not. But in all creoles such ambiguity is impossible. In Hawaiian creole the person who bought a shirt would say, 'I bin go store go buy shirt', while the person who failed to buy a shirt would say, 'I bin go store for buy shirt.' The distinction is crucial.

So creoles are not in any way inferior. In fact, it is worth remembering that many fully-fledged languages – the Afrikaans of South Africa, the Chinese of Macao, and the Swahili of east Africa – were originally creoles.

In studying creoles, Bickerton noticed that they are very similar in structure to the language of children between the ages of two and four. At that age, children are prone to make certain basic errors in their speech, such as using double negatives and experiencing confusion with irregular plurals so that they say 'feets' and 'sheeps'. At the same time, certain fairly complicated aspects of grammar, which we might reasonably expect to befuddle children, cause them no trouble at all. One is the ability to distinguish between stative and nonstative verbs with a present participle. Without getting too technical about it, this means that with certain types of verbs we use a present participle to create sentences like 'I am going for a walk' but with other verbs we dispense with the present participle, which is why we say 'I like you' and not 'I am liking you'. Very probably you have never thought about this before. The reason you have never thought about it is that it is seemingly instinctive. Most children have mastered the distinction between stative and nonstative verbs by the age of two and are never troubled by it again. Intriguingly, all creole languages make precisely the same distinction.

All of this would seem to suggest that certain properties of language are innate. Moreover, as we have seen, it appears that the earth's languages may be more closely related than once thought. The links between languages – between, say, German *Bruder*, English *brother*, Gaelic *bhrathair*, Sanskrit *bhrata*, and Persian *biradar* – seem self-evident to us today but it hasn't always been so. The science of historical linguistics, like so much else, owes its beginnings to the work of an amateur enthusiast, in this case an Englishman named Sir William Jones.

Dispatched to India as a judge in 1783, Jones whiled away his evenings by teaching himself Sanskrit. On the face of it this was an odd and impractical thing to do, since Sanskrit was a dead language and had been for many centuries. That so much of it survived at all was in large part due to the efforts of priests, who memorized its sacred hymns, the Vedas, and passed them on from one generation to the next for hundreds of years even though the words had no meaning for them. These texts represent some of the oldest writings in any Indo-European language. Jones noticed many striking similarities between Sanskrit and European languages – the Sanskrit word for birch, for instance, was *bhurja*. The Sanskrit for king, *raja*, is close to the Latin *rex*. The Sanskrit for ten, *dasa*, is reminiscent of the Latin *decem*. And so on. All of these clearly suggested a common historical parentage. Jones looked at other languages and discovered further similarities. In a landmark speech to the Asiatick Society in Calcutta he proposed that many of the classical languages – among them Sanskrit, Greek, Latin, Gothic, Celtic, and Persian – must spring from the same source. This was a bold assertion since nothing in recorded history would encourage such a conclusion, and it excited great interest among scholars all over Europe. The next century saw a feverish effort to track down the parent language, Indo-European, as it was soon called. Scores of people became involved, including noted scholars such as the Germans Friedrich von Schlegel and Jacob Grimm (yes, he of the fairy tales, though philology was his first love) and the splendidly

named Franz Bopp. But, once again, some of the most important breakthroughs were the work of inspired amateurs, among
them Henry Rawlinson, an official with the British East India
Company, who deciphered ancient Persian more or less single-
handed, and, somewhat later, Michael Ventris, an English
architect who deciphered the famously difficult Linear B script
of ancient Minoa, which had flummoxed generations of academics.

These achievements are all the more remarkable when you
consider that often they were made using the merest fragments
– of ancient Thracian, an important language spoken over a
wide area until as recently as the Middle Ages, we have just
twenty-five words – and in the face of remarkable indifference
on the part of the ancient Greeks and Romans, neither of
whom ever bothered to note the details of a single other
language. The Romans even allowed Etruscan, a language
that had greatly contributed to their own, to be lost, so that
today Etruscan writings remain tantalizingly untranslated.

Nor can we read any Indo-European writings, for the simple
reason that not a scrap exists. Everything we know – or, to be
more precise, think we know – is based on conjecture, on
finding common strands in modern-day languages and tracing
these strands to a hypothetical mother tongue, Proto-Indo-
European, which may never even have existed. The lack of
documentary evidence isn't too surprising when you bear in
mind that we are going back an awfully long time. The early
Indo-Europeans were Neolithic – that is, late Stone Age –
people who can be dated back to about 7000 B.C. The descended languages of Indo-European almost always show some
kind of kinship in their names for primary family relationships,
such as mother and father; for parts of the body, such as eye,
foot, heart, and ear; for common animals, such as goat and ox;
and for natural elements, such as snow, thunder, and fire. We
can deduce something about how these people lived from these
cognates. They had a common word for snow and cold, so the
climate obviously was not tropical, and yet they appear to
have had no common word for sea. Those tribes that reached

the sea each came up with words of their own, so presumably they began their migration from a point well inland. Among the other words held in common are *oak*, *beech*, *birch*, *willow*, *bear*, *wolf*, *deer*, *rabbit*, *sheep*, *goat*, *pig*, and *dog*. They had no common word for horse or window. By studying the known range of certain flora and fauna, linguists have placed their original homeland in various places: the Russian steppes, Scandinavia, central Europe, the Danube valley, Asia Minor – indeed, almost everywhere.

Their common existence is thought to have ended between 3500 and 2500 B.C., when they began to fan out across Europe and Asia. For the most part these were probably not great exoduses but rather gradual encroachments as each new generation sought new pastures and hunting grounds. Over the millennia they spread over wide areas – even reaching China. Explorers at the turn of the century were astonished to find a cache of Buddhist documents written in two related but unknown languages in what is now the Chinese province of Sinkiang, along the Old Silk Road. The languages, which they called Tocharian, were clearly Indo-European, as can be seen, for instance, in their words for the number three: *tre* and *trai*. As the centuries passed, the original Indo-European language split into a dozen broad groups: Celtic, Germanic, Greek, Indo-Iranian, Slavonic, Thraco-Illyrian, and so on. These further subdivided into literally scores of new languages, ranging from Swedish to Faeroese to Parthian to Armenian to Hindi to Portuguese. It is remarkable to reflect that people as various as a Gaelic-speaking Scottish Highlander and a Sinhalese-speaking Sri Lankan both use languages that can be traced directly back to the same starting point. With this in mind, it is perhaps little wonder that the Greeks and Romans had no idea that they were speaking languages that were cousins of the barbarian tongues all around them. The notion would have left them dumbfounded. Just within Europe the degree of divergence is so great that only relatively recently have two languages, Albanian and Armenian, been identified as being Indo-European.

Of all the Indo-European languages, Lithuanian is the one that has changed the least – so much so that it is sometimes said that a Lithuanian can understand simple phrases in Sanskrit. At the very least, Lithuanian has preserved many more of the inflectional complexities of the original Indo-European language than others of the family.

English is part of the Germanic family, which gradually split into three branches. These were North Germanic, consisting of the Scandinavian languages; West Germanic, consisting principally of English, German, and Dutch (but also Frisian, Flemish, and other related dialects); and East Germanic, whose three component languages, Burgundian, Gothic, and Vandalic, died off one by one. Many other European languages disappeared over time, among them Cornish, Manx, Gaulish, Lydian, Oscan, Umbrian, and two that once dominated Europe, Celtic and Latin.

Celtic, I must hasten to add, is not dead. Far from it. It is still spoken by half a million people in Europe. But they are scattered over a wide area and its influence is negligible. At its height, in about 400 B.C., Celtic was spoken over a vast area of the continent, a fact reflected in scores of place names from Belgrade to Paris to Dundee, all of which commemorate Celtic tribes. But from that point on, its dominions have been constantly eroded, largely because the Celts were a loose collection of tribes and not a great nation state, so they were easily divided and conquered. Even now the various branches of Celtic are not always mutually comprehensible. Celtic speakers in Scotland, for instance, cannot understand the Celtic speakers of Wales a hundred miles to the south. Today Celtic survives in scattered outposts along the westernmost fringes of Europe – on the bleak Hebridean Islands and coastal areas of Scotland, in shrinking pockets of Galway, Mayo, Kerry, and Donegal in Ireland, in mostly remote areas of Wales, and on the Brittany peninsula of northwest France. Everywhere it is a story of inexorable decline. At the turn of the century Cape Breton Island in Nova Scotia had 100,000 Gaelic speakers – most of them driven there by the forced clearances of the

Scottish highlands – but now Gaelic is extinct there as a means of daily discourse.

Latin, in distinct contrast, didn't so much decline as evolve. It became the Romance languages. It is not too much to say that French, Italian, Spanish, Portuguese, and Romanian (as well as a dozen or so minor languages/dialects like Provençal and Catalan) are essentially modern versions of Latin. If we must fix a date for when Latin stopped being Latin and instead became these other languages, the year 813 is a convenient milestone. It was then that Charlemagne ordered that sermons throughout his realm be delivered in the 'lingua romana rustica' and not the customary 'lingua latina'. But of course you cannot draw a line and say that the language was Latin on this side and Italian or French on that. As late as the thirteenth century, Dante was still regarding his own Florentine tongue as Latin. And indeed it is still possible to construct long passages of modern Italian that are identical to ancient Latin.

The Romance languages are not the outgrowths of the elegant, measured prose of Cicero, but rather the language of the streets and of the common person, the Latin vulgate. The word for horse in literary Latin was *equus*, but to the man in the street it was *caballus*, and it was from this that we get the French *cheval*, the Spanish *caballo*, and the Italian *cavallo*. Similarly, the classical term for head was *caput* (from which we get *capital* and *per capita*), but the street term was *testa*, a kind of pot, from which comes the French *tête* and the Italian *testa* (though the Italians also use *capo*). Cat in classical Latin was *felix* (whence *feline*), but in the vulgate it was *cattus*. Our word salary comes literally from the vulgar Latin *salarium*, 'salt money' – the Roman soldier's ironic term for what it would buy. By the same process the classical *pugna* (from which we much later took *pugnacious*) was replaced by the slangy *battualia* (from which we get *battle*), and the classical *urbs*, meaning 'city' (from which we get *urban*), was superseded by *villa* (from which the French get their name for a city, *ville*, and we take the name for a place in the country).

24

The grammar of the vulgate also became simplified as Latin spread across the known world and was adopted by people from varying speech backgrounds. In classical Latin word endings were constantly changing to reflect syntax: a speaker could distinguish between, say, 'in the house' and 'to the house' by varying the ending on 'house'. But gradually people decided that it was simpler to leave house uninflected and put *ad* in front of it for 'to', *in* for 'in', and so on through all the prepositions and by this means the case endings disappeared. An almost identical process happened with English later.

Romanians often claim to have the language that most closely resembles ancient Latin. But in fact, according to Mario Pei, if you wish to hear what ancient Latin sounded like, you should listen to Lugudorese, an Italic dialect spoken in central Sardinia, which in many respects is unchanged from the Latin of 1,500 years ago.

Many scholars believe that classical Latin was spoken by almost no one – that it was used exclusively as a literary and scholarly language. Certainly such evidence as we have of everyday writing – graffiti on the walls of Pompeii, for example – suggests that classical Latin was effectively a dead language as far as common discourse was concerned long before Rome fell. And, as we shall see, it was that momentous event – the fall of Rome – that helped to usher in our own tongue.

3

GLOBAL LANGUAGE

All languages have the same purpose – to communicate thoughts – and yet they achieve this single aim in a multiplicity of ways. It appears there is no feature of grammar or syntax that is indispensable or universal. The ways of dealing with matters of number, tense, case, gender, and the like are wondrously various from one tongue to the next. Many languages manage without quite basic grammatical or lexical features, while others burden themselves with remarkable complexities. Finnish has fifteen case forms, so every noun varies depending on whether it is nominative, accusative, allative, inessive, comitative, or one of ten other grammatical conditions. Imagine learning fifteen ways of spelling *cat*, *dog*, *house*, and so on. English, by contrast, has abandoned case forms, except for possessives, where we generally add *'s*, and with personal pronouns which vary by no more than three ways (e.g. *they, their, them*). Similarly, in English *ride* has just five forms (*ride, rides, rode, riding, ridden*); the same verb in German has sixteen. In Russian, nouns can have up to twelve inflections and adjectives as many as sixteen. In English adjectives have just one invariable form with but, I believe, one exception: *blond/-blonde*.

Sometimes languages fail to acquire what may seem to us quite basic terms. The Romans had no word for grey. To them it was another shade of dark blue or dark green. Irish Gaelic possesses no equivalent of *yes* or *no*. They must resort to roundabout expressions such as 'I think not' and 'This is so'. Italians cannot distinguish between a niece and a granddaughter or between a nephew and a grandson. The Japanese have no definite or indefinite articles corresponding to the English *a*, *an*, or *the*, and they do not distinguish between singular and plural as we do with, say, *ball/balls* and *child/children* or as the French do with *château/châteaux*. This may seem strange until you reflect that we don't make a distinction with a lot of words – *sheep, deer, trout, Swiss, scissors* – and it scarcely ever causes us trouble. We could probably well get by without it for all words. But it is harder to make a case for the absence in Japanese of a future tense. To them *Tokyo e yukimasu* means both 'I go to Tokyo' and 'I will go to Tokyo'. To understand which sense is intended, you need to know the context. This lack of explicitness is a feature of Japanese – even to the point that they seldom use personal pronouns like *me*, *my*, and *yours*. Such words exist, but the Japanese employ them so sparingly that they might as well not have them. Over half of all Japanese sentences have no subject. They dislike giving a straightforward yes or no. It is no wonder that they are so often called inscrutable.

Not only did various speech communities devise different languages, but also different cultural predispositions to go with them. Speakers from the Mediterranean region, for instance, like to put their faces very close, relatively speaking, to those they are addressing. A common scene when people from southern Europe and northern Europe are conversing, as at a cocktail party, is for the latter to spend the entire conversation stealthily retreating, to try to gain some space, and for the former to keep advancing to close the gap. Neither speaker may even be aware of it. There are more of these speech conventions than you might suppose. English speakers dread silence. We are all familiar with the uncomfortable feeling that overcomes us when a conversation palls. Studies have shown that when a pause reaches four seconds, one or more of the conversationalists will invariably blurt something – a fatuous comment on the weather, a startled cry of 'Gosh, is that the time?' – rather than let the silence extend to a fifth second.

27

A vital adjunct to language is the gesture, which in some cultures can almost constitute a vocabulary all its own. Modern Greek has more than seventy common gestures, ranging from the chopping off the forearm gesture, which signifies extreme displeasure, to several highly elaborate ones, such as placing the left hand on the knee, closing one eye, looking with the other into the middle distance and wagging the free hand up and down, which means 'I don't want anything to do with it'. According to Mario Pei, the human anatomy is capable of producing some 700,000 'distinct elementary gestures' of this type. We have nothing remotely like that number in English, but we have many more than you might at first think – from wagging a finger in warning at a child, to squeezing the nose and fanning the face to indicate a noisome smell, to putting a hand to the ear as if to say, 'I can't hear you'.

Estimates of the number of languages in the world usually fix on a figure of about 2,700, though almost certainly no one has ever made a truly definitive count. In many countries, perhaps the majority, there are at least two native languages, and in some cases – as in Cameroon and Papua New Guinea – there are hundreds. India probably leads the world, with more than 1,600 languages and dialects (it isn't always possible to say which is which). The rarest language as of 1984 was Oubykh, a highly complex Caucasian language with eighty-two consonants but only three vowels, once spoken by 50,000 people in the Crimea. But as of July 1984 there was just one living speaker remaining and he was eighty-two years old.

The number of languages naturally changes as tribes die out or linguistic groups are absorbed. Although new languages, particularly creoles, are born from time to time, the trend is towards absorption and amalgamation. When Columbus arrived in the New World, there were an estimated 1,000 languages. Today there are about 600.

Almost all languages change. A rare exception is written Icelandic, which has changed so little that modern Icelanders can read sagas written a thousand years ago. In English, by contrast, the change has been much more dramatic. Almost any untrained person looking at a manuscript from the time of, say, the Venerable Bede would be hard pressed to identify it as being in English – and in a sense he or she would be right. Today we have not only a completely different vocabulary and system of spelling, but even a different structure.

Nor are languages any respecters of frontiers. If you drew a map of Europe based on languages it would bear scant resemblance to a conventional map. Switzerland would disappear, becoming part of the surrounding dominions of French, Italian, and German but for a few tiny pockets for Romansh (or Romantsch or Rhaeto-Romanic as it is variously called), which is spoken as a native language by about half the people in the Graubünden district (or Grisons district – almost everything has two names in Switzerland) at the country's eastern edge. This steep and beautiful area, which takes in the ski resorts of St Moritz, Davos, and Klosters, was once effectively isolated from the rest of the world by its harsh winters and forbidding geography. Indeed, the isolation was such that even people in neighbouring valleys began to speak different versions of the language, so that Romansh is not so much one language as five fragmented and not always mutually intelligible dialects. A person from the valley around Sutselva will say, 'Vagned nà qua' for 'Come here', while in the next valley he will say, 'Vegni neu cheu'.[1] In other places people will speak the language in the same way but spell it differently depending on whether they are Catholic or Protestant.

German would cover not only its traditional areas of Germany, Austria, and much of Switzerland, but would spill into Belgium, Czechoslovakia, Romania, Hungary, the Soviet Union, and Poland, and it could be further divided into high and low German, which have certain notable differences in terms of vocabulary and syntax. In Bavaria, for instance, *Samstag* is the name for Saturday, but in Berlin it is *Sonnabend*; a plumber in Bavaria is a *Spengler*, but a *Klempner* in Berlin.

Italy, too, would appear on the map not as one language entity but as a whole variety of broadly related but often mutually incomprehensible dialects. Italian, such as it is, is not a national language, but really only the dialect of Florence and Tuscany, which has slowly been gaining pre-eminence over other dialects. Not until 1979 did a poll show for the first time that Italian was the dialect spoken at home by more than 50 per cent of Italians.

Much the same would be the position in the Soviet Union, which would dissolve into 149 separate languages. Almost half the people in the country speak some language other than Russian as a native tongue, and a full quarter of the people do not speak Russian at all.

Such pockets would be everywhere. Even Latin would make an appearance: it is still the official language of the Vatican City.

All these languages blend and merge and variously affect each other. French normally puts the adjective after the noun it is modifying (as in *l'auto rouge* rather than *le rouge auto*), but in Alsace and other Rhineland regions influenced by Germany, the locals have a tendency to reverse the normal order. In a similar way, in the Highlands of Scotland, English speakers, whether or not they understand Gaelic, have developed certain speech patterns clearly influenced by Gaelic phrasings, saying 'take that here' rather than 'bring that here' and 'I'm seeing you' in preference to 'I see you'. In border areas, such as between Holland and West Germany or between West Germany and Denmark, the locals on each side often understand each other better than they do their own compatriots.

Some languages are not so distinct as we are sometimes led to believe. Spanish and Portuguese are closely enough related that the two can read each other's newspapers and books, though they have more difficulty understanding speech. Finns and Estonians can freely understand each other. Danes, Swedes, and Norwegians often insist that their languages are quite distinct and yet, as Mario Pei puts it, there are greater differences between Italian dialects such as Sicilian and Piedmontese than there are between any of the three main Scandinavian languages. Romanian and Moldavian, spoken in the Soviet Union, are essentially the same language with different names. So are Serbian and Croatian, the only real difference being that Serbian uses the Cyrillic alphabet and Croatian uses Western characters.

In many countries people use one language for some activities and a second language for others. In Luxembourg, the inhabitants use French at school, German for reading newspapers, and Luxemburgish, a local Germanic dialect, at home. In Paraguay, people conduct business in Spanish, but tell their jokes in Guarani, the native Indian tongue. In Greece for a long time children were schooled only in Katharevousa, a formal language so archaic that it was (and indeed still is) no longer spoken anywhere in the country. The language for common discourse was Dhimotiki, yet perversely this everyday language was long held in such low esteem that when the Old Testament was published in Dhimotiki for the first time in 1903, riots broke out all over the country.[2]

In countries where two or more languages coexist, confusion often arises. In Belgium, many towns have two quite separate names, one recognized by French speakers, one by Dutch speakers, so that the French Tournai is the Dutch Doornik, while the Dutch Luik is the French Liège. The Dutch Bergen is the French Mons, the Dutch Kortrijk is the French Courtrai, and the city that to all French-speaking people (and indeed most English-speaking people) is known as Bruges (and pronounced 'broozsh') is to the locals called Brugge and pronounced 'broo-guh'. Although Brussels is officially bilingual, it is in fact a French-speaking island in a Flemish lake.

Language is often an emotive issue in Belgium and has brought down many governments. Part of the problem is that there has been a reversal in the relative fortunes of the two main language groups. Wallonia, the southern French-speaking half of Belgium, was long the economic powerhouse of the country, but with the decline of traditional heavy industries such as steel and coal, the economic base has moved north to the more populous, but previously backward, region of Flanders. During the period of the Walloon ascendancy, the Dutch dialect, Flemish, or Vlaams, was forbidden to be spoken

31

in parliament, courts, and even in schools. This naturally caused lingering resentment among the Dutch-speaking majority.

The situation is so hair-triggered that when a French-speaking group of villages in Flanders known as the Fourons elected a French-speaking mayor who refused to conduct his duties in Dutch, the national government was brought down twice and the matter clouded Belgian politics for a decade.

Even more bitter has been the situation in French-speaking Canada. In 1976, the separatist Parti Québecois, under the leadership of René Lévesque, introduced a law known as Bill 101, which banned languages other than French on commercial signs, restricted the number of admissions to English schools (and required the children of immigrants to be schooled in French even if both parents spoke English), and made French the language of the workplace for any company employing more than fifty people. The laws were enforced by a committee with the ominous name of the Commission de Surveillance de la Langue Française. Fines of up to $760 were imposed by 400 'language police'. All of this was a trifle harsh on the 800,000 Quebec citizens who spoke English, and a source of considerable resentment, as when 'Merry Christmas' greetings were ordered to be taken down and 15,000 Dunkin' Donuts bags were seized. In December 1988, the supreme court of Canada ruled that parts of Bill 101 were illegal. According to the court, Quebec could order that French be the primary language of commerce, but not the only one. As an immediate response, 15,000 francophones marched in protest through the streets of Montreal and many stores that had bilingual signs were vandalized, often by having the letters FLQ (for Front de Libération de Québec) spray-painted across their windows. One was firebombed.

But even 1,000 miles from Quebec linguistic ill-feeling sometimes surfaces. Because Canada is officially bilingual, a national law states that all regions of the country must provide services in both French and English, but this has caused sometimes bitter resentment in non-French-speaking areas such as Manitoba, where there are actually more native speakers of German and Ukrainian than of French. French Canadians are a shrinking proportion of the country, falling from 29 per cent of the total population in 1961 to 24 per cent today and forecast to fall to 20 per cent by early in the next century.

People can feel incredibly strongly about these matters. As of February 1989, the Basque separatist organization ETA (short for Euskadi To Azkatasuna, 'Basque Nation and Liberty') had committed 672 murders in the name of linguistic and cultural independence. Even if we are repelled by the violence, it is easy to understand the feelings of resentment that arise among linguistic minorities. Under Franco, you could be arrested and imprisoned just for speaking Basque in public. Catalan, a language midway between Spanish and French, spoken by 250,000 people principally in Catalonia but also as far afield as Roussillon in France, was likewise long banned in Spain. In France for decades letters addressed in Breton were returned with the message *Adresse en Breton interdite* ('Address in Breton forbidden'). Hitler and Mussolini even went so far as to persecute Esperanto speakers.

Suppression is still going on. In the Soviet Union in the 1980s, Azerbaijanis and other linguistic minorities rioted, and sometimes lost their lives, for the right to have newspapers and schoolbooks in their own languages. In Romania there exists a group of people called Szeklers who speak what is said to be the purest and most beautiful form of Hungarian. But for thirty years before the fall of Nicolae Ceausescu the Romanian government systematically eradicated their culture, closing down schools, forcing the renowned Hungarian-language Bolyai University to merge with a lesser-known Romanian one, even bulldozing whole villages, all in the name of linguistic conformity.

On the whole, however, governments these days take a more enlightened view of their minority languages. Nowhere perhaps has this reversal of attitudes been more pronounced than in Wales. Once practically banned, the Welsh language is now officially protected by the government. It is a language of rich but daunting beauty. Try getting your tongue around this sentence, from a car park in Gwynedd, the most deter-minedly Welsh-speaking of Wales's eight counties: 'A ydych wedi talu a dodi eich tocyn yn y golwg?' It translates as 'Did you remember to pay and display?' and, yes, it is about as unpronounceable as it looks. In fact, more so because Welsh pronunciations rarely bear much relation to their spellings when viewed from an English-speaking perspective. The town of Dolgellau, for instance, is pronounced 'doll-geth-lee', while Llandudno is 'hlan-did-no'. And those are the easy ones. There are also scores of places that bring tears to the eyes of outsiders: Llwchmynydd, Bwlchtocyn, Dwygyfylchi, Cwmystwyth, Pontrhydfendigaid, and Cnwch Coch.

Given such awesome phonics it is perhaps little wonder that Prince Charles had endless difficulties mastering the language before his investiture as Prince of Wales in 1969. In this he is not alone. Almost 80 per cent of all Welsh people do not speak Welsh. Although the country is officially bilingual and all public signs are in Welsh as well as English, the Welsh language is spoken hardly at all in the south, around the main industrial cities of Swansea, Cardiff, and Newport, and elsewhere it tends to exist only in pockets in the more remote inland areas.

That it has survived at all is a tribute to the character of the Welsh people. Until well into this century Welsh was all but illegal. It was forbidden in schools, in the courts, and at many places of work. Children who forgot themselves and shouted it on the playground were often forced to undergo humiliating punishments. Now all that has changed. Since the 1960s the British government has allowed Welsh to become an official language, has permitted its use in schools in predominantly Welsh-speaking areas, allowed people to give court evidence in Welsh, and set up a Welsh television station. Welsh, according to the *Economist*, is now 'the most subsidized minority language in the world'. Discussing the advent of S4C, the Welsh-language television station, it observed: 'Never mind that it costs £43 million a year to broadcast to the 20 per cent of the population of Wales who speak Welsh, who in turn make up only 1 per cent of the population of Britain.'

All of this was secured for the Welsh people only after a long campaign of vandalism, in which road signs were painted over, television masts torn down, and weekend cottages owned by English people set alight. More than a hundred people were imprisoned during the campaign. Today, although still very much a minority tongue, Welsh is more robust than many other small European languages – certainly in much better health than the Breton language of France, its closest relation. (Breton and Welsh are so close that speakers from the two regions can converse, though they have lived apart for 1,500 years.) Its numbers are falling, but it is still spoken by half a million people.

The position is somewhat less buoyant for the Gaelic of Ireland. There too the government has been a generous defender of the language, but with less visible success. Ireland is not even officially an English-speaking country. Yet 94 per cent of her citizens speak only English and just 1 per cent use Gaelic as their preferred language. Ireland is the only member of the Common Market that does not insist on having its own language used in community business, largely because it would be pointless. The dearth of Gaelic speakers does convey certain advantages to those who have mastery of the tongue. The *Spectator* magazine noted in 1986 how Dr Conor Cruise O'Brien would respond to an awkward question in the Dáil, or lower house of parliament, by emitting a mellifluous flurry of Gaelic, which most of the members of his audience could but admire if not even faintly understand.

The Irish-speaking area of Ireland, called the Gaeltacht, has been inexorably shrinking for a long time. Even before the potato famine of 1845 drove hundreds of thousands of people from the land, only a quarter of the population spoke Gaelic. Today Gaelic clings to a few scattered outposts, mostly along the rocky and underpopulated west coast. This has long been one of the most depressed, if fabulously scenic, areas of Europe. The government has tried to shore up the perennially faltering economy by bringing in tourists and industry, but this has put an inevitable strain on the local culture. In the 1970s the population of Donegal, the main Irish-speaking area, increased by a fifth, but the newcomers were almost entirely English speakers who not only cannot speak Gaelic but have little desire to learn a language that is both difficult and so clearly doomed.

All the evidence suggests that minority languages shrink or thrive at their own ineluctable rate. It seems not to matter greatly whether governments suppress them brutally or support them lavishly. Despite all the encouragement and subsidization given to Gaelic in Ireland, it is spoken by twice as many people in Scotland, where there has been negligible government assistance. Indeed, Scottish Gaelic is one of the few minority languages in the world to be growing. Gaelic was introduced to Scotland by invaders from Ireland thirteen centuries ago and long held sway in the more remote islands and glens along the western side of the country. From 80,000 speakers in 1960 the number has now crept up to a little over 90,000 today. Even so, Gaelic speakers account for just 2.5 per cent of the Scottish population.

But almost everywhere else the process is one of slow, steady, and all too often terminal decline. The last speaker of Cornish as a mother tongue died 200 years ago, and though constant efforts are made to revive the language, no more than fifty or sixty people can speak it fluently enough to hold a conversation. It survives only in two or three dialect words, most notably *emmets* ('ants'), the word locals use to describe the tourists who come crawling over their gorgeous landscape each summer. A similar fate befell Manx, a Celtic language spoken on the Isle of Man, whose last native speakers died in the 1960s.

The Gaelic of Ireland may well be the next to go. In 1983, Bord na Gaelige, the government body charged with preserving the language, wrote: 'There is very little hope indeed that Irish will survive as a community language in the Gaeltacht beyond the end of the century' – an uncharacteristically downbeat, if sadly realistic, assessment.

We naturally lament the decline of these languages, but it is not an altogether undiluted tragedy. Consider the loss to English literature if Joyce, Shaw, Swift, Yeats, Wilde, Synge, Behan, and Ireland's other literary masters had written in what is inescapably a fringe language. Their works would be as little known to us as those of the poets of Iceland or Norway, and that would be a tragedy indeed. No country has given the world more incomparable literature per head of population than Ireland, and for that reason alone we might be excused a small, selfish celebration that English was the language of her greatest writers.

4

THE FIRST THOUSAND YEARS

In the country inns of a small corner of northern Germany, in the spur of land connecting Schleswig-Holstein to Denmark, you can sometimes hear people talking in what sounds eerily like a lost dialect of English. Occasional snatches of it even make sense, as when they say that the 'veather ist cold' or inquire of the time by asking, 'What ist de clock?' According to Professor Hubertus Menke, head of the German Department at Kiel University, the language is 'very close to the way people spoke in Britain more than 1,000 years ago'.[1] This shouldn't entirely surprise us. This area of Germany, called Angeln, was once the seat of the Angles, one of the Germanic tribes that 1,500 years ago crossed the North Sea to Britain, where they displaced the native Celts and gave the world what would one day become its most prominent language.

Not far away, in the marshy headlands of northern Holland and western Germany, and on the long chain of wind-battered islands strung out along their coasts, live a group of people whose dialect is even more closely related to English. These are the 300,000 Frisians, whose Germanic tongue has been so little altered by time that many of them can, according to the linguistic historian Charlton Laird, still read the medieval epic *Beowulf* 'almost at sight'. They also share many striking similarities of vocabulary: the Frisian for boat is *boat* (as compared to the Dutch and German *boot*), rain is *rein* (German and Dutch *regen*), and goose is *goes* (Dutch and German *gans*).

In about A.D. 450, following the withdrawal of Roman troops from Britain, these two groups of people and two other related groups from the same corner of northern Europe, the Saxons and Jutes, began a long exodus to Britain. It was not so much an invasion as a series of opportunistic encroachments taking place over several generations. The tribes settled in different parts of Britain, each bringing its own variations in speech, some of which persist in Britain to this day, and they variously merged and subdivided until they had established seven small kingdoms and dominated most of the island, except for Wales, Scotland, and Cornwall, which remained Celtic strongholds.

That is about as much as we know – and much of that is supposition. We don't know exactly when or where the invasion began or how many people were involved. We don't know why the invaders gave up secure homes to chance their luck in hostile territory. Above all, we are not sure how well – or even if – the conquering tribes could understand each other. What is known is that although the Saxons continued to flourish on the continent, the Angles and Jutes are heard of there no more. They simply disappeared. Although the Saxons were the dominant group, the new nation gradually came to be known as England and its language as English, after the rather more obscure Angles. Again, no one knows quite why this should be.

The early Anglo-Saxons left no account of these events for the simple reason that they were, to use the modern phrase, functionally illiterate. They possessed a runic alphabet, which they used to scratch inscriptions on ceremonial stones called runes (hence the term *runic*) or occasionally as a means of identifying valued items, but they never saw their alphabet's potential as a way of communicating thoughts across time. In 1982, a gold medallion about the size of a 10p piece was found in a field in Suffolk. It had been dropped or buried by one of the very earliest of the intruders, sometime between A.D. 450 and 480. The medallion bears a runic inscription which says (or at least is thought to say): 'This she-wolf is a reward to my kinsman.' Not perhaps the most profound of statements, but it is the earliest surviving example of Anglo-Saxon writing in

Britain. It is, in other words, the first recorded sentence in English.

Not only were the Anglo-Saxons relatively uncultured, they were also pagan, a fact quaintly preserved in the names of four of our weekdays, Tuesday, Wednesday, Thursday, and Friday, which respectively commemorate the gods Tiw, Woden, and Thor, and Woden's wife, Frig. (Saturday, Sunday, and Monday, to complete the picture, take their names from Saturn, the sun, and the moon.)

It is difficult to conceive of the sense of indignity that the Celts must have felt at finding themselves overrun by primitive, unlettered warriors from the barbaric fringes of the Roman empire. For the Celts, without any doubt, were a sophisticated people. As Laird notes: 'The native Celts had become civilized, law-abiding people, accustomed to government and reliable police, nearly as helpless before an invading host as most modern civilian populations would be.' Many of them enjoyed aspects of civilization – running water, central heating – which were quite unknown to the conquering hordes and indeed would not become common again in Britain for nearly 1,500 years. For almost four centuries they had been part of the greatest civilization the world had known, and enjoyed the privileges and comforts that went with it. A tantalizing glimpse into the daily life and cosmopolitan nature of Roman Britain surfaced in 1987 with the discovery of a hoard of curse tablets in Bath near a spring once dedicated to the goddess Sulis Minerva. It was the practice of aggrieved citizens at that time to scratch a curse on a lead tablet and toss it with a muttered plea for vengeance into the spring. The curses were nothing if not heartfelt. A typical one went: 'Docimedes has lost two gloves and asks that person who has stolen them should lose his minds and his eyes.' The tablets are interesting in that they show that people of Roman Britain were just as troubled by petty thievery (and, not incidentally, just as prone to misspellings and lapses of grammar) as we are today, but also they underline the diversity of the culture. One outstandingly suspicious victim of some minor pilferage meticulously listed the eighteen people he thought most likely to have perpetrated the deed. Of these eighteen names, two are Greek, eight Latin, and eight Celtic. It is clear that after nearly four centuries of living side by side, and often intermarrying,* relations between the Romans and Celts had become so close as to be, in many respects, indistinguishable.

In 410, with their empire crumbling, the Roman legions withdrew from Britain and left the Celts to their fate. Under the slow pagan onslaught, many Celts were absorbed or slaughtered. Others fled to the westernmost fringes of the British Isles or across the Channel to France, where they founded the colony of Brittany and reintroduced Celtic to mainland Europe. Some Celts stayed and fought – among them the semi-legendary King Arthur – and there is evidence from place names to suppose that pockets of Celtic culture survived for some time in England (around Shaftesbury in northeast Dorset, for example). But little is known for sure. This was the darkest of the dark ages, a period when history blends with myth and proof grows scant.

The first comprehensive account of the period is *The Ecclesiastical History of the English People*, written in Latin by the Venerable Bede, a monk at Jarrow in Northumbria. Although it is thought to be broadly accurate, Bede's history was written almost 300 years after the events it describes – which is rather like us writing a history of Elizabethan England based on hearsay.

Despite their long existence on the island – the Romans for 367 years, the Celts for at least 1,000 – they left precious little behind. Many English place names are Celtic in origin (Avon and Thames, for instance) or Roman (the *-chester* in Manchester and the *-caster* in Lancaster both come from the Roman word for camp), but in terms of everyday vocabulary it was almost as if they had never been. In Spain and Gaul the Roman

---

*To take a notable but little-known example, Saint Patrick, the patron saint of Ireland, was the son of a Roman official and his British wife. Far from being Irish, as is commonly supposed, Saint Patrick was Welsh. The only reason he ended up in Ireland was that he was kidnapped at the age of sixteen and taken there by Irish pirates.

occupation resulted in entirely new languages, Spanish and French, but in Britain they left barely five words,[2] while the Celts left no more than twenty – mostly geographical terms to describe the more hilly and varied British landscape.

This singular lack of linguistic influence is all the more surprising when you consider that the Anglo-Saxons had freely, and indeed gratefully, borrowed vocabulary from the Romans on the continent before coming to the British Isles, taking such words as *street, pillow, wine, inch, mile, table*, and *chest*, among many others. The list of mundane items for which they lacked native terms underlines the poverty of their culture.

And yet for all their shortcomings, the Anglo-Saxons possessed a language that was, in the phrase of Otto Jespersen, 'rich in possibilities', and once literacy was brought to them, it flowered with astonishing speed. The main bringer of literacy, and of Christianity, was St Augustine, who travelled to Britain with forty missionaries in 597 and within a year had converted King Ethelbert of Kent at his small provincial capital, Canterbury (which explains why the head of the English church is called the Archbishop of Canterbury, even though he resides in London). With that initial victory, Christianity quickly spread over the island, towing literacy in its wake. In only a little over 100 years England became a centre of culture and learning as great as any in Europe.

No one, of course, can say at what point English became a separate language, distinct from the Germanic dialects of mainland Europe. What is certain is that the language the invaders brought with them soon began to change. Like the Indo-European from which it sprang, it was a wondrously complex tongue. Nouns had three genders and could be inflected for up to five cases. As with modern European languages, gender was often arbitrary. *Wheat*, for example, was masculine, while *oats* was feminine and *corn* neuter,[3] just as in modern German *police* is feminine while *girl* is neuter. Modern English, by contrast, has essentially abandoned cases except with personal pronouns where we make distinctions between *I / me / mine, he / him / his*, and so on.

Old English had seven classes of strong verbs and three of weak, and their endings altered in relation to number, tense, mood, and person (though, oddly, there was no specific future tense). Adjectives and pronouns were also variously inflected. A single adjective like *green* or *big* could have up to eleven forms. Even something as basic as the definite article *the* could be masculine, feminine, or neuter, and had five case-forms as a singular and four as a plural. It is a wonder that anyone ever learned to speak it.

And yet for all its grammatical complexity Old English is not quite as remote from modern English as it sometimes appears. *Scip*, *bæð*, *bricg*, and *þæt* might look wholly foreign but their pronunciations – respectively 'ship', 'bath', 'bridge', and 'that' – have not altered in a thousand years. Indeed, if you take twenty minutes to familiarize yourself with the differences in Old English spelling and pronunciation – learning that *i* corresponds to the modern 'ee' sound, that *e* sounds like 'ay' and so on – you can begin to pick your way through a great deal of abstruse-looking text. You also find that in terms of sound values Old English is a much simpler and more reliable language with every letter distinctly and invariably related to a single sound. There were none of the silent letters or phonetic inconsistencies that bedevil modern English spelling.

There was, in short, a great deal of subtlety and flexibility built into the language, and once the Anglo-Saxons learned to write, their literary outpouring was both immediate and astonishingly assured. This cultural flowering found its sharpest focus in the far northern kingdom of Northumbria. Here, on the outermost edge of the civilized world, sprang forth England's first great poet, the monastic Cædmon; its first great historian, the Venerable Bede; and its first great scholar, Alcuin of York, who became head of Charlemagne's palace school at Aachen and was one of the progenitors of the Renaissance. 'The light of learning then shone more brightly in Northumbria than anywhere else in Europe,' Simeon Potter noted without hyperbole in *Our Language*. Had it not been for Alcuin much of our ancient history would almost certainly have been lost. 'People don't always realize,' wrote Kenneth Clark, 'that only three or four antique manuscripts of the Latin authors are still in existence: our whole knowledge of ancient literature is due to the collecting and copying that began under Charlemagne.'[4]

Barely had this cultural revival begun than England and her infant language were under attack again – this time by Viking raiders from Scandinavia and Denmark. These were people who were related to the Anglo-Saxons by both blood and language. In fact, they were so closely related that they could probably broadly understand each other's languages, though this must have been small comfort to the monks, farmers, and ravaged women who suffered their pillaging. These attacks on Britain were part of a huge, uncoordinated, and mysterious expansion by the Vikings (or Norsemen or Danes, as history has variously called them). No one knows why these previously mild and pastoral people suddenly became aggressive and adventurous, but for two centuries they were everywhere – in Russia, Iceland, Britain, France, Ireland, Greenland, even North America. At first, in Britain, the attacks consisted of smash-and-grab raids, mostly along the east coast. The famous monastery of Lindisfarne was sacked in 793 and the nearby monastery of Jarrow, where Bede had laboured, fell the following year.

Then, just as mysteriously, the raids ceased and for half a century the waters around the British Isles were quiet. But this was, to dust off that useful cliché, the calm before the storm, a period in which the inhabitants must have watched the coast with unease. In 850 their worst fears were confirmed when some 350 heavily laden Viking ships sailed up the Thames, setting off a series of battles for control of territory that went on for years, rolling across the British landscape rather like two wrestlers, with fortune favouring first one side and then the other. Finally, after an unexpected English victory in 878, a treaty was signed establishing the Danelaw, a line running roughly between London and Chester, dividing control of Britain between the English in the south and the Danes in the north. To this day it remains an important linguistic dividing line between northern and southern dialects.

The Danish influence in the north was enormous. The scale of their settlements can be seen from the fact that more than 1,400 place names in northern England are of Scandinavian origin. For a long time, the people in some places spoke only Old English while in other places, often on the next hillside, they spoke only Old Norse. Occasionally this arrangement lasted for years – in the Shetland Islands it lasted for centuries, with the people speaking a Norwegian dialect called Norn until well into the 1700s, of which some 1,500 dialect words survive to this day – but for the most part the two linguistic sides underwent a relaxed and peaceful merger. A great many Scandinavian terms were adopted, without which English would clearly be the poorer: *freckle, leg, skull, meek, rotten, clasp, crawl, dazzle, scream, trust, lift, take, husband, sky*. Sometimes these replaced Old English words, but often they took up residence alongside them, adding a useful synonym to the language, so that today in English we have both *craft* and *skill*, *wish* and *want*, *raise* and *rear*, and many other doublets. Sometimes the words came from the same source but had grown slightly different in pronunciation, as with *shriek* and *screech*, *no* and *nay*, or *ditch* and *dike*, and sometimes they went a further step and acquired slightly different meanings, as with *scatter* and *shatter*, *skirt* and *shirt*, *whole* and *hale*, *bathe* and *bask*, *stick* and *stitch*, *hack* and *hatch*, *wake* and *watch*, *break* and *breach*.

But most remarkably of all, the English adopted certain grammatical forms. The pronouns *they, them*, and *their* are Scandinavian. This borrowing of basic elements of syntax is highly unusual, perhaps unique among developed languages, and an early demonstration of the remarkable adaptability of English speakers.

One final cataclysm awaited the English language: the Norman conquest of 1066. The Normans were Vikings who had settled in northern France 200 years before. Like the Celtic Britons before them, they had given their name to a French province, Normandy. But unlike the Celts, they had

45

abandoned their language and much of their culture and become French in manner and speech. So totally had they given up their language, in fact, that not a single Norse word has survived in Normandy, apart from some place names. That is quite remarkable when you consider that the Normans bequeathed 10,000 words to English. The variety of French the Normans spoke was not the speech of Paris, but a rural dialect, and its divergence from standard French became even more pronounced when it took root in England – so much so that historians refer to it not as French, but as Anglo-Norman. This, as we shall see in a moment, had important consequences for the English language of today and may even have contributed to its survival.

No king of England spoke English for the next 300 years. It was not until 1399, with the accession of Henry IV, that England had a ruler whose mother tongue was English. One by one English earls and bishops were replaced by Normans (though in some instances not for several years). French-speaking craftsmen, designers, cooks, scholars, and scribes were brought to Britain. Even so, for the common people life went on. They were almost certainly not alarmed that their rulers spoke a foreign tongue. It was commonplace in the past. Canute from the century before was Danish, and even Edward the Confessor, the last but one Anglo-Saxon king, spoke French as his first tongue. As recently as the eighteenth century, England happily installed a German king, George I, even though he spoke not a word of English and reigned for thirteen years without mastering his subjects' language. Common people did not expect to speak like their masters any more than they expected to live like them.

Norman society had two tiers: the French-speaking aristocracy and the English-speaking peasantry. Not surprisingly, the linguistic influence of the Normans tended to focus on matters of court, government, fashion, and high living. Meanwhile, the English peasant continued to eat, drink, work, sleep, and play in English. The breakdown can be illustrated in two ways. First, the more humble trades tended to have Anglo-Saxon names (baker, miller, shoemaker), while the more skilled trades adopted French names (mason, painter, tailor). At the same time, animals in the field usually were called by English names (sheep, cow, ox), but once cooked and brought to the table, they were generally given French names (beef, mutton, veal, bacon).*

Anglo-Norman differed from the standard French of Paris in several ways. For one thing, Parisian French, called Francien, tended to avoid the 'w' sound. So while the Normans pronounced *quit, question, quarter*, and other such words as if they were spelled *kwit, kwestion*, and *kwarter*, Parisians pronounced them with a hard 'k' sound. Equally, standard French used *cha-* in some constructions where the Normans used *ca-*. Thus we have such differences as *carry/charrier, cauldron/chaudron, cattle/chattel*. (Our word *chattel* was adopted later.) The Normans used the suffixes *-arie* and *-orie*, while the French used *-aire* and *-oire*, which gives us such pairings as *victory/victoire* and *salary/salaire*. Anglo-Norman kept the *s* in words such as *August, forest*, and *beast*, while Francien gradually forsook them for a circumflex: *Août, forêt, bête*.[5]

Norman French, like the Germanic tongues before it, made a lasting impact on English vocabulary. Of the 10,000 words adopted from Norman French, some three-quarters are still in use – among them *justice, jury, felony, traitor, petty, damage, prison, marriage, sovereign, parliament, govern, prince, duke, viscount, baron*. In fact, nearly all our words relating to jurisprudence and government are of French origin, as are many of the ranks of aristocracy, such as *countess, duke, duchess*, and *baron*, but not – perhaps a bit oddly – *king* and *queen*. At the same time, many English words were adopted into French. Sometimes it is not possible to tell who was borrowing from whom – whether, for example, we took *aggressive* from the Normans or they took

*It should be noted that Burchfield, in *The English Language*, calls this distinction between field names and food names 'an enduring myth' on the grounds that the French terms were used for living animals as well (he cites Samuel Johnson referring to a cow as 'a beef'), but even so I think the statement above is a reasonable generalization.

their *aggressif* from us, or whether the English *intensity* came before or after the Norman *intensité*. In other matters, such as syntax, their influence was less dramatic. Only a few expressions like *court martial*, *attorney general*, and *body politic* reflect the habits of French word ordering.

Because English had no official status, for three centuries it drifted. Without a cultural pivot, some place to set a standard, differences in regional usage became more pronounced rather than less. As C. L. Barber notes: 'Early Middle English texts give the impression of a chaos of dialects, without many common conventions in pronunciation or spelling, and with wide divergences in grammar and vocabulary.'[6]

And yet it survived. If there is one uncanny thing about the English language, it is its incredible persistence. In retrospect it seems unthinkable to us now that it might have been otherwise, but we forget just how easily people forsake their tongues – as the Celts did in Spain and France, as the Vikings did in Normandy, and as the Italians, Poles, Africans, Russians, and countless others all did in America. And yet in Britain, despite the constant buffetings of history, English survived. It is a cherishable irony that a language that succeeded almost by stealth, treated for centuries as the inadequate and second-rate tongue of peasants, should one day become the most important and successful language in the world.

Its lowly position almost certainly helped English to become a simpler, less inflected language. As Baugh and Cable note: 'By making English the language mainly of uneducated people, the Norman conquest made it easier for grammatical changes to go forward unchecked.' In Old English, as we have seen, most verbs were not only highly inflected, but also changed consonants from one form to the next, but these were gradually regularized and only one such form survives to this day – *was/were*. An explicit example of this simplification can be seen in the *Peterborough Chronicle*, a yearly account of Anglo-Saxon life kept by the monks at Peterborough. Because of turmoil in the country, work on the chronicle was suspended for twenty-three years between 1131 and 1154, just at the period when

English was beginning to undergo some of its most dramatic changes. In the earlier section, the writing is in Old English. But when the chronicle resumes in 1154, the language is immeasurably simpler – gender is gone, as are many declensions and conjugations, and the spelling has been greatly simplified. To modern eyes, the earlier half looks to be a foreign language; the later half is unmistakably English. The period of Middle English had begun.

Several events helped. One was the loss of Normandy to the French crown by the hapless King John in 1204. Isolated from the rest of Europe by the English Channel, the Norman rulers gradually came to think of themselves not as displaced Frenchmen but as Englishmen. Intermarrying between Normans and British contributed to the sense of Englishness. The children of these unions learned French from their fathers, but English from their mothers and nannies. Often they were more comfortable with English. The Normans, it must be said, were never hostile to English. William the Conqueror himself tried to learn it, though without success, and there was never any campaign to suppress it.

Gradually, English reasserted itself. French remained, until 1362, the language of Parliament and, for somewhat longer, of the courts, but only for official purposes – rather like Latin in the Catholic church. For a time, at least up until the age of Chaucer, the two coexisted. Barnett notes that when the Dean of Windsor wrote a letter to Henry IV the language drifted unselfconsciously back and forth between English and French. This was in 1403, three years after the death of Chaucer, so it is clear that French lingered. And yet it was doomed.

By the late twelfth century some Norman children were having to be taught French before they could be sent away to school. By the end of the fourteenth century Oxford University introduced a statute ordering that students be taught at least partly in French 'lest the French language be entirely disused'. In some court documents of this period the syntax makes it clear that the judgements, though rendered in French, had been thought out in English. Those who could afford it

WHAT'S WRONG NOW?

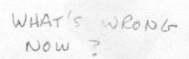

sent their children to Paris to learn the more fashionable Central French dialect, which had by this time become almost a separate language. There is telling evidence of this in *The Canterbury Tales*, when Chaucer notes that one of his pilgrims, the Prioress, speaks a version of French known only in London, 'For Frensh of Paris was to hir unknowe'.

/ The harsh, clacking, guttural Anglo-French had become a source of amusement to the people of Paris, and this provided perhaps the ultimate – and certainly the most ironic – blow to the language in England. Norman aristocrats, rather than be mocked for persevering with an inferior dialect that many of them spoke badly anyway, began to take an increasing pride in English. So total was this reversal of attitude that when Henry V was looking for troops to fight with him at Agincourt in 1415, he used the French threat to the English language as a rallying cry. /

So English triumphed at last, though of course it was a very different language – in many ways a quite separate language – from the Old English of Alfred the Great. In fact, Old English would have seemed as incomprehensible to Geoffrey Chaucer as it does to us, so great had been the change in the time of the Normans. It was simpler in grammar, vastly richer in vocabulary. Alongside the Old English *motherhood*, we now had *maternity*, with *friendship* we had *amity*, with *brotherhood, fraternity*, and so on.

Under the long onslaught from the Scandinavians and Normans, Anglo-Saxon had taken a hammering. According to one estimate,[7] about 85 per cent of the 30,000 Anglo-Saxon words died out under the influence of the Danes and Normans. That meant that only about 4,500 Old English words survived – about 1 per cent of the total number of words in the *Oxford English Dictionary*. And yet those surviving words are among the most fundamental words in English: *man, wife, child, brother, sister, live, fight, love, drink, sleep, eat, house*, and so on. They also include most of the short 'function' words of the language: *to, for, but, and, at, in, on*, and so forth. As a result, at least half the words in almost any sample of modern English writing will be of Anglo-Saxon origin. According to another study cited by McCrum,[8] every one of the 100 most common words in English is Anglo-Saxon. To this day we have an almost instinctive preference for the older Anglo-Saxon phrases. As Simeon Potter has neatly put it: 'We feel more at ease getting a *hearty welcome* than after being granted a *cordial reception*.'

It is sometimes suggested that our vocabulary is vast because it was made to be, simply because of the various linguistic influences that swept over it. But in fact this love of variety of expression runs deeper than that. It was already evident in the early poetry of the Anglo-Saxons that they had an intuitive appreciation of words sufficient to ensure that even if England had never been invaded again her language would have been rich with synonyms. As Jespersen notes, in *Beowulf* alone there are thirty-six words for hero, twelve for battle, eleven for ship – in short, probably more than exist today.

It is true that English was immeasurably enriched by the successive linguistic waves that washed over the British Isles. But it is probably closer to the truth to say that the language we speak today is rich and expressive not so much because new words were imposed on it as because they were welcomed.

Thanks to the proliferation of English dialects during the period of Norman rule, by the fifteenth century people in one part of England often could not understand people in another part. William Caxton, the first person to print a book in English, noted the sort of misunderstandings that were common in his day in the preface to *Eneydos* in 1490 in which he related the story of a group of London sailors heading down the 'tamyse' for Holland who found themselves becalmed in Kent. Seeking food, one of them approached a farmer's wife and 'axed for mete and specyally he axyd after eggys' but was met with blank looks by the wife who answered that she 'coude speke no frenshe'. The sailors had travelled barely fifty miles and yet their language was scarcely recognizable to another speaker of English. In Kent, eggs were *eyren* and would remain so for at least another fifty years.

A century later the poet George Puttenham noted that the English of London stretched not much more than sixty miles from the city. But its influence was growing all the time. The size and importance of London guaranteed that its dialect would eventually triumph, though other factors helped – such as the fact that the East Midlands dialect (its formal if somewhat misleading name) had fewer grammatical extremes than other dialects and that the East Midlands area was the seat of the two main universities, Oxford and Cambridge, whose graduates naturally tended to act as linguistic missionaries.

Chaucer's was the language of London – and therefore comparatively easy for us to follow. We may not instantly comprehend all the words, but when we see the prologue of *The Canterbury Tales* we can at the very least recognize it as English:

> Whan that Aprille with his shoures sote
> The droghte of Marche hath perced to the rote,
> And bathed every veyne in swich licour,
> Of which vertu engendred is the flour.

Compare that with this passage in the Kentish dialect written at about the same time: 'And vorlet ous oure yeldinges: ase and we vorleteþ oure yelderes, and ne ous led naȝt, in-to vondinge, ac vri ous vram queade.' Recognize it? It's the last sentence of the Lord's Prayer, beginning, 'And forgive us our trespasses . . .' As the Chaucer authority David Burnley notes, many of the poet's contemporaries outside London were still using spellings and phrasings that 'make their works scarcely intelligible to us without special study'.[9] Some of the dialects of the north were virtually foreign languages – and indeed can sometimes still seem so.

This was a period of the most enormous and rapid change in English, as Caxton himself noted when he wrote: 'And certaynly our langage now used varyeth ferre [far] from that which was used and spoken when I was borne.' Caxton was born just twenty-two years after Chaucer died, yet in the space of that time the English of London moved from being medieval to modern. The difference is striking. Where even now we can understand Chaucer only with a fair lavishing of footnotes, Caxton can be as easily followed as Shakespeare. Caxton's spellings often look curious to us today, but the vocabulary is little changed, and we can read him at more or less normal speed, as when he writes: 'I was sittyng in my study [when] to my hands came a lytle booke in frenshe, which late was translated oute of latyn by some noble clerke of fraunce . . .'

Even so, English by Chaucer's time had already undergone many consequential changes. The most notable is that it had lost most of its inflections. Gender had disappeared in the north of England and was on its knees in the south. Adjectives, which had once been inflected up to eleven ways, now had just two inflections, for singular and plural (e.g. a fressh floure, but fresshe floures), but even here there was a growing tendency to use one form all the time, as we do today.

Sometimes words were modified in one grammatical circumstance but left untouched in another. That is why we have *knife* with an *f* but *knives* with a *v*. Other such pairs are *half/halves, grass/graze, grief/grieve, calf/calves*. Sometimes there was a spelling change as well, as with the second vowel in *speech* and *speak*. Sometimes the pronunciation changed, as between *bath* and *bathe* and as with the 's' in *house* becoming a 'z' in *houses*. And sometimes, to the eternal confusion of non-English speakers, these things happened all together, so that we have not only the spelling doublet *life/lives* but also the pronunciation doublet 'līves' and 'lĭves' as in 'a cat with nine lives lives next door'. Sometimes, too, conflicting regional usages have left us with two forms of the word, such as *fox* with an *f*, but *vixen* with a *v*, or given us two spellings for words, such as *phial* and *vial*. And sometimes, as we shall see later, it left us with some of the most wildly unphonetic spellings of any language in the world.

Although East Midlands was the pre-eminent dialect, not all East Midlands forms triumphed. The practice in London of placing *-n* or *-en* on the end of present indicative verbs was gradually driven out by the southern practice of using *-th*, so that *loven* became *loveth*, for instance, and this in turn was eventually driven out by the northern -*s* or -*es* ending, as in the modern form *loves*. Why this northern provincialism should gradually have taken command of a basic verb form is an enduring mystery. It may simply be that the -*s* form made for smoother spoken English. In any case, by Shakespeare's time it was much more common in speech than in writing, though Shakespeare himself freely used both forms, sometimes employing *goes*, sometimes *goeth*.

Casualness of usage and style was a hallmark of the Middle and early Modern English periods. Chaucer sometimes used *doughtren* for the plural of *daughters* and sometimes *doughtres*, sometimes *yeer* and sometimes *yeres*. Like other writers of the period, he appeared to settle on whichever form first popped into his head, even at the risk of being inconsistent from one paragraph to the next.

But, I must quickly interject, a problem with interpreting Chaucer is that not one of his original manuscripts survives. Everything we have of his was copied by medieval scribes, who sometimes took extraordinary liberties with the text, seeing themselves more as editors than as copyists. At the same time, they were often strikingly careless. For example, the Clerk's Tale contains the line 'Ther stood a throop of site delitable', but in various manuscripts *site* is rendered as *sighte*, *syth*, *sigh*, and *cite*. It is impossible at this remove to know which was the word Chaucer intended. Literally scores of such confusions and inconsistencies clutter the manuscripts of most poets of the age, which makes an analysis of changes in the language problematic. It is often noted that Chaucer's spelling was wildly inconsistent: *cunt*, if you will forgive an excursion into crudity (as we so often must when dealing with Chaucer), is spelled in at least five ways in his works, ranging from *kent* to *quainte*. So it isn't possible to say whether the inconsistency lies with Chaucer or his copyists or both.

Other forms, such as plural pronouns, had yet to settle. Chaucer used *hi*, *hem*, and *her* for *they*, *them*, and *their* (*her* for *their* survived up to the time of Shakespeare, who used it at least twice in his plays). Similarly *his*, where we now use *its*, was the usual form until about 1600, which is why the King James Bible is full of constructions like 'If the salt has lost his savour, wherewith shall it be salted?' Similarly, *which* was until about the same time often applied to animate things as well as inanimate, as in the Lord's Prayer: 'Our Father which art in heaven'.

In Old English there were at least six endings that denoted plurals, but by Shakespeare's time these had by and large shrunk to two: *-s* and *-en*. But even then the process was nowhere near complete. In the Elizabethan Age, people sometimes said *shoes* and sometimes *shoen*, sometimes *houses* and sometimes *housen*. It is interesting to reflect that had the seat of government stayed in Winchester, rather than moved the sixty miles or so to London, we would today very probably be talking of six housen and a pair of shoen. Today just three of these old weak plurals remain: *children*, *brethren*, and *oxen*. However, even though *-s* (or *-es* after an *-sh* spelling) has become the standard form for plurals, traces of the complex Old English system lurk in the language in plurals such as *men*, *women*, *feet*, *geese*, and *teeth*.

Similarly, verbs have undergone a long and erratic process of regularization. Chaucer could choose between *ached* and *oke*, *climbed* and *clomb*, *clew* or *clawed*, *shaved* and *shove*. In Shakespeare's time *forgat* and *digged* were legitimate past tenses. In fact, until well into the seventeenth century *digged* was the more common (as in Shakespeare's 'two kinsmen digg'd their grave with weeping'). As recently as 1751, Thomas Gray's famous poem was published as 'Elegy Wrote in a Country Churchyard'. Seventy years later the poet John Keats could write, 'Let my epitaph be: here lies one whose name was writ on water.' So the invariable pattern we use today – *write*, *wrote*, *written* – is really quite recent.

The common pattern in these changes was for the weak verbs to drive out the strong ones, but sometimes it worked the other way, so that today we have *torn* instead of *teared* and *knew* rather than *knowed*. Many of these have become regularized, but there are still 250 irregular verbs in English, and a surprising number of these are still fluid – so that even now most of us are not always sure whether we should say *dived* or *dove*, *sneaked* or *snuck*, *hove* or *heaved*, *wove* or *weaved*, *strived* or *strove*, *swelled* or *swollen*.

Other words underwent changes, particularly those beginning with *n*, where there was a tendency for this letter to drift away from the word and attach itself to the preceding indefinite article. The process is called metanalysis. Thus a *napron* became an *apron*, a *nauger* became an *auger*, and an *ekename* became (over time) a *nickname*. By a similar process, the nicknames Ned, Nell, and Nan are thought to be corruptions of 'mine Edward', 'mine Ellen', and 'mine Ann'.[10]

But there were losses along the way. Today we have two demonstrative pronouns, *this* and *that*, but in Shakespeare's day there was a third, *yon*, which denoted a further distance than *that*. You could talk about this hat, that hat, and yon hat. Today the word survives as a colloquialism, *yonder*, but our speech is fractionally impoverished for its loss.

(Other languages possess even further degrees of thatness. As Pei notes, 'The Cree Indian language has a special *that* [for] things just gone out of sight, while Ilocano, a tongue of the Philippines, has three words for *this* referring to a visible object, a fourth for things not in view and a fifth for things that no longer exist.')[11]

Some of the changes since Shakespeare's time are obvious. *Thee* and *thou* had already begun a long decline (though they still exist in some dialects of northern England). Originally *thou* was to *you* as in French *tu* is to *vous*. *Thou* signified either close familiarity or social inferiority, while *you* was the more impersonal and general term. In European languages to this day choosing between the two forms can present a very real social agony. As Jespersen, a Dane who appreciated these things, put it: 'English has thus attained the only manner of address worthy of a nation that respects the elementary rights of each individual.'[12]

The changing structure of English allowed writers the freedom to express themselves in ways that had never existed

56

before, and none took up this opportunity more liberally than Shakespeare, who happily and variously used nouns as verbs, as adverbs, as substantives, and as adjectives – often in ways they had never been employed before. He even used adverbs as adjectives, as with 'that bastardly rogue,' in *Henry IV*, a construction that must have seemed as novel then as it does now. He created expressions that could not grammatically have existed previously – such as 'breathing one's last' and 'backing a horse'.

No one in any tongue has ever made greater play of his language. He coined some 2,000 words – an astonishing number – and gave us countless phrases. As a phrasemaker there has never been anyone to match him. Among his inventions: one fell swoop, in my mind's eye, more in sorrow than in anger, to be in a pickle, bag and baggage, vanish into thin air, budge an inch, play fast and loose, go down the primrose path, the milk of human kindness, remembrance of things past, the sound and the fury, to thine own self be true, to be or not to be, cold comfort, to beggar all description, salad days, flesh and blood, foul play, tower of strength, to be cruel to be kind, and on and on and on and on. And on. He was so wildly prolific that he could put two in one sentence, as in Hamlet's observation: 'Though I am native here and to the manner born, it is a custom more honoured in the breach than the observance.' He could even mix metaphors and get away with it, as when he wrote: 'Or to take arms against a sea of troubles.'

It is terrifying to think that had not two faithful followers, the actors John Hemming and Henry Condell, taken the considerable trouble of assembling an anthology of his work, the famous First Folio, in 1623, seven years after his death, sixteen of his plays would very probably have been lost to us for ever. As it is two have been: *Cardenio* and *Love's Labour's Won*.

Not a single Shakespeare manuscript survives, so, as with Chaucer, we cannot be sure how closely the work we know is really Shakespeare's. Hemming and Condell consulted any

number of sources to produce their folio – printers' manuscripts, actors' promptbooks, even the memories of other actors.
But from what happened to the work of other authors it is
probable that they have been changed a lot. One of Shakespeare's publishers was Richard Field and it is known from
extant manuscripts that when Field published the work of the
poet John Harrington he made more than a thousand changes
to the spelling and phrasing. It is unlikely that he did less with
Shakespeare, particularly since Shakespeare himself seemed
singularly unconcerned with what became of his work after his
death. As far as is known, he did not bother to save any of his
poems and plays – a fact that is sometimes taken as evidence
that he didn't write them.

There have been many other more subtle changes in English
since Shakespeare's day. One has been the rise of the progressive verb form. Where we would say, 'What are you
reading?' Shakespeare could only say, 'What do you read?' He
would have had difficulty expressing the distinctions contained
in 'I am going', 'I was going', 'I have been going', and 'I will
(or shall) be going'. The passive progressive construction, as in
'The house is being built', was quite unknown to him. Yet it
goes without saying that this scarcely slowed him down.

Even in its greatest flowering English was still considered in
many respects a second-rate language. Newton's *Principia* and
Bacon's *Novum Organum* were both published in Latin. Sir
Thomas More wrote *Utopia* in Latin. William Harvey wrote
his treatise on the circulation of blood (written in 1616, the
year of Shakespeare's death) in Latin. Edward Gibbon wrote
his histories in French and then translated them into English.
As Baugh and Cable note, 'The use of English for purposes of
scholarship was frankly experimental.'

Moreover in Shakespeare's day English had yet to conquer
the whole of the British Isles. It was the language of England
and lowland Scotland, but it had barely penetrated into Wales,
Ireland, and the Scottish Highlands and islands – and would
not for some time. (As recently as this century Britain was able
to elect a prime minister whose native tongue was not English:

to wit, the Welsh-speaking David Lloyd George.) In 1582, the scholar Richard Mulcaster noted glumly: 'The English tongue is of small account, stretching no further than this island of ours, nay not there over all.'

He had no way of knowing that within less than a generation English would be transported to the New World, where it would begin its inexorable rise to becoming the foremost language of the world.

WHERE WORDS COME FROM

If you have a morbid fear of peanut butter sticking to the roof of your mouth, there is a word for it: *arachibutyrophobia*. There is a word to describe the state of being a woman: *muliebrity*. And there's a word for describing a sudden breaking off of thought: *aposiopesis*. If you harbour an urge to look through the windows of the homes you pass, there is a word for the condition: *crytoscopophilia*. When you are just dropping off to sleep and you experience that sudden sensation of falling, there is a word for it: it's a *myoclonic jerk*. If you want to say that a word has a circumflex on its penultimate syllable, without saying flat out that it has a circumflex there, there is a word for it: *properispomenon*. There is even a word for a figure of speech in which two connotative words linked by a conjunction express a complex notion that would normally be conveyed by an adjective and a substantive working together. It is a *hendiadys*. (But of course.) In English, in short, there are words for almost everything.

Some of these words deserve to be better known. Take *velleity*, which describes a mild desire, a wish or urge too slight to lead to action. Doesn't that seem a useful term? Or how about *slubberdegullion*, a seventeenth-century word signifying a worthless or slovenly fellow? Or *ugsome*, a late medieval word meaning loathsome or disgusting? It has lasted half a millennium in English, was a common synonym for *horrid* until well into the last century, and can still be found tucked away forgotten at the back of most unabridged dictionaries. Isn't it a shame to let it slip away? Our dictionaries are full of such words – words describing the most specific of conditions, the most improbable of contingencies, the most arcane of distinctions.

And yet there are odd gaps. We have no word for coolness corresponding to warmth. There is no word for the indentation on your upper lip. We are strangely lacking in middling terms – words to describe with some precision the middle ground between hard and soft, near and far, big and little. We have a possessive impersonal pronoun *its* to place alongside *his*, *her*, and *their*, but no equivalent impersonal pronoun to contrast with the personal *whose*. Thus we have to rely on inelegant constructions such as 'the house whose roof' or resort to periphrasis. We have a word to describe all the work you find waiting for you when you return from vacation, *backlog*, but none to describe all the work you have to do before you go. Why not *forelog*? And we have a large number of negative words – *inept, dishevelled, incorrigible, ruthless, unkempt* – for which the positive form is missing. English would be richer if we could say admiringly of a tidy person, 'She's *so* shevelled', or praise a capable person for being full of ept or an energetic one for having heaps of ert. Many of these words did once have positive forms. *Ruthless* was companioned by *ruth*, meaning compassion. One of Milton's poems contains the well-known line, 'Look homeward, Angel, now, and melt with ruth'. But, as with many such words, one form died and another lived. Why this should be is beyond explanation. Why should we have lost *demit* (send away) but saved *commit*? Why should *impede* have survived while the once equally common and seemingly just as useful *expede* expired? No one can say.

Despite these gaps and casualties, English retains probably the richest vocabulary, and most diverse shading of meanings, of any language. We can distinguish between house and home (as, for instance, the French cannot), between continual and continuous, sensual and sensuous, forceful and forcible, childish and childlike, masterly and masterful, assignment and assignation, informant and informer. For almost every word we have a multiplicity of synonyms. Something is not just big, it is large, immense, vast, capacious, bulky, massive, whopping. No other language has so many words all saying the same thing. It has been said that English is unique in possessing a synonym for each level of our culture: popular, literary, and scholarly – so that we can, according to our background and cerebral attainments, rise, mount, or ascend a stairway, shrink in fear, terror, or trepidation, and think, ponder, or cogitate upon a problem. This abundance of terms is often cited as a virtue. And yet a critic could equally argue that English is an untidy and acquisitive language, cluttered with a plethora of needless words. After all, do we really need *fictile* as a synonym for *mouldable*, *glabrous* for *hairless*, *sternutation* for *sneezing*? Jules Feiffer once drew a strip cartoon in which the down-at-heel character observed that first he was called poor, then needy, then deprived, then underprivileged, and then disadvantaged, and concluded that although he still didn't have a dime he sure had acquired a fine vocabulary. There is something in that. A rich vocabulary carries with it a concomitant danger of verbosity, as evidenced by our peculiar affection for redundant phrases, expressions that say the same thing twice: *beck and call, law and order, assault and battery, null and void, safe and sound, first and foremost, trials and tribulations, hem and haw, spick-and-span, kith and kin, dig and delve, hale and hearty, peace and quiet, vim and vigour, pots and pans, cease and desist, rack and ruin, without let or hindrance, to all intents and purposes, various different.*

Despite this bounty of terms, we have a strange – and to foreigners it must seem maddening – tendency to load a single word with a whole galaxy of meanings. *Fine*, for instance, has fourteen definitions as an adjective, six as a noun and two as an adverb. In the *Oxford English Dictionary* it fills two full pages and takes 5,000 words of description. We can talk about fine art, fine gold, a fine edge, feeling fine, fine hair, and a court fine and mean quite separate things. The condition of having many meanings is known as *polysemy*, and it is very common. *Sound* is another polysemic word. Its vast repertory of meanings can suggest an audible noise, a state of healthiness (sound mind), an outburst (sound off), an inquiry (sound out), a body of water (Puget Sound), or financial stability (sound economy), among many others. And then there's *round*. In the *OED*, *round* alone (that is without variants like *rounded* and *roundup*) takes 7½ pages to define, or about 15,000 words of text – about as much as is contained in the first forty pages of this book. Even when you strip out its obsolete senses, *round* still has twelve uses as an adjective, nineteen as a noun, seven as a transitive verb, five as an intransitive verb, one as an adverb, and two as a preposition. But the polysemic champion must be *set*. Superficially it looks a wholly unassuming monosyllable, the verbal equivalent of the single-celled organism. Yet it has 58 uses as a noun, 126 as a verb, and 10 as a participial adjective. Its meanings are so various and scattered that it takes the *OED* 60,000 words – the length of a short novel – to discuss them all. A foreigner could be excused for thinking that to know *set* is to know English.

Generally, polysemy happens because one word sprouts a variety of meanings, but sometimes it is the other way round – similar but quite separate words evolve identical spellings. *Boil* in the sense of heating a pan of water and *boil* in the sense of an irruption of the skin are two unrelated words that simply happen to be spelled the same way. So are *policy* in the sense of a strategy or plan and the *policy* in a life insurance policy. *Excise*, meaning 'to cut', is quite distinct in origin from *excise* in the sense of a customs duty.

Sometimes, just to heighten the confusion, the same word ends up with contradictory meanings. This kind of word is called a *contronym*. *Sanction*, for instance, can either signify permission to do something or a measure forbidding it to be done. *Cleave* can mean cut in half or stick together. A *sanguine* person is either hotheaded and bloodthirsty or calm and cheerful. Something that is *fast* is either stuck firmly or moving quickly. A door that is *bolted* is secure, but a horse that has *bolted* has taken off. If you *wind up* a meeting you finish it; if you *wind up* a watch, you start it. To *ravish* means to rape, but equally it means to enrapture. *Quinquennial* describes something that lasts for five years or happens only once in five years.

Trying one's best is a good thing, but *trying* one's patience is a bad thing. A *blunt* instrument is dull, but a *blunt* remark is pointed. Occasionally when this happens the dictionary makers give us different spellings to differentiate the two meanings – as with *flour* and *flower*, *discrete* and *discreet* – but such orthological thoughtfulness is rare.

So where do all these words come from? According to the great Danish linguist Otto Jespersen words are for the most part formed in one of four ways: by adding to them, by subtracting from them, by making them up, and by doing nothing to them. Neat as that formula is, I would venture to suggest that it overlooks two other prolific sources of new words: borrowing them from other languages and creating them by mistake. Let us look at each in turn.

1. WORDS ARE CREATED BY ERROR. One sort is called ghost words. The most famous of these perhaps is *dord*, which appeared in the 1934 *Merriam-Webster International Dictionary* as another word for density. In fact, it was a misreading of the scribbled 'D or d', meaning that 'density' could be abbreviated either to a capital or lower-case letter. The people at Merriam-Webster quickly removed it, but not before it found its way into other dictionaries. Such occurrences are more common than you might suppose. According to the First Supplement of the *OED*, there are at least 350 words in English dictionaries that owe their existence to typographical errors or other misrenderings. For the most part they are fairly obscure. One such is *messuage*, a legal term used to describe a house, its land and buildings. It is thought to be simply a careless transcription of the French *ménage*.

Many other words owe their existence to mishearings. *Button-hole* was once buttonhold. *Sweetheart* was originally *sweetard*, as in *dullard* and *dotard*. *Bridegroom* was in Old English *bryd-guma*, but the context made people think of *groom* and an *r* was added. By a similar process an *l* found its way into *belfrey*, even though, etymologically, the word has nothing to do with bells. *Asparagus* was for 200 years called *sparrow-grass*. *Pentice* became *penthouse*. *Shamefaced* was originally *shamefast* (*fast* here having the sense of lodged firmly, as in 'stuck fast'). The process can still be seen today in the tendency among many people to turn, for example, *chaise longue* into *chaise lounge*.

Sometimes words are created by false analogy or back-formation. One example of this is the word *pea*. Originally the word was *pease*, as in the nursery rhyme 'pease porridge hot, pease porridge cold'. But this was mistakenly thought to signify a plural and the word *pea* was back-formed to denote singularity. A similar misunderstanding gave us *cherry* (from *cerise*). Etymologically *cherries* ought to be both singular and plural – and indeed it once was. The words *grovel* and *sidle* similarly came into English because the original adjectives, *grovelling* and *sideling*, were assumed to contain the participles *-ing*, as in *walking* and *seeing*. In fact, it was the suffix *-ling*, but this did not stop people from adding a pair of useful verbs to the language. Other back-formations are *laze* (from *lazy*), *rove*, *burgle*, *greed* (from *greedy*), *beg* (from *beggar*), and *difficult* (from *difficulty*). Given the handiness and venerability of the process, it is curious to note that language authorities still generally squirm at the addition of new ones to the language. Among those that still attract occasional opprobrium are *enthuse* and *donate*.

Finally, erroneous words are sometimes introduced by respected users of the language who simply make a mistake. Shakespeare thought *illustrious* was the opposite of *lustrous* and thus for a time gave it a sense that wasn't called for. Rather more alarmingly, the poet Robert Browning caused considerable consternation by including the word *twat* in one of his poems, thinking it an innocent term. The work was *Pippa Passes*, written in 1841 and now remembered for the line 'God's in His heaven, all's right with the world'. But it also contains this disconcerting passage:

> Then, owls and bats,
> Cowls and twats,
> Monks and nuns, in a cloister's moods,
> Adjourn to the oak-stump pantry!

Browning had apparently somewhere come across the word *twat* – which meant precisely the same then as it does now – but somehow took it to mean a piece of headgear for nuns. The verse became a source of twittering amusement for generations of schoolboys and a perennial embarrassment to their elders, but the word was never altered and Browning was allowed to live out his life in wholesome ignorance because no one could think of a suitably delicate way of explaining his mistake to him.

2. WORDS ARE ADOPTED. This is of course one of the glories of English – its willingness to take in words from abroad, rather as if they were refugees. We take words from almost anywhere – *shampoo* from India, *chaparral* from the Basques, *caucus* from the Algonquin Indians, *ketchup* from China, *potato* from Haiti, *sofa* from Arabia, *boondocks* from the Tagalog language of the Philippines, *slogan* from Gaelic. You can't get much more eclectic than that. And we have been doing it for centuries. According to Baugh and Cable[1] as long ago as the sixteenth century English had already adopted words from more than fifty other languages – a phenomenal number for the age. Sometimes the route these words take is highly circuitous. Many Greek words became Latin words, which became French words, which became English words. *Garbage*, which has had its present meaning of food waste since the Middle Ages, was brought to England by the Normans, who had adapted it from an Italian dialectal word, *garbuzo*, which in turn had been taken from the Old Italian *garbuglio* (a mess), which ultimately had come from the Latin *bullire* (to boil or bubble).

Sometimes the same word reaches us at different times, having undergone various degrees of filtering, and thus can exist in English in two or more related forms, as with *canal* and *channel*, *regard* and *reward*, *poor* and *pauper*, *catch* and *chase*, *cave* and *cage*, *amiable* and *amicable*. Often these words have been so modified in their travels that their kinship is all but invisible. Who would guess that *coy* and *quiet* both have the same grand-parent in the Latin *quietus*, or that *sordid* and *swarthy* come jointly from the Latin *sordere* (to be soiled or dirty), or that *entirety* and *integrity* come from the Latin *integritas* (completeness, purity)?

Occasionally a single root gave birth to triplets, as with *cattle*, *chattel*, and *capital*, *hotel*, *hostel*, and *hospital*, and *strait*, *straight*, and *strict*. There is at least one quadruplet – *jaunty*, *gentle*, *gentile*, and *genteel*, all from the Latin *gentilis* – though there may be more. But the record holder is almost certainly the Latin *discus*, which has given us *disk*, *disc*, *dish*, *desk*, *dais*, and, of course, *discus*. (But having said that, one native Anglo-Saxon root, *bear*, has given birth to more than forty words, from *birth* to *born* to *burden*.)

Often words change meanings dramatically as they pass from one nation to another. The Latin *bestia* has become variously *biscia* (snake) in Italy, *bitch* (female dog) in England, *biche* (female deer) in France, and *bicho* (insect) in Portugal.[2]

We in the English-speaking world are actually sometimes better at looking after our borrowed words than the parents were. Quite a number of words that we've absorbed no longer exist in their place of birth. For instance, the French do not use *nom de plume*, *double entendre*, *panache*, *bon viveur*, *legerdemain* (literally 'light of hand'), or *R.S.V.P.* for répondez s'il vous plaît. (Instead they write: 'Prière de répondre.') The Italians do not use *brio* and although they do use *al fresco*, to them it signifies not being outside but being in prison.

Many of the words we take in are so artfully anglicized that it can be a surprise to learn they are not native. Who would guess that our word *puny* was once the Anglo-Norman *puis né* or that *curmudgeon* may once have been the French *cœur méchant* (evil heart), or that *breeze*, so English-sounding, was taken from the Spanish *briza*, or that the distress signal *mayday* was lifted from the French cry *m'aider* (meaning 'help me')? *Chowder* came directly from the French *chaudière* (cauldron), while *bankrupt* was taken literally from the Italian expression *banca rotta*, meaning 'broken bench'. In the late Middle Ages, when banking was evolving in Italy, transactions were conducted in open-air markets. When a banker became insolvent his bench was broken up. Sometimes the foreign words came quietly, but other times they needed a good pummelling before they assumed anything like a native shape, as when the Gaelic *sionnachuighim* was knocked into *shenanigan* and the Amerind *raugroughcan* became *raccoon*.

This tendency to turn foreign sounds into native speech is common. In New York, Flatbush was originally Vlacht Bos and Gramercy Park was originally De Kromme Zee. British soldiers in World War I called Ypres Wipers and in the 1950s, American soldiers in Japan converted the song 'Shi-i-Na-Na Ya-Ru' into 'She Ain't Got No Yo-Yo'.

One of our more inexplicable habits is the tendency to keep the Anglo-Saxon noun but to adopt a foreign form for the adjectival form. Thus fingers are not fingerish; they are digital. Eyes are not eyeish; they are ocular. English is unique in this tendency to marry a native noun to an adopted adjective. Among other such pairs are *mouth/oral, book/literary, water/ aquatic, house/domestic, moon/lunar, son/filial, sun/solar, town/urban*. This is yet another perennial source of puzzlement for anyone learning English. Sometimes, a Latinate adjective was adopted but the native one kept as well, so that we can choose between, say, *earthly* and *terrestrial, motherly* and *maternal, timely* and *temporal*.

Although English is one of the great borrowing tongues – deriving at least half of its common words from non-Anglo-Saxon stock – others have been even more enthusiastic in adopting foreign terms. In Armenian, only 23 per cent of the words are of native origin, while in Albanian the proportion is just 8 per cent. A final curious fact is that although English is a Germanic tongue and the Germans clearly were one of the main founding groups of America, there is almost no language from which we have borrowed fewer words than German. Among the very few are *kindergarten* and *hinterland*. We have borrowed far more words from every other European language, and probably as many from several smaller and more obscure languages such as Inuit. No one has yet come up with a plausible explanation for why this should be.

3. WORDS ARE CREATED. Often they spring seemingly from nowhere. Take *dog*. For centuries the word in English was *hound* (or *hund*). Then suddenly in the late Middle Ages, *dog* – a word etymologically unrelated to any other known word – displaced it. No one has any idea why. This sudden arising of words happens more often than you might think. Among others without known pedigree are *jaw, bad, jam, big, gloat, fun, crease, pour, put, niblick* (the golf club), *noisome, numskull, jalopy,* and countless others. *Blizzard* suddenly appeared in the nineteenth century in America (the earliest use is attributed to Davy Crockett) and *rowdy* appeared at about the same time. Recent examples of this phenomenon are *yuppie* and *sound bites,* which seem to have burst forth spontaneously and spread with remarkable rapidity throughout the English-speaking world.

Other words exist in the language for hundreds of years, either as dialect words or as mainstream words that have fallen out of use, before suddenly leaping to prominence – again quite mysteriously. *Scrounge* and *seep* are both of this type. They have been around for centuries and yet neither, according to Robert Burchfield,[3] came into general use before 1900.

Many words are made up by writers. According to apparently careful calculations, Shakespeare used 17,677 words in his writings, of which at least one tenth had never been used before. Imagine if every tenth word you wrote were original. It is a staggering display of ingenuity. But then Shakespeare lived in an age when words and ideas burst upon the world as never before or since. For a century and a half, from 1500 to 1650, English flowed with new words. Between 10,000 and 12,000 words were coined, of which about half still exist. Not until modern times would this number be exceeded, but even then there is no comparison. The new words of today represent an explosion of technology – words like *lunar module* and *myocardial infarction* – rather than of poetry and feeling. Consider the words that Shakespeare alone gave us, *barefaced, critical, leapfrog, monumental, castigate, majestic, obscene, frugal, radiance, dwindle, countless, submerged, excellent, fretful, gust, hint, hurry, lonely, summit, pedant, obscene,* and some 1,685 others. How would we manage without them? He might well have created even more except that he had to bear in mind the practicalities of being instantly comprehended by an audience. Shakespeare's vocabulary changed considerably as he aged. Jespersen notes that some 200 to 300 words are found in the early plays that are never repeated. Many of these were provincialisms that he later shed, but which independently made their way into the language later – among them *cranny, beautified, homicide, aggravate,* and *forefathers.* It has also been observed by scholars that the new terms of his younger years appeal directly to the senses (*snow-white, fragrant, brittle*) while the coinages of the later years are more often concerned with psychological considerations.

Shakespeare was at the centre of this remarkable verbal outburst but not alone in it. Ben Jonson gave us *damp, defunct, clumsy,* and *strenuous* among many other useful terms. Isaac Newton coined *centrifugal* and *centripetal.* Sir Thomas More came up with *absurdity, acceptance, exact, explain,* and *exaggerate.* The classical scholar Sir Thomas Elyot fathered, among others, *animate, exhaust,* and *modesty.* Coleridge produced *intensify,* Jeremy Bentham produced *international* (and apologized for its inelegance), Thomas Carlyle gave us *decadent* and *environment.* George Bernard Shaw thought up *superman.*

Many new coinages didn't last – often for obvious reasons. Jonson's less inspired efforts included *ventositous* and *obstupefact.* Shakespeare gave us the useful *gloomy,* but failed with *barky* and *brisky* (formed after the same pattern but somehow never catching on) and failed equally with *conflux, vastidity,* and *tortive.* Milton found no takers for *inquisiturient,* while, later still, Dickens tried to give the world *vocular.* The world didn't want it.

Sometimes words are made up for a specific purpose. The U.S. Army in 1974 devised a food called *funistrada* as a test word during a survey of soldiers' dietary preferences. Although no such food existed, funistrada ranked higher in the survey than lima beans and eggplant (which seems about right to me, at least as far as the lima beans go).

According to Mary Helen Dohan, in *Our Own Words*, the military vehicle the tank got its name because during its secretive experimental phase people were encouraged to think it was a storage receptacle – hence a tank. The curiously nautical terminology for its various features – *hatch, turret, hull, deck* – arises from the fact that it was developed by the British Admiralty rather than the Army.

4. WORDS CHANGE BY DOING NOTHING. That is, the word stays the same but the meaning changes. Surprisingly often the meaning becomes its opposite or something very like it. *Counterfeit* once meant a legitimate copy. *Brave* once implied cowardice – as indeed *bravado* still does. (Both come from the same source as *depraved*.) *Crafty*, now a disparaging term, originally was a word of praise, while *enthusiasm*, which is now a word of praise, was once a term of mild abuse. *Zeal* has lost its original pejorative sense, but *zealot* curiously has not. *Garble* once meant to sort out, not to mix up. A *harlot* was once a boy, and a *girl* in Chaucer's day was any young person, whether male or female. *Manufacture*, from the Latin root for hand, once signified something made by hand; it now means virtually the opposite. *Politician* was originally a sinister word (perhaps, on second thoughts, it still is), while *obsequious* and *notorious* simply meant flexible and famous. Simeon Potter notes that when James II first saw St Paul's Cathedral he called it amusing, awful, and artificial, and meant that it was pleasing to look at, deserving of awe, and full of skilful artifice.

This drift of meaning, technically called *catachresis*, is as widespread as it is curious. *Egregious* once meant eminent or admirable. In the sixteenth century, for no reason we know of, it began to take on the opposite sense of badness and unworthiness (it is in this sense that Shakespeare employs it in *Cymbeline*) and has retained that sense since. Now, however, it seems that people are increasingly using it in the sense not of

71

bad or shocking, but of simply being pointless and un-constructive.

According to Mario Pei, more than half of all words adopted into English from Latin now have meanings quite different from their original ones. A word that shows just how wide-ranging these changes can be is *nice*, which is first recorded in 1290 with the meaning of stupid and foolish. Seventy-five years later Chaucer was using it to mean lascivious and wanton. Then at various times over the next 400 years it came to mean extravagant, elegant, strange, slothful, unmanly, luxur-ious, modest, slight, precise, thin, shy, discriminating, dainty, and – by 1769 – pleasant and agreeable. The meaning shifted so frequently and radically that it is now often impossible to tell in what sense it was intended, as when Jane Austen wrote to a friend, 'You scold me so much in a nice long letter . . . which I have received from you.'

Sometimes the changing connotations of a word can give a new and startling sense to literary passages, as in *The Mayor of Casterbridge* where Thomas Hardy has one of his characters gaze upon 'the unattractive exterior of Farfrae's erection' or in *Bleak House* where Dickens writes that 'Sir Leicester leans back in his chair, and breathlessly ejaculates.'[4]

This drift of meaning can happen with almost anything, even our clothing. There is a curious but not often noted tendency for the names of articles of apparel to drift around the body. This is particularly apparent to Britons in America (and vice versa) who discover that the names for clothes have moved around at different rates and now often signify quite separate things. A Briton going into a New York department store with a shopping list consisting of vest, knickers, sus-penders, jumper and pants would in each instance be given something dramatically different from what he expected. (To wit, a British vest is an American undershirt. An American vest is a British waistcoat. Where the British use braces to hold up their trousers, the Americans use suspenders to hold up their pants. They never use *pants* to signify underwear, nor do they use *knickers* except as a term for the kind of knee-length trousers that golfers used to wear. *Jumper* as another word for sweater is quite unknown in America; there *jumper* means a pinafore dress.)

Sometimes an old meaning is preserved in a phrase or expression. *Neck* was once widely used to describe a parcel of land, but that meaning has died out except in the expression 'neck of the woods'. *Tell* once meant to count. This meaning died out but is preserved in the expression *bank teller* and in the term for people who count votes. When this happens, the word is called a *fossil*. Other examples of fossils are the italicized words in the following list:

short *shrift*
hem and *haw*
rank and *file*
raring to go
not a *whit*
out of *kilter*
new*fangled*
at *bay*
spick-and-span
to and *fro*
kith and kin

Occasionally, because the sense of the word has changed, fossil expressions are misleading. Consider the oft-quoted statement 'the exception proves the rule'. Most people take this to mean that the exception confirms the rule, though when you ask them to explain the logic in that statement, they usually cannot. After all, how *can* an exception prove a rule? It can't. The answer is that an earlier meaning of *prove* was to test (a sense preserved in *proving ground*) and with that meaning the statement suddenly becomes sensible – the exception tests the rule. A similar misapprehension is often attached to the statement 'the proof of the pudding is in the eating'.

Sometimes words change by becoming more specific. *Starve* originally meant to die before it took on the more particular sense of to die by hunger. A *deer* was once any animal (it still is in the German *tier*) and *meat* was any food (the sense is preserved in 'meat and drink' and in mincemeat, which contains various fruits but no meat in the sense that we now use it). A *forest* was any area of countryside set aside for hunting, whether or not it was covered with trees. (In England to this day, the Forest of Bowland in Lancashire is largely treeless, as are large stretches of the New Forest in Hampshire.) And *worm* was a term for any crawling creature, including snakes.

5. WORDS ARE CREATED BY ADDING OR SUBTRACTING SOMETHING. English has more than a hundred common prefixes and suffixes – *-able, -ness, -ment, pre-, dis-, anti-*, and so on – and with these it can form and re-form words with a facility that yet again sets it apart from other tongues. For example, we can take the French word *mutin* (rebellion) and turn it into *mutiny, mutinous, mutinously, mutineer*, and many others, while the French have still just the one form, *mutin*.

We are astonishingly indiscriminate in how we form our compounds, sometimes adding an Anglo-Saxon prefix or suffix to a Greek or Latin root (*plainness, sympathizer*), and sometimes vice versa (*readable, disbelieve*).[5] This inclination to use affixes and infixes provides gratifying flexibility in creating or modifying words to fit new uses, as strikingly demonstrated in the word *incomprehensibility*, which consists of the root *-hen-* and eight affixes and infixes: *in, -com-, -pre-, -s-, -ib-, -il-, -it-*, and *-y*. Even more melodic is the musical term *quasihemidemisemiquaver*, which describes a note that is equal to 128th of a semibreve.

As well as showing flexibility it also promotes confusion. We have six ways of making *labyrinth* into an adjective: *labyrinthian, labyrinthean, labyrinthal, labyrinthine, labyrinthic*, and *labyrinthical*. We have at least six ways of expressing negation with prefixes: *a-, anti-, in-, il-, im-, ir-, un-*, and *non-*. It is arguable whether this is a sign of admirable variety or just untidiness. It must be exasperating for foreigners to have to learn that a thing unseen is not unvisible, but invisible, while something that cannot be reversed is not inreversible but irreversible and that a thing

74

not possible is not nonpossible or antipossible but impossible. Furthermore, they must learn not to make the elementary mistake of assuming that because a word contains a negative suffix or prefix it is necessarily a negative word. *In-*, for instance, almost always implies negation but not with *invaluable*, while *-less* is equally negative, as a rule, but not with *priceless*. Things are so confusing that even native users have shown signs of mental fatigue and left us with two forms meaning the same thing: *flammable* and *inflammable*, *iterate* and *reiterate*, *ebriate* and *inebriate*, *habitable* and *inhabitable*, *durable* and *perdurable*, *fervid* and *perfervid*, *gather* and *forgather*, *ravel* and *unravel*.

Some word endings are surprisingly rare. If you think of *angry* and *hungry*, you might conclude that *-gry* is a common ending, but in fact it occurs in no other common words in English. Similarly *-dous* appears in only *stupendous*, *horrendous*, *tremendous*, *hazardous*, and *jeopardous*, while *-lock* survives only in *wedlock* and *warlock* and *-red* only in *hatred* and *kindred*. *Forgiveness* is the only example of a verb + *-ness* form. Equally some common-seeming prefixes are actually more rare than superficial thought might lead us to conclude. If you think of *forgive*, *forget*, *forgo*, *forbid*, *forbear*, *forlorn*, *forsake*, and *forswear*, you might think that *for-* is a common prefix, but in fact it appears in no other common words, though once it appeared in scores of others. Why certain forms like *-ish*, *-ness*, *-ful*, and *-some* should continue to thrive while others like *-lock* and *-gry* that were once equally popular should fall into disuse is a question without a good answer.

Fashion clearly has something to do with it. The suffix *-dom* was long in danger of disappearing, except in a few established words like *kingdom*, but it underwent a resurgence (largely instigated in America) in the last century, giving us such useful locutions as *officialdom* and *boredom* and later more contrived forms like *best-sellerdom*. The ending *-en* is today one of the most versatile ways we have of forming verbs from adjectives (*harden*, *loosen*, *sweeten*, etc.) and yet almost all such words are less than 300 years old.

Nor is there any discernible pattern to help explain why a

particular affix attaches itself to a particular word or why some creations have thrived while others have died of neglect. Why, for instance, should we have kept *disagree* but lost *disadorn*, retained *impede* but banished *expede*, kept *inhibit* but rejected *cohibit*?[6]

The process is still perhaps the most prolific way of forming new words and often the simplest. For centuries we had the word *political*, but by loading the single letter *a* on to the front of it, a new word, *apolitical*, joined the language in 1952.

Still other words are formed by lopping off their ends. *Mob*, for example, is a shortened form of *mobile vulgus* (fickle crowd). *Exam*, *gym*, and *lab* are similar truncations, all of them dating only from the last century when syllabic amputations were the rage. Yet the impulse to shorten words is an ancient one. Indeed, many of our most common words are contractions of whole phrases – for instance, *goodbye*, a shortening of God-be-with-you, and *hello*, which was in Old English *hal beo thu* or 'whole be thou'.[7]

Finally, but no less importantly, English possesses the ability to make new words by fusing compounds – *airport*, *seashore*, *footwear*, *wristwatch*, *landmark*, *flowerpot*, and so on almost endlessly. All Indo-European languages have the capacity to form compounds. Indeed, German and Dutch do it, one might say, to excess. But English does it more neatly than most other languages, eschewing the choking word chains that bedevil other Germanic languages and employing the nifty refinement of making the elements reversible, so that we can distinguish between a houseboat and a boathouse, between basketwork and a workbasket, between a casebook and a bookcase. Other languages lack this facility.

— 6 —

PRONUNCIATION

What is the most common vowel sound in English? Would you say it is the *o* of *hot*, the *a* of *cat*, the *e* of *red*, the *i* of *in*, the *u* of *up*? In fact, it is none of these. It isn't even a standard vowel sound. It is the colourless murmur of the schwa, represented by the symbol [ə] and appearing as one or more of the vowel sounds in words without number. It is the sound of *i* in *animal*, of *e* in *enough*, of the middle *o* in *orthodox*, of the second, fourth, fifth, and sixth vowels in *inspirational*, and of at least one of the vowels in almost every multisyllabic word in the language. It is everywhere.

This reliance of ours on one drab phoneme is a little odd when you consider that English contains as lush a mixture of phonics as any language in the world. We may think we're pretty tame when we encounter such tongue twisters as the Czech *vrch pln mlh* (meaning 'a hill in the fog') or Gaelic agglomerations like *pwy ydych chwi* (Welsh for 'who are you?'), but on the other hand we possess a number of sounds that other languages find treacherous and daunting, most notably the 'th' sound of *the* and *think*, which is remarkably rare in the world at large, or the 'l' sound that Orientals find so deeply impossible. (I once worked with a Chinese fellow in England who when things went wrong would mutter darkly, 'Bruddy hairo!' which I took to be some ancient Cantonese invective; it was not until many months later that I realized he was just saying, 'Bloody hell'.)

If there is one thing certain about English pronunciation it is that there is almost nothing certain about it. No other language in the world has more words spelled the same way and yet pronounced differently. Consider just a few:

heard – beard
road – broad
five – give
early – dearly
beau – beauty
steak – streak
ache – moustache
low – how
doll – droll
scour – four
grieve – sieve
paid – said
break – speak

In some languages, such as Finnish, there is a neat one-to-one correspondence between sound and spelling. A *k* to the Finns is always 'k', an *l* eternally and comfortingly 'l'. But in English pronunciation is so various – one might say random – that not one of our twenty-six letters can be relied on for constancy. Either they clasp to themselves a variety of pronunciations, as with the *c* in *race, rack*, and *rich*, or they sulk in silence, like the *b* in *debt*, the *a* in *bread*, the second *t* in *thistle*. In combinations they become even more unruly and unpredictable, most famously in the letter cluster *ough*, which can be pronounced in any of eight ways – as in *through, though, thought, tough, plough, thorough, hiccough*, and *lough* (an Irish-English word for lake or loch, pronounced roughly as the latter). The pronunciation possibilities are so various that probably not one English speaker in a hundred could pronounce with confidence the name of a crowlike bird called the chough. (It's chuff.) Two words in English, *hegemony* and *phthisis*, have nine pronunciations each. But perhaps nothing speaks more clearly for the absurdities of English pronunciation than that the word for the study of pronunciation in English, *orthoepy*, can itself be pronounced two ways.

Every language has its quirks and all languages, for whatever reason, happily accept conventions and limitations that aren't necessarily called for. In English, for example, we don't have words like *fwost* or *zpink* or *abtholve* because we never normally combine those letters to make those sounds, though there's no reason why we couldn't if we wanted to. We just don't. Chinese takes this matter of self-denial to extremes, particularly in the variety of the language spoken in the capital, Peking. All Chinese dialects are monosyllabic – which can itself be almost absurdly limiting – but the Pekingese dialect goes a step further and demands that all words end in an 'n' or 'ng' sound. As a result, there are so few phonetic possibilities in Pekingese that each sound must represent on average seventy words. Just one sound, 'yi', can stand for 215 separate words. Partly the Chinese get around this by using rising or falling pitches to vary the sounds fractionally, but even so in some dialects a falling 'i' can still represent almost forty unrelated words. We use pitch in English to a small extent, as when we differentiate between 'oh' and 'oh?' and 'oh!' but essentially we function by relying on a pleasingly diverse range of sounds. Almost everyone agrees that English possesses more sounds than almost any other language, though few agree on just how many sounds that might be. The British authority Simeon Potter says there are forty-four distinct sounds – twelve vowels, nine diphthongs (a kind of gliding vowel), and twenty-three consonants. The International Phonetic Alphabet, perhaps the most widely used, differentiates between fifty-two sounds used in English, divided equally between consonants and vowels, while the *American Heritage Dictionary* lists forty-five for purely English sounds, plus a further half dozen for foreign terms. Italian, by contrast, uses only about half as many sounds, a mere twenty-seven, while Hawaiian gets by with just thirteen. So whether the number in English is forty-four or fifty-two or something in between, it is quite a lot. But having said that, if you listen carefully, you will find that there are many more than this.

The combination 'ng', for example, is usually treated as one discrete sound, as in *bring* and *sing*. But in fact we make two sounds with it – employing a soft 'g' with *singer* and a hard 'g' with *finger*. We also tend to vary its duration, giving it fractionally more resonance in descriptive or onomatopoeic words like *zing* and *bong* and rather less in mundane words like *something* and *rang*. We make another unconscious distinction between the hard 'th' of *those* and the soft one of *thought*. Many dictionaries fail to note this distinction and yet it makes all the difference between *mouth* as a noun and *mouth* as a verb, and between the noun *thigh* and the adjective *thy*. More subtly still, when we use a 'k' sound at the start of a word, we put a tiny puff of breath behind it (as in *kitchen* and *conquer*) but when the 'k' follows an *s* (as in *skill* or *skid*) we withhold the puff. When we make an everyday observation like 'I have some homework to do', we pronounce the word 'hav'. But when we become emphatic about it – 'I *have* to go now' – we pronounce it 'haff'.

Each time we speak we make a multitude of such fractional adjustments, most of which we are wholly unaware of. But these only begin to hint at the complexity of our phonetics. An analysis of speech at the Bell Telephone Laboratories by Dr John R. Pierce detected more than ninety separate sounds just for the letter *t*.

We pronounce many words – perhaps most – in ways that are considerably at variance with the ways they are spelled and often even more so with the ways we *think* we are saying them. We may believe we say 'ladies', but it's more probably 'laties' or even, in the middle of a busy sentence, 'lays'. *Handbag* comes out as 'hambag'. We constantly allow sounds to creep into words where they have no real business. We introduce a 'p' between 'm' and 't' or 'm' and 's' sounds, so that we really say 'warmpth' and 'sompthing'. We can't help ourselves. We similarly put a 't' between 'n' and 's' sounds, which is why it is nearly impossible for us to distinguish between *mints* and *mince* or between *prints* and *prince*. Occasionally these intruders become established in the spellings. *Glimpse* (coming from the same source as *gleam*) was originally *glimsen*, with no 'p', but the curious desire to put one there proved irresistible over time. *Thunder* originally had no 'd' (German *donner* still doesn't) and *stand* had no 'n'. One was added to *stand*, but not, oddly, to *stood*. *Messenger* never had an 'n' (*message* still doesn't), *pageant* never had a 't', and *sound* no 'd'.

We tend to slur those things most familiar to us, particularly place names. Australians will tell you they come from "stralia', while Torontoans will tell you they come from 'Tronna'. In Iowa its 'Iwa' and in Ohio it's 'Hia'. People from Milwaukee say they're from 'Mwawkee'. In Louisville it's 'Loovul', in Newark it's 'Nerk', and in Indianapolis it's 'Naplus'. People in Philadelphia don't come from there; they come from 'Fuhluffia'. The amount of slurring depends on the degree of familiarity and frequency with which the word is spoken. The process is well illustrated by the street in London called Marylebone Road. Visitors from abroad often misread it as 'Marleybone'. Provincial Britons tend to give it its full phonetic value: 'Mary-luh-bone'. Londoners are inclined to slur it to 'Mairbun' or something similar while those who live or work along it slur it even further to something not far off 'Mbn'.

For the record, when bits are nicked off the front end of words it's called *aphesis*, when off the back it's called *apocope*, and when from the middle it's *syncope*. A somewhat extreme example of the process is the naval shortening of *forecastle* to *fo'c'sle*, but the tendency to compress is as old as language itself. *Daisy* was once *day's eye*, *shepherd* was *sheep herd*, *lord* was *loafward*, *every* was *everich*, *fortnight* was a *fourteen-night*.

The British are particularly good at lopping syllables off words as if with a sword, turning *immediately* into 'meejutly', *necessary* into 'nessree', *library* into 'libree'. The process was brought to a kind of glorious consummation with a word that is now all but dead – *halfpennyworth*. With the disappearance of the halfpenny, the English are now denied the rich satisfaction of compressing *halfpennyworth* into *haypth*. They must instead content themselves with giving their place names a squeeze – turning Barnoldswick into 'Barlick', Wymondham to 'Windum', Cholmondeston into 'Chumson'. (Of which much more in Chapter 13.)

Americans like to think their diction more precise. To be sure, they do give full value to each syllable in words like *necessary*, *immediate*, *dignatory*, *lavatory*, and (very nearly) *laboratory*. On the other hand, they more freely admit a dead schwa into *-ile* words such as *fragile*, *hostile*, and *mobile* (though not, perversely, into *infantile* and *mercantile*) where the British are, by contrast, scrupulously phonetic. And both, I would submit, are equally prone to slur phrases – though not necessarily the same ones. Where the British will say *howjado* for 'how do you do', an American will say *jeetjet* for 'have you taken sustenance recently?' and *lesskweet* for 'in that case, let us retire to a convivial place for a spot of refreshment'.

This tendency to compress and mangle words was first formally noted in a 1949 *New Yorker* article by one John Davenport who gave it the happy name of Slurvian. In American English, Slurvian perhaps reaches its pinnacle in Baltimore, a city whose citizens have long had a particular gift for chewing up the most important vowels, consonants, and even syllables of most words and converting them into a kind of verbal compost, to put it in the most charitable terms possible. In Baltimore (pronounced Balamer), an eagle is an 'iggle', a tiger is a 'tagger', water is 'wooder', a power mower is a 'paramour', a store is a 'stewer', clothes are 'clays', orange juice is 'arnjoos', a bureau is a 'beero', and the Orals (Orioles) are the local baseball team. Whole glossaries have been composed to help outsiders interpret these and the many hundreds of other terms that in Baltimore pass for English. Baltimoreans may be masters at this particular art, but it is one practised to a greater or lesser degree by people everywhere.

All of this is by way of coming around to the somewhat paradoxical observation that we speak with remarkable laxness and imprecision and yet manage to express ourselves with wondrous subtlety – and simply breathtaking speed. In normal conversation we speak at a rate of about 300 syllables a minute. To do this we force air up through the larynx – or supralaryngeal vocal tract, to be technical about it – and, by variously pursing our lips and flapping our tongue around in our mouth rather in the manner of a freshly landed fish, we shape each passing puff of air into a series of loosely differentiated plosives, fricatives, gutturals, and other minor atmospheric disturbances. These emerge as a more or less continuous blur of sound. People don't talk like this, theytalklikethis. Syllables, words, sentences run together like a watercolour left in the rain. To understand what anyone is saying to us we must separate these noises into words and the words into sentences so that we might in our turn issue a stream of mixed sounds in response. If what we say is suitably apt and amusing, the listener will show his delight by emitting a series of uncontrolled high-pitched noises, accompanied by sharp intakes of breath of the sort normally associated with a seizure or heart failure. And by these means we converse. Talking, when you think about it, is a very strange business indeed.

And yet we achieve the process effortlessly. We absorb and interpret spoken sounds more or less instantaneously. If I say to you, 'Which do you like better, peas or carrots?' it will take you on average less than a fifth of a second – the length of an eye blink – to interpret the question, consider the relative merits of the two vegetables, and formulate a reply. We repeat this process hundreds of times a day, generally with such speed that often we have our answer ready before the person has even finished the question.

As listeners we can distinguish between the most subtle gradations of emphasis. Most people, if they are reasonably attentive, can clearly detect the difference between *that's tough* and *that stuff*, between *I love you* and *isle of view*, and between *grey day* and *Grade A* even though the phonics could hardly be more similar. Sometimes, however, precise diction proves elusive, particularly when there is no direct eye contact. (It is remarkable the extent to which we read lips – or at least facial expressions.) Every newspaper person has his or her favourite story involving slip-ups resulting from misheard dictation. I remember once while working on an evening newspaper in southern England receiving a wire service story that made absolutely no sense until a correction was sent a few minutes later saying: 'In the preceding story, for "Crewe Station" read "crustacean".' In a similar way, pilots long had difficulty in distinguishing between *five* and *nine* until someone thought to start using the more distinct *fiver* and *niner*. Germans, suffering a similar problem with *zwei* and *drei*, introduced the nonce word *zwo*, for two, to deal with such misunderstandings.

Despite these occasional drawbacks, listening is something we do remarkably well. Speech, by contrast, is a highly inefficient process. We are all familiar with the feeling of not being able to get the words out fast enough, of mixing up sounds into spoonerisms, of stumbling over phonetically demanding words like *statistics* and *proprietorial*. The fact is that we will never be able to speak as quickly as we can hear.

Hence the tendency to slur. There has been a clear trend over time to make our pronunciations less precise, to let letters lapse into silence or allow sounds to merge and become less emphatic. This happened with *-ed* endings. In Chaucer's day, *helped* was pronounced not 'helpt' but 'hel-pud', with the two syllables clearly enunciated. By Shakespeare's time, poets could choose between the two to suit their cadence – writing *helped* to indicate the historic pronunciation or *help'd* to signify the modern one.

Such pronunciation changes are a regular feature of language. Sometimes they occur with the speed of centuries, sometimes with seemingly hell-for-leather haste. They appear from time to time in all languages for reasons that no one really understands. German had one not long after the departure of the Angles and Saxons to Britain, which resulted in the division of German into High and Low varieties. (High German refers not, as is commonly supposed, to the part of the country at the top of the map, but rather to the area at the bottom around Bavaria because the land there is more elevated.) In the German shift, northern speakers came to place *s*'s where before they had put *t*'s, and to put *f*'s where previously they had employed *p*'s. These changes were of course too late to affect English, and thus explain the differences in many modern English and German words, such as *water* and *wasser* and *open* and *offen*. Such changes are by no means unique to English or even the Germanic languages. Latin underwent a prolonged series of changes. In the fourth century, to take one example, the Latin *centum* (hundred) began to be pronounced in various ways – a fact reflected in the modern French *cent*, 'sahnt', Spanish *ciento*, 'thiento', and Italian *cento*, 'chento'. By such means did the Romance languages grow.

In England the Great Vowel Shift, as it is generally and somewhat misleadingly called, happened later, roughly around the time of Chaucer. Textbook discussions of the shift can sometimes leave us with the impression that people pronounced their vowels in one way up to a certain date and then suddenly, as if on a whim, began pronouncing them in an altogether different way. But of course it was never as simple as that. Many of the pronunciation changes reflected shifts that had begun centuries before in the time of King Alfred and some of them are not complete to this day. (*Shove* and *move* may one day be pronounced in the same way; it would make sense.) So, although it is true to say that these constituted some of the most sudden and dramatic changes English had ever undergone, we should not lose sight of the fact that we are talking about a period that spanned, even at its most rapid, a couple of generations. When Chaucer died in 1400, people still pronounced the *e* on the end of words. One hundred years later not only had it become silent, but scholars were evidently unaware that it ever *had* been pronounced. In short, changes that seem historically to have been almost breathtakingly sudden will often have gone unnoticed by those who lived through them.

No one knows why this vowel shift happened. As Charlton Laird has succinctly put it: 'For some reason, Englishmen started shoving tense vowels forward in their mouths. Then they stopped. And they have remained stopped. Nobody knows why they started or why they stopped.' For whatever reasons, in a relatively short period the long vowel sounds of English (or tense vowels as Laird called them) changed their values in a fundamental and seemingly systematic way, each of them moving forward and upward in the mouth. There was evidently a chain reaction in which each shifting vowel pushed the next one forward: the 'o' sound of *spot* became the 'a' sound of *spat*, while *spat* became *speet*, *speet* became *spate*, and so on. The 'aw' sound of *law* became the 'oh' sound of *close*, which in turn became the 'oo' sound of *food*. Chaucer's *lyf*, pronounced 'leef', became Shakespeare's *life*, pronounced 'lafe', became our *life*. Not all vowel sounds were affected. The short *e* of *bed* and the short *i* of *hill*, for instance, were unmoved, so that we pronounce those words today just as the Venerable Bede said them 1,200 years ago.

There were other changes as well – most notably the loss of the Old English sound χ, which, in technical terms, was a voiceless labiodental fricative – or to you and me the throat-clearing sound of the *ch* in the Scottish *loch* or the German *ach*. The loss of this sound from English meant that others rushed to fill the vacuum, as in the Old English word *burχ* (place) which became variously *burgh* as in Edinburgh, *borough* as in Gainsborough, *brough* as in Middlesbrough, and *bury* as in Canterbury.

Before the shift *house* was pronounced 'hoose' (it still is in Scotland), *mode* was pronounced 'mood', and *home* rhymed with 'gloom', which is why Domesday Book is pronounced and sometimes called Doomsday. (The word has nothing to do with the modern word *doom*, incidentally. It is related to the *domes-* in *domestic*.) But as with most things, shifting vowel sounds were somewhat hit and miss, often because regional variations disrupted the pattern. This is most notably demonstrated with the 'oo' sound. In Chaucer's day in London, all double *o* words were pronounced to rhyme with the modern word *food*. But once the pattern was broken, all kinds of other variations took hold, giving us such anomalies as *blood*, *stood*, *rood*, and so on. Most of these words were pronounced in different ways by different people from different places until they gradually settled into their modern forms, although some have never truly settled, such as *roof* and *poof*, which some people rhyme with *goof* and others pronounce with the sound in *foot*. A similar drift with 'ove' accounts for the different sounds of *shove*, *move*, and *hove*.

Since obviously there is no one around who heard English as it was spoken in the time of Chaucer and Caxton, how do we know all this? The answer is that for the most part we cannot know for sure. Most of it is based on supposition. But scholars can get a good idea of what English must have sounded like by looking at the rhymes and rhythms of historic verse and by examining the way words were spelled in letters and other snatches of informal writing. In this respect we owe a huge debt to bad spellers. It is from misspellings in letters of the seventeenth, eighteenth, and nineteenth centuries that we can be pretty certain that *boiled* was pronounced *byled*, that *join* was *gine*, that *merchant* was *marchant*, and so on. From the misspellings of Queen Elizabeth we know that *work* was once pronounced 'wark', *person* was 'parson', *heard* was 'hard', and *defer* was 'defar', at least at court.[1] In the same period, short vowels were often used interchangeably, so that *not* was sometimes written *nat* and *when* sometimes appeared as *whan*. Relics of this variability include *strap* and *strop*, *taffy* and *toffy*, *God* and *gad*.

Rhymes too tell us much. We know from Shakespeare's rhymes that *knees*, *grease*, *grass*, and *grace* all rhymed (at least more or less) and that *clean* rhymed with *lane*. (The modern pronunciation was evidently in use but considered substandard.) Shakespeare also made puns suggesting a similar pronunciation between *food* and *ford* and between *reason* and *raising*. The *k* in words like *knight* and *knave* was still sounded in Shakespeare's day, while words like *sea* and *see* were still pronounced slightly differently – *sea* being something roughly halfway between *see* and *say* – as were other pairs involving *ee* and *ea* spellings, such as *peek* and *peak*, *seek* and *speak*, and so on. All of this is of particular interest to us because it was in this period that America began to be colonized, so it was from this stock of pronunciations that American English grew. For this reason, it has been said that Shakespeare probably sounded more American than English. Well, perhaps. But in fact if he and his compatriots sounded like anything modern at all it was more probably Irish, though even here there are so many exceptions as to make such suggestions dubious.

For example, the Elizabethans, unlike modern English speakers, continued to pronounce many *er* words as *ar* ones, rhyming *serve* with *carve* and *convert* with *depart*. In England, some of these pronunciations survive, particularly in place names, such as Derby, Berkeley, and Berkshire, though there are many exceptions and inconsistencies, as with the town of Berkhamsted, Hertfordshire, in which the first word is pronounced 'birk-', but the second is pronounced 'hart-'. It also survives in a very few everyday words in Britain, notably *derby*, *clerk*, and – with an obviously modified spelling – *heart*, though not in *jerk*, *kerb*, *nerve*, *serve*, *herd*, *heard*, or almost any others of the type. In America, it has been even more consistently abandoned and survives only in *heart*. But the change is more recent than you might suppose. Well into the nineteenth century, Noah Webster was still castigating those who would say *marcy* for *mercy* and *marchant* for *merchant*. And then of course there's that favourite word of Yosemite Sam's, *varmint*, which is simply a variant of *vermin*. In both Britain and America the problem was sometimes resolved by changing the spelling: thus Hertford, Connecticut, became Hartford, while in Britain Barclay and Carr became acceptable variants for Berkeley and Kerr. In at least three instances this problem between 'er' and 'ar' pronunciation has left us with modern doublets: *person* and *parson*, *university* and *varsity*, and *perilous* and *parlous*.

It is probable, though less certain, that words such as *herd*, *birth*, *hurt*, and *worse*, which all today carry an identical 'er' sound – and which, entirely incidentally, is a sound that appears to be unique to English – had slightly different pronunciations up to Shakespeare's day and perhaps beyond. All of these pronunciation changes have continued up until fairly recent times. As late as the fourth decade of the eighteenth century Alexander Pope was rhyming *obey* with *tea*, *ear* with

88

repair, give with *believe, join* with *divine*, and many others that jar against modern ears. The poet William Cowper, who died in 1800, was still able to rhyme *way* with *sea. July* was widely pronounced 'Julie' until about the same time. *Gold* was pronounced 'gould' until well into the nineteenth century (hence the family name) and *merchant* was still often 'marchant' long after Webster's death.

Sometimes changes in pronunciation are rather more subtle and mysterious. Consider, for example, changes in the stress on many of those words that can function as either nouns or verbs – words like *defect, reject, disguise,* and so on. Until about the time of Shakespeare all such words were stressed on the second syllable. But then three exceptions arose – *outlaw, rebel,* and *record* – in which the stress moved to the first syllable when they were used as nouns (e.g. we re bel' against a reb'el; we re ject' a re'ject). As time went on, according to one authority,[2] the number of words of this type was doubling every hundred years or so, going from 35 in 1700 to 70 in 1800 and to 150 by this century, spreading to include such words as *object, subject, convict,* and *addict.* Yet there are still a thousand words which remain unaffected by this 400-year trend, among them *disdain, display, mistake, hollow, bother,* and *practice.* Why should this be? No one can say.

What is certain is that just as English spellings often tell us something about the history of our words, so do some of our pronunciations, at least where French terms are concerned. Words adopted from France before the seventeenth century have almost invariably been anglicized, while those coming into the language later usually retain a hint of Frenchness. Thus older *ch-* words have developed a distinct 'tch' sound as in *change, charge,* and *chimney,* while the newer words retain the softer 'sh' sound of *champagne, chevron, chivalry,* and *chaperone. Chef* was borrowed twice into English, originally as *chief* with a hard *ch* and later as *chef* with a soft *ch.* A similar tendency is seen in *-age,* the older forms of which have been thoroughly anglicized into an 'idge' sound (*bandage, cabbage, language*) while the newer imports keep a Gallic 'azh' flavour (*badinage,* *camouflage*). There has equally been a clear tendency to move the stress to the first syllable of older adopted words, as with *mutton, button,* and *baron,* but not with newer words such as *balloon* and *cartoon.* Presumably because of their proximity to France (or, just as probably, because of their long disdain for things French) the British have a somewhat greater tendency to disguise French pronunciations, pronouncing *garage* as 'gar-ridge', *fillet* as 'fill-ut', and putting a clear first-syllable stress on *café, buffet, ballet,* and *pâté.* (Some Britons go so far as to say 'buffy' and 'bally'.)

Spelling and pronunciation in English are very much like trains on parallel tracks, one sometimes racing ahead of the other before being caught up. An arresting example of this can be seen in the slow evolution of verb forms in the sixteenth and seventeenth centuries that turned *hath* into *has* and *doth* into *does.* Originally *-th* verbs were pronounced as spelled. But for a generation or two during the period from (roughly) 1600 to 1650 they became pronounced as if spelled in the modern way, even when the spelling was unaltered. So, for example, when Oliver Cromwell saw *hath* or *chooseth,* he almost certainly read them as 'has' or 'chooses' despite their spellings. Only later did the spellings catch up.[3]

Often, however, the process has worked the other way around, with pronunciation following spelling. *Atone* was once pronounced 'at one' (the term from which it sprang), while *atonement* was 'at one-ment'. Many people today pronounce that *t* in *often* because it's there (even though they would never think to do it with *soften, fasten,* or *hasten*) and I suspect that a majority of people in the English-speaking world would be surprised to learn that the correct (or at least historic) pronunciation of *waistcoat* is 'wess-kit', of *victuals* is 'vittles', of *forehead* is 'forrid', and of *comptroller* is 'controller' (the one is simply a fancified spelling of the other). In all of these the sway of spelling is gradually proving irresistible.

Quite a few of these spelling-induced pronunciation changes are surprisingly recent. At the time of the American Revolution, *husband* was pronounced 'husban', *soldier* was 'sojur', and *pavement* was 'payment', according to Burchfield.[4] Until well into the nineteenth century, *zebra* was pronounced 'zebber', *chemist* was 'kimmist', and *Negro*, despite its spelling, was 'negger' (hence the insulting term *nigger*). Burchfield goes on to point out that until the nineteenth century *swore* was spoken with a silent *w* (as *sword* still is) as were *Edward* and *upward*, giving 'Ed'ard' and 'up'ard'.

Much of this would seem to fly in the face – indeed, *does* fly in the face – of what we were saying earlier, namely that pronunciations tend to become slurred over time. Although that is generally true, there are constant exceptions. Language, never forget, is more fashion than science, and matters of usage, spelling, and pronunciation tend to wander around like hemlines. People say things sometimes because they are easier or more sensible, but sometimes simply because that's the way everyone else is saying them. *Bounteous*, for instance, was in Noah Webster's day pronounced 'bountchus' – a clear case of evolutionary slurring – but for some reason purists took exception to it and *bountchus* quickly became a mark of ignorance. It is for the same reason precisely that in modern England it is considered more refined to pronounce *ate* as 'et'.

But without doubt the most remarkable example of pronunciation change arising purely as a whim of fashion was the sudden tendency in eighteenth-century upper-class southern England to pronounce words like *dance*, *bath*, and *castle* with a broad *a*, as if they were spelled *dahnce*, *bahth*, and *cahstle*. In the normal course of things, we might have expected the pronunciations to drift back. But for some reason they stuck (at least they have so far), helping to underscore the social, cultural, and orthoepic differences between not only Britons and Americans but even between Britons and Britons. The change was so consequential and far-reaching that it is not so much a matter of pronunciation as of dialect. And that rather neatly takes us to the topic of our next chapter.

7

VARIETIES OF ENGLISH

No place in the English-speaking world is more breathtakingly replete with dialects than Great Britain. According to Robert Claiborne, there are 'no less than thirteen' quite distinct dialects in Britain. Mario Pei puts the number of dialects at forty-two – nine in Scotland, three in Ireland and thirty in England and Wales, but even that is probably an underestimate. If we define dialect as a way of speaking that fixes a person geographically, then it is scarcely an exaggeration to say that in Britain there are as many dialects as there are hills and valleys. In the six northernmost counties of England alone, seventeen separate pronunciations just for the word *house* have been recorded.

Professor Higgins boasted in *Pygmalion* that he could place any man in London within two miles, 'sometimes within two streets', but others claim even more specificity than that. I live in a dale in Yorkshire that is just five miles long, but locals insist they can tell whether a person comes from up the dale or down the dale by how he speaks. In a nearby village that lies half in Lancashire and half in Yorkshire, people claim to be able to tell which side of the high street a person was born on. There may be some exaggeration attached to that, but certainly Yorkshire people can tell in an instant whether someone comes from Bradford or Leeds, even though the two cities are contiguous. Certain features of British dialects can be remarkably localized. In *Trust an Englishman*, John Knowler notes that he once knew a man whose odd pronunciation of the letter *r* he took to be a speech impediment until he happened to visit the man's childhood village in an isolated part of Northumberland and discovered that *everyone* there pronounced *r* in the same way.

The systematic study of dialects is a recent phenomenon, so no one can say just how many rich and varied forms of speech died before anyone got round to recording them. One of the first people to think of doing so was, perhaps somewhat surprisingly, J. R. R. Tolkien, later to become famous as the author of the Hobbit trilogy, but at the time a professor of English at the University of Leeds. His idea was to try to record, in a comprehensive and orderly way, the dialect words of England before they disappeared for ever. Tolkien moved on to Oxford before the work got under way, but he was succeeded by another enthusiast, Harold Orton, who continued the painstaking work. Fieldworkers were sent to 313 areas, mainly rural, to interview people who were elderly, illiterate, and locally born (i.e. not contaminated by too much travel or culture), in an effort to record the everyday terms for practically everything, from cooking utensils to slang terms for breaking wind. The work took from 1948 to 1961. The result was *The Linguistic Atlas of England*.

The research threw up many surprising anomalies. The Berkshire villages of Kintbury, Boxford, and Cold Ash are within about eight miles of each other, yet in each they call the outer garment of clothing by a different name – respectively greatcoat, topcoat, and overcoat. In the whole of the north topcoat is the usual word, but in Shropshire there is one small and inexplicable island of overcoat wearers. In Oxfordshire, meanwhile, there is a lozenge-shaped linguistic island where people don't drink their drinks, they sup them. Why the northern English word for drinking should be used in an area of a few square miles in a southern county by people who employ no other northern expressions is a mystery to which there is no logical answer. No less mysterious is the way the terms 'twenty-one' and 'one-and-twenty' move up the country in alternating bands. In London people say 'twenty-one', but if you move forty miles to the north they say 'one-and-twenty'. Forty miles north of *that* and they say 'twenty-one' again. And so it goes right the way up to Scotland, changing from one to the other every forty miles or so. Just to complicate things, in Boston, in Lincolnshire, they say that a person is twenty-one years old, but that he has one-and-twenty marbles, while twenty miles away in Louth, they say the very opposite.

Sometimes relatively obscure British dialect words have been carried overseas, where they have unexpectedly prospered. The usual American word for stealing a look, *peek*, was originally a dialect word in England, existing in only three pockets of East Anglia, but that was the area from which many of the first immigrants came. In the same way, the usual word in America for the cylinder around which thread is wound, *spool*, is indigenous to two compact areas of the Midlands. The casual affirmative word *yeah* was also until fairly recently a quaint localism confined to small areas of Kent, Surrey, and south London. The rest of Britain would say *yes*, *aye*, or *ar*. Much the same thing seems to have happened elsewhere in the British empire. Three of the most pervasive Australianisms, *fair dinkum*, *cobber*, and *no worries*, appear to have their roots in English dialectal expressions.

Taken together, these variations of vocabulary and pronunciation add up to what linguists call our idiolect. A paradox of accents is that in England, where people from a common heritage have been living together in a small area for thousands of years, there is still a huge variety of accents, whereas in America, where people from a great mix of backgrounds have been living together in a vast area for a relatively short period, people speak with just a few voices. As Simeon Potter puts it: 'It would be no exaggeration to say that greater differences in pronunciation are discernible in the north of England between Trent and Tweed than in the whole of North America.'[1] Surely we should expect it to be the other way around? In England, the prolonged proximity of people ought to militate against differences in accent, while in America the relative isolation of many people ought to encourage regional accents. And yet people as far apart as New York state and Oregon speak with largely identical voices. According to some estimates almost two-thirds of the American population, living on some 80 per cent of the land area, speak with the same accent – a quite remarkable degree of homogeneity.

Some authorities have suggested that once there was much greater diversity in American speech than now. As evidence, they point out that in *Huckleberry Finn* Mark Twain needed seven dialects to reflect the speech of various characters all from the same area of the Midwest. That would not be necessary, or even possible, today. On the other hand it may simply be that thousands of regional accents exist in America, but that linguists have not been as alert to them as they might be.

As in Britain, the study of dialects in America was a relatively neglected field until fairly recently. The American Dialect Society was founded as long ago as 1889, but a systematic survey of American speech patterns did not begin until well into this century. Much of the most important initial work was done by Professor Hans Kurath of the University of Michigan, who produced the seminal *A Word Geography of the Eastern United States* in 1949. Kurath carefully studied the minute variations in speech to be found along the eastern seaboard – differences in vocabulary, pronunciation, and the like – and drew lines called isoglosses that divided the country into four main speech groups: Northern, Midland, Southern, and New England. Later work by others enabled these lines to be extended as far west as Texas and the prairie states. Most authorities since then have accepted these four broad divisions.

If you followed Kurath's isoglosses carefully enough, you could go to a field in, say, northern Iowa and stand with one foot in the Northern dialect region and the other foot in the Midland region. But if you expected to find that people on one side of the line spoke a variety of American English distinctively different from people on the other side, you would be disappointed. It is not as simple as that. Isoglosses are notional conveniences for the benefit of geographical linguists. There is no place where one speech region begins and another ends. You could as easily move the line in that Iowa field 200 yards to the north or fourteen miles or perhaps even 100 miles and be no less accurate. It is true that people on the Northern side of the line *tend* to have characteristics of speech that distinguish them from people on the Midland side, but that's about as far as you can take it. Even within a single region speech patterns blur and blur again into an infinitude of tiny variations. A person in Joliet, Illinois, sounds quite different from a person in Texarkana, Texas, yet they are both said to live in the Midland speech area. Partly to get round this problem, Midland is now usually subdivided into North Midland and South Midland, but we are still dealing with huge generalities.

So only in the very baldest sense can we divide American speech into distinct speech areas. Nonetheless, these speech areas do have certain characteristics that set them apart from one another. People from the Northern states call cake topping *frosting*. To southerners it's *icing*. Northerners say 'greesy'. Others say 'greezy'. In the eastern United States groceries are put in a bag, in the south in a poke and everywhere else in a sack – except in one small part of Oregon where they rather mysteriously also say *poke*. Northerners tend to prefer the 'oo' sound to the 'ew' sound in words like *duty*, *Tuesday*, and *newspaper*, saying 'dooty' instead of 'dewty' and so on. The Northern and Northern Midland accents are further distinguished by a more clipped pattern, as evidenced by a pronounced tendency to drop words at the beginning of sentences, as in 'This your house?' and 'You coming?' People from the same area have less ability to distinguish between rounded vowel sounds like 'ŏ' and 'ah' such as exist between *cot* and *caught*. In the South, on the other hand, there is a general reluctance or inability to distinguish clearly between *fall* and *foal*, *oil* and *all*, *poet* and *pour it*, *morning* and *moaning*, *peony* and *penny*, *fire* and *far*, *sawer* and *sour*, *courier* and *Korea*, *ahs* and *eyes*, *are* and *hour*, and many others.

Sometimes these speech preferences can pinpoint speakers to a quite specific area. People in South Carolina, for instance, say 'vegetubbles', but in North Carolina it's 'vegetibbles'. North Carolinians also give themselves away when they say,

'She's still in the bed' and 'Let's do this one at the time'. People in Philadelphia don't say *attitude*, they say 'attytude', and they don't have a 'downtown', they have a 'center city', which is divided not into blocks but squares. If you call a soft drink tonic, you come from Boston. People in New England call a small, naturally occurring object a stone rather than a rock, while in Rhode Island they don't refer to the playground toy in which a long plank balances on a fulcrum as a seesaw or teeter-totter as they do elsewhere in America, but as a dandle.

These linguistic pockets are both distinct and surprisingly numerous. In southern Utah, around St George, there is a pocket where people speak a peculiar dialect called (no one seems quite sure why) Dixie, whose principal characteristics are the reversal of 'ar' and 'or' sounds, so that a person from St George doesn't park his car in a carport, but rather porks his core in a corepart. The bright objects in the night sky are stores, while the heroine of *The Wizard of Oz* is Darthy. When someone leaves a door open, Dixie speakers don't say, 'Were you born in a barn?' They say, 'Were you barn in a born?'

Perhaps the most famous of all American dialectal studies is that of the *Dictionary of American Regional English* (or *DARE*), which began as recently as 1963, under the direction of Frederic Cassidy. A hundred fieldworkers, armed with stacks of questionnaires, were sent to 1,000 carefully selected communities to interview 2,777 informants. Each questionnaire contained 1,847 questions divided into forty-one categories, designed to tease out local or regional names for practically everything. The researchers collected a phenomenal 2.5 million items. They found more than 100,000 variations in terminology and pronunciation throughout the country, including seventy-nine names for dragonfly, 130 names for oak trees, and 176 names for dust balls under the bed. (In our house, they were just dustballs under the bed.) Something of the colossal scale of the undertaking is indicated by the fact that nearly a century elapsed between the book's being proposed and the publication of Volume 1 (A to C) in 1985, which itself takes up 1,056 pages. Five volumes altogether are planned.

It seems churlish to say it when so many years of dedicated work have gone into *DARE*, but it is hard to escape the conclusion that it is not truly comprehensive. In Iowa not one informant was from Des Moines, the state capital, and not one was black. Yet the speech patterns and vocabulary of people raised in Des Moines are quite distinct from those of people brought up in rural areas of the state, and this division is almost certainly even more pronounced among black people. However, a more exhaustive approach would not necessarily guarantee a more accurate survey. Since 1931 diligent scholars have been collecting data for the much more thorough *Linguistic Atlas of the United States and Canada*, but they are not finished yet. In 1939 the first volume, the *Linguistic Atlas of New England*, was produced, and the work has been proceeding westward ever since. The problem is that by the time the westernmost states are dealt with, more than half a century will have elapsed and the early volumes will be largely out of date.

Although the main dialect boundaries run from east to west in America, dividing the country into a kind of linguistic layer cake, some important speech differences contrarily go in the opposing direction. People along the eastern seaboard, for instance, tend to pronounce words such as *foreign* and *horrible* as 'fahrun' and 'harruble', whereas people further west, whether from the North or South, tend to say 'forun' (or 'forn') and 'horruble'. People along much of the east coast can distinguish between words that are elsewhere in America strictly homonyms – *horse* and *hoarse*, *morning* and *mourning*, *for* and *four*.[2]

Kurath was aware that his four main speech divisions were not adequate. He subdivided the four regions into eighteen further speech areas, and we should remember that he was dealing only with the eastern states as far south as South Carolina. If we were to project those divisions on to the rest of the country (and bearing in mind that regional differences tend to diminish as we move west) we could expect to find perhaps fifty or sixty sub-areas. But it may be that a really thorough study would show that there are hundreds, even thousands, of regional speech divisions.

A sufficiently sophisticated computer could probably place with reasonable accuracy, sometimes to within a few miles, almost any English-speaking person in the world depending on how he pronounced the following ten words: *cot, caught, cart, bomb, balm, oil, house, horse, good,* and *water.* Just four of these words – *bomb, balm, cot,* and *caught* – could serve as broad regional shibboleths for almost every American, according to the dialectologist W. Nelson Francis.

What accounts for all these regional variations? Why do people in Boston call white coffee 'regular' when everywhere else regular coffee is black? Why do people in Texas say 'arn' for *iron*? Why do so many people in New York say 'doo-awg' for *dog*, 'oo-awf' for *off*, 'kee-ab' for *cab*, 'thoid' for *third*, 'erster' for *oyster*? There is certainly no shortage of theories, some of which may be charitably described as being less than half-baked. Charlton Laird, generally a shrewd and reliable observer of the vagaries of English, writes in *The Miracle of Language*: 'The New York City variant of *doy* for *die*, *boy* for *buy*, *thoid* for *third* suggests forms in Yorkshire, which are reflections of the strong influence of old York upon the New York.' That is just nonsense; people in Yorkshire simply do not speak that way and never have. Robert Hendrickson in *America Talk* cites the interesting theory that the New York accent may come from Gaelic. The hallmark of this accent is of course the 'oi' diphthong as in 'thoidy-thoid' for *thirty-third* and 'moider' for *murder*, and Hendrickson points out that *oi* appears in many Gaelic words, such as *taoiseach* (the Irish term for prime minister). However, there are one or two considerations that suggest this theory may need further work. First, *oi* is not pronounced 'oy' in Gaelic; *taoiseach* is pronounced 'tea-sack'. Second, there is no tradition of converting 'ir' sounds to 'oi' ones in Ireland, such as would result in *murder* becoming 'moider'. And third, most of the Irish immigrants to New York didn't speak Gaelic anyway.

But there are other factors at work, such as history and geography. The colonists along the eastern seaboard naturally had closer relationships with England than those colonists who moved inland. That explains at least partly why the English of the eastern seaboard tends to have so much in common with British English – the tendency to put a 'yew' sound into words like *stew* and *Tuesday*, the tendency to have broader and rounder 'a' and 'o' sounds, the tendency to suppress 'r' sounds in words like *car* and *horse*. There are also similarities of vocabulary. *Queer* is still widely used in the South in the sense of strange or odd. *Common* still has a pejorative flavour (as in 'She's so common') that it lacks elsewhere in America. Ladybugs, as they are known in the North, are still called ladybirds in the South and sidewalks in some areas are called pavements, as they are in Britain. All of these are a result of the closer links between Britain and east coast cities such as Boston, Savannah, and Charleston.

Fashion comes into it too. When the custom arose in eighteenth-century Britain of pronouncing words like *bath* and *path* with a broad *a* rather than a flat one, the practice was imitated along the eastern seaboard, but not further inland, where people were clearly less susceptible to considerations of what fashionable society thought of them. In Boston, the new fashion was embraced to such an extent that up to the middle of the last century, according to H. L. Mencken, people used the broad *a* in such improbable words as *apple*, *hammer*, *practical*, and *Saturday*.

Related to all these factors is probably the most important, and certainly the least understood, factor of all, social bonding, as revealed in a study by William Labov of the University of Pennsylvania, probably America's leading dialectologist. Labov studied the accents of New York City and found that they were more complicated and diverse than was generally assumed. In particular he studied the sound of *r* in words like *more*, *store*, and *car*. As recently as the 1930s such *r*'s were never voiced by native New Yorkers, but over the years they have come increasingly to be spoken – but only sometimes. Whether or not people voiced the *r* in a given instance was thought to be largely random. But Labov found that there was actually much more of a pattern to it. In a word, people were using *r* as

a way of signalling their social standing, rather like the flicker-
ings of fireflies. The higher one's social standing, the more
often the r's were flickered, so to speak. Upper-middle-class
speakers pronounced the r about 20 per cent of the time in
casual speech, about 30 per cent of the time in careful speech
and 60 per cent of the time in highly careful speech (when
asked to read a list of words). The comparable figures for
lower-class speakers were 10 per cent for the first two and 30
per cent for the third. More than that, Labov found, used or
disregarded the r as social circumstances demanded. He found
that sales assistants in department stores tended to use many
more r's when addressed by middle-class people than when
speaking with lower-class customers. In short, there was very
little randomness involved.

Even more interestingly, Labov found that certain vowel
sounds were more specific to one ethnic group or another. For
instance, the tendency to turn *bag* into something more like
'be-agg' and *bad* into 'be-add' was more frequent among second
generation Italians, while the tendency (and I should stress
that it was no more than that) among lower-class Jewish
speakers was to drawl certain 'o' sounds, turning *dog* into 'doo-
awg', *coffee* into 'coo-awfee'. The suggestion is that this is a
kind of hypercorrection. The speakers are unconsciously trying
to distance themselves from their parents' foreign accents.
Yiddish speakers tended to have trouble with certain unfamiliar English vowel sounds. They tended to turn *cup of coffee*
into 'cop of coffee'. The presumption is that their children
compensated for this by overpronouncing those vowels. Hence
the accent.

So while certain distinctive pronunciations like 'doo-er' (or
'doo-ah') for *door*, 'oo-off' for *off*, 'kee-ab' for *cab*, 'moider' for
murder and so on are all features of the New York accent,
almost no native New Yorker uses more than a few of them.

Outside New York, regional accents play an important
part in binding people together – sometimes in unexpected
ways. On Martha's Vineyard the 'ou' sound of *house* and *loud*
was traditionally pronounced 'həus' and 'ləud'. With the

rise of tourism, the normal, sharper American 'house' pronunciation was introduced to the island and for a while
threatened to drive out the old sound. But a study reported
by Peter Trudgill in *Sociolinguistics*[3] found that the old pronunciation was on the increase, particularly among people
who had left the island to work and later come back. They
were using the old accent as a way of distinguishing themselves
from off-islanders.

Dialects are not just matters of localities and regions. There
are also occupational dialects, ethnic dialects, and class dialects.
It is not too much to say, given all the variables, that dialects
vary from house to house, indeed from room to room within
each house, that there are as many dialects in a language as
there are speakers. As Mario Pei has noted, no two people in
any language speak the same sounds in precisely the same
way. That is of course what enables us to recognize a person
by his voice. In short, we each have our own dialect.

National dialects can develop with remarkable speed.
Within only a generation or so of its colonization, visitors to
Australia were beginning to notice a distinctive accent. In
1965, one 'Afferbeck Lauder' published a book called *Let Stalk
Strine*, which wittily celebrated the national accent. Among
the words dealt with were *scona*, a meteorological term, as in
'Scona rine'; *dimension*, defined as the customary response to
'thank you'; and *air fridge*, a synonym for ordinary, middling.
Other Strinisms noted by Lauder and others are 'Emma chisit'
for 'How much is it?', 'emma necks' for what you have for
breakfast, and 'fairairs' for a long time, as in 'I waited fairairs
and airs'. A striking similarity between Australia and America
is the general uniformity of speech compared with Britain.
There are one or two differences in terminology across the
country – a tub of ice cream is called a bucket in New South
Wales and a pixie in Victoria – but hardly more than that. It
appears that size and population dispersal have little to do
with it. It is far more a matter of cultural identity.*

*However, unlike America, Australia has three layers of social accent:
cultivated, used by about 10 per cent of people and sounding very like

When the first inhabitants of the continent arrived in Botany Bay in 1788 they found a world teeming with flora, fauna, and geographical features such as they had never seen. 'It is probably not too much to say,' wrote Otto Jespersen, 'that there never was an instance in history when so many new names were needed.' Among the new words the Australians devised, many of them borrowed from the aborigines, were *billabong* for a brackish body of water, *didgeridoo* for a kind of trumpet, *bombora* for a navigable stretch of river containing dangerous rocks, and of course *boomerang*, *koala*, *outback*, and *kangaroo*. The new natives also quickly showed a gift for colourful slang: *tucker* for food, *slygrogging* for sneaking a drink, *bonzer* for excellent, *nong* for an idiot, *having the shits* for being irritable, and, more recently, *technicolour yawn* for throwing up. Often these are just everyday words shortened: *postie* for postman, *footy* for football, *arvo* for the afternoon, *roo* for kangaroo, *compo* for compensation. And then of course there are all those incomparable Australian expressions: 'scarce as rocking-horse manure', 'about as welcome as a turd in a swimming pool', 'don't come the raw prawn' (don't try to fool me), 'rattle your dags' (get a move on).

Although historically tied to Britain, linguistically Australia has been as receptive to American influences as to British ones. In Australia, people eat cookies, not biscuits; politicians run for office and not stand, as in Britain; they drive station wagons rather than estate cars; give their money to a teller rather than a cashier in a bank; wear cuffs on their pants, not turn-ups on their trousers; say mail, not post; and cover small injuries with a Band-Aid rather than a plaster. They spell many words in the American way – *labor* rather than *labour*, for instance – and, perhaps most significantly, the national currency is the dollar, not the pound.

Canada, too, exhibits a fair measure of hybridization, preserving some British words – *tap* (for faucet), *scones*, *porridge*, *zed*

British English; broad, a working-class accent used by a similar number of people (notably Paul Hogan); and general, an accent falling between the two and used by the great mass of people.

as the pronunciation for the last letter of the alphabet – that are largely unknown in America. At least one term, *riding*, for a political constituency, is now pretty well unknown even in Britain. There are said to be 10,000 Canadianisms – words like *skookum* (meaning strong) and *reeve* (a mayor), though the bulk of these are used only in small areas and are not necessarily familiar even to other Canadians.

With all their grammatical intricacies and deviations from standard vocabulary, dialects can sometimes become almost like separate languages. Indeed, a case is sometimes made that certain varieties *are* separate languages. A leading contender in this category is Scots, the variety of English used in the lowlands of Scotland (and not to be confused with Scottish Gaelic, which really *is* a separate language). As evidence, its supporters point out that it has its own dictionary, *The Concise Scots Dictionary*, as well as its own body of literature, most notably the poems of Robert Burns, and it is full of words that would leave most other English speakers darkly baffled: *swithering* for hesitating, *shuggle* for shake, *niffle-naffle* for wasting time, *gontrum niddles* for a cry of joy, and countless others. Although Scots, or Lallans as it is sometimes also called, is clearly based on English, it is often all but incomprehensible to other English speakers. A few lines from Burns's poem *To a Haggis* may give some idea of its majestic unfathomability:

> Fair fa' your honest sonsie face,
> Great chieftain o' the puddin'-race!
> Aboon them a' ye tak your place,
> Painch, trip, or thaim:
> Weel are ye wordy o' a grace
> As lang's my arm.

In America, a case is sometimes made to consider Cajun a separate tongue. Cajun is still spoken by a quarter of a million people (or more, depending on whose estimates you follow) in parts of Louisiana. The name is a corruption of *Acadian*, the adjective for the French-speaking inhabitants of Acadia (based on Nova Scotia, but taking in parts of Quebec and Maine), who settled there in 1604 but were driven out by the British in the 1750s. Moving to the isolated bayous of southern Louisiana, they continued to speak French but were cut off from their linguistic homeland and thus forced to develop their own vocabulary to a large extent. Often it is more colourful and expressive than the parent tongue. The Cajun for humming-bird, *sucfleur* ('flower-sucker'), is clearly an improvement on the French *oiseaumouche*. Other Cajun terms are *rat du bois* ('rat of the woods') for a possum and *sac à lait* ('sack of milk') for a type of fish. The Cajun term for the language they speak is Bougalie or Yats, short for 'Where y'at?' Their speech is also peppered with common French words and phrases: *merci, adieu, c'est vrai* ('it's true'), *qu'est-ce que c'est* ('what is it?'), and many others. The pronunciation has a distinctly Gallic air, as in their way of turning long 'a' sounds into 'eh' sounds, so that *bake* and *lake* become 'behk' and 'lehk'. And finally, as with most adapted languages, there's a tendency to use non-standard grammatical forms: *bestest* and *don't nobody know*.

A similar argument is often put forward for Gullah, still spoken by up to a quarter of a million people mostly on the Sea Islands of Georgia and South Carolina. It is a peculiarly rich and affecting blend of West African and English. Gullah (the name may come from the Gola tribe of West Africa) is often called Geechee by those who speak it, though no one knows why. Those captured as slaves suffered not only the tragedy of having their lives irretrievably disrupted but also the further misfortune of coming from one of the most linguistically diverse regions of the world, so that communication between slaves was often difficult. If you can imagine yourself torn from your family, shackled to some Hungarians, Russians, Swedes, and Poles, taken halfway around the world, dumped in a strange land, worked like a dog, and shorn for ever of the tiniest shred of personal liberty and dignity, then you can perhaps conceive the background against which creoles like Gullah arose. Gullah itself is a blend of twenty-eight separate African tongues. So it is hardly surprising if at first glance such languages seem rudimentary and unrefined. As Robert

Hendrickson notes in his absorbing book *American Talk*, 'the syntactic structure, or underlying grammar, of Gullah is . . . extraordinarily economical, making the language quickly and readily accessible to new learners'. But although it is simple, it is not without subtlety. Gullah is as capable of poetry and beauty as any other language.

One of the first serious investigations into Gullah was undertaken by Joel Chandler Harris, known for his Uncle Remus stories. Harris, born in 1848 in Eatonton, Georgia, was a painfully shy newspaperman with a pronounced stammer who grew up deeply ashamed that he was illegitimate. He became fascinated with the fables and language of former slaves during the period just after the Civil War, and recorded them with exacting diligence in stories that were first published in the *Atlanta Constitution* and later compiled into books that enjoyed a considerable popularity both during Harris's lifetime and after it. The formula was to present the stories as if they were being told by Uncle Remus to the small son of a plantation owner. Among the best known were *Nights With Uncle Remus* (1881), *The Tar Baby* (1904), and *Uncle Remus and Br'er Rabbit* (1906). All of these employed the patois spoken by mainland blacks. But Harris also produced a series of Gullah stories, based around a character called Daddy Jack. This was a considerably different dialect, though Harris thought it simpler and more direct. It had – indeed still has – no gender and no plurals. *Dem* can refer to one item or to hundreds. Apart from a few lingering West African terms like *churrah* for splash, *dafa* for fat, and *yeddy* or *yerry* for hear, the vocabulary is now almost entirely English, though many of the words don't exist in mainstream English. *Dayclean*, for instance, means dawn and *trut mout* (literally 'truth mouth') means a truthful speaker. Other words are truncated and pronounced in ways that make them all but unidentifiable to the uninitiated. *Nead* is Gullah for underneath. Learn is *lun*, thirsty is *tusty*, the other is *turrer*, going is *gwan*.

Without any doubt, the most far-flung variety of English is that found on Tristan da Cunha, a small group of islands in mid-Atlantic roughly halfway between Africa and South America. Tristan is the most isolated inhabited place in the world, 1,500 miles from the nearest landfall, and the local language reflects the fact. Although the inhabitants have the dark looks of the Portuguese who first inhabited the islands, the family names of the 300-odd islanders are mostly English, as is their language – though with certain quaint differences reflecting their long isolation from the rest of the world. It is often endearingly ungrammatical. People don't say 'How are you?' but 'How you is?' It also has many wholly local terms. *Pennemin* is a penguin; *watrem* is a stream. But perhaps most strikingly, spellings are often loose. Many islanders are called Donald, but the name is always spelled Dondall. Evidently one of the first users misspelled it that way generations ago and the spelling stuck.

8

SPELLING

The mainland of Europe never produced an alphabet of its own. Our own alphabet has its roots in pictographs. Our letter *A* comes from the Semitic aleph, meaning 'ox', and originally was a rough depiction of an ox's head. *B* comes from the Semitic bēth, meaning 'house'. But the people of the Near East, unlike those of the Far East, made an important leap in thought of almost incalculable benefit to us. They began to use their pictographs to represent sounds rather than things. The Egyptian symbol for the word *re* began to stand not just for sun but for any syllable pronounced 'ray'.

To appreciate the wonderfully simplifying beauty of this system you have only to look at the problems that bedevil the Chinese and Japanese languages. There are two ways of rendering speech into writing. One is with an alphabet, such as we have, and the other is with a pictographic-ideographic system, such as the Chinese use. The basic unit of the Chinese written word is the radical. The radical for earth is ± and for small is ﾉﾚ. All words in Chinese are formed from these and 212 other radicals. Radicals can stand alone or be combined to form other words. Eye and water make *teardrop*. Mouth and bird make *song*. Two women means *quarrel* and three women means *gossip*.

Since every word requires its own symbol, Chinese script is immensely complicated. It possesses some 50,000 characters, of which about 4,000 are in common use. Chinese typewriters are enormous and most trained typists cannot manage more than about ten words a minute. But even the most complex

Chinese typewriter can manage only a fraction of the characters available. If a standard Western typewriter keyboard
were expanded to take in every Chinese ideograph it would
have to be about fifteen feet long and five feet wide – about the
size of two ping-pong tables pushed together.

Dictionaries, too, are something of a nightmare. Without an
alphabet, how do you sensibly arrange the words? The answer
is that in most dictionaries the language is divided into 214
arbitrary clusters based on their radicals, but even then you
must hunt randomly through each section until you stumble
across the spelling you seek.

The consequences of not having an alphabet are considerable. There can be no crossword puzzles, no games like Scrabble, no palindromes, no anagrams, no Morse code. In the age
of telegraphy, to get around this last problem, the Chinese
devised a system in which each word in the language was
assigned a number. *Person*, for instance, was 0086. This process
was equally cumbersome, but it did have the advantage that
an American or Frenchman who didn't know a word of
Chinese could translate any telegram from China simply by
looking in a book. To this day in China, and other countries
such as Japan where the writing system is also ideographic,
there is no logical system for organizing documents. Filing
systems often exist only in people's heads. If the secretary dies,
the whole office can fall apart.

However, Chinese writing possesses one great advantage
over other languages. It can be read everywhere. Chinese is
not really a language at all, but more a family of loosely
related dialects. A person from Fukien can no more understand
the speech of the people of Shanghai than a Londoner can
understand what people are saying in Warsaw or Stockholm.
In some places one dialect is spoken over a very wide area, but
in other parts of the country, particularly in the deep south,
the dialects can change every two or three miles. Yet although
the person from Fukien couldn't talk to anyone from Canton,
he could read their newspapers because the written language
is the same everywhere. The ideographs are pronounced differ-

ently in different areas but read the same – rather in the way that 1, 2, 3 means the same to us as it does to a French person even though we see it as 'one, two, three' while they see it as 'un, deux, trois'.

An equally useful advantage of written Chinese is that people can read the literature of 2,500 years ago as easily as yesterday's newspapers, even though the spoken language has changed beyond recognition. If Confucius were to come back to life today, no one apart from scholars would understand what he was saying, but if he scribbled a message people could read it as easily as they could a shopping list.

Even more complicated is Japanese, which is a blend of three systems: a pictographic system of 7,000 characters called *kanji* and two separate syllabic alphabets each consisting of 48 characters. One of these alphabets, *katakana* (sometimes shortened to *kana*), is used to render words and names (such as Dunkin' Donuts and Egg McMuffin) that the ancient devisers of *kanji* failed to foresee. Since many of the *kanji* characters have several pronunciations and meanings – the word *ka* alone has 214 separate meanings – a second syllabic alphabet was devised. Called *hiragana* and written as small symbols above the main text, it tells the reader which of the many possible interpretations of the *kanji* characters is intended.

All this is so immensely complicated that until the mid-1980s most Japanese had to learn English or some other Western language in order to use a personal computer. The Japanese have now managed to get around the pictographic problem by using a keyboard employing *katakana* syllables which are converted on the screen into *kanji* characters, rather as if we were to write *twenty per cent* by striking three keys – '20', 'per', and 'cent' – and then seeing on the screen one symbol: '20%'. Despite this advance, the Japanese still suffer two considerable problems. First, they have no tradition of keyboard writing, so that typing is a bewildering new skill to many of them, and, second, each computer must be immensely more powerful than a Western model just to deal with the fact that it takes 7,000 symbols to write Japanese (against a hundred or so for most Western languages) and that whereas Western letters can be represented on computer screens by as few as 35 dots of light, Japanese characters can require up to 576 dots to be clearly distinguishable.

It is a disarming reflection of their determination and ingenuity that they have become such a technological powerhouse with such a patently inefficient system of orthography.

In comparison the Western way of writing begins to look admirably simple and well ordered. And yet in its way it is itself a pretty imperfect system for converting sounds into thoughts. English is particularly hit and miss. We have some forty sounds in English, but more than 200 ways of spelling them. We can render the sound 'sh' in up to fourteen ways (*shoe, sugar, passion, ambitious, ocean, champagne,* etc.); we can spell 'ō' in more than a dozen ways (*go, beau, stow, sew, doe, though, escargot,* etc.) and 'ā' in a dozen more (*hey, stay, make, maid, freight, great,* etc.). If you count proper nouns, the word in English with the most varied spellings is *air* with a remarkable thirty-eight: *Aire, Ayr, heir, e'er, ere,* and so on.

Spellings in English are so treacherous, and opportunities for flummoxing so abundant, that the authorities themselves sometimes stumble. The first printing of the second edition of *Webster's New World Dictionary* had *millennium* spelled *millenium* in its definition of that word, while in the first edition of the *American Heritage Dictionary* you can find *vichysoisse* instead of *vichyssoise.* In *The English Language,*[1] Robert Burchfield, called by William Safire the 'world's most influential lexicographer', talks about grammatical prescriptivists who regard 'innovation as dangerous or at any rate resistable'. It should be *resistible.* In *The Story of Language,* Mario Pei writes *flectional* on page 114 and *flexional* just four pages later. And in *The Treasure of Our Tongue,* Lincoln Barnett laments the decline of spelling by noting: 'An English examination at New Jersey's Fairleigh Dickinson University disclosed that less than one quarter of the freshmen class could spell *professor* correctly.' I wonder, for my part, how many of them could spell *freshman class*?

Just as a quick test, see if you can tell which of the following words are mispelled.

> supercede
> conceed
> procede
> idiosyncracy
> concensus
> accomodate
> dexterous
> impressario
> rhythym
> opthalmologist
> diptheria
> anamoly
> afficianado
> caesarian
> grafitti

In fact, they all are. So was *misspelled* at the end of the preceeding paragraph. So was *preceding* just there. I'm sorry, I'll stop. But I trust you get the point that English can be a maddeningly difficult language to spell correctly.

Some people contend that English orthography is not as bad as all that – that it even has some strengths. Simeon Potter believed that English spelling possessed three distinguishing features that offset its other shortcomings. The consonants are fairly regular in their pronunciation, the language is blessedly free of the diacritical marks that complicate other languages – the umlauts, cedillas, circumflexes, and so on – and, above all, English preserves the spelling of borrowed words, so that people of many nations 'are immediately aware of the meanings of thousands of words which would be unrecognizable if written phonetically'. We might dare to quibble with the first of these observations. Potter evidently was not thinking of the *c* in *bloc*, *race*, and *church* or the *s* in *house*, *houses*, and *mission*, or the *t* in *think*, *tinker*, and *mention*, or the *h* in *host*, *hour*, *thread*, and *cough*, or the two *g*'s in *garage* and *gauge*, or indeed most of the other syllables when he praised their regularity of pronunciation. To be fair, English does benefit from the absence of diacritical marks. These vary from language to language, but in some they play a crucial, and often confusing, role. In Hungarian, for instance, *tőke* means capital, but *töke* means testicles. *Szár*, on the other hand, means stem, but take away the accent and it becomes the sort of word you say when you hit your thumb with a hammer. David Crystal in *The English Language* observes that there are only 400 or so irregular spellings in English (only?), and, rather more persuasively, notes that 84 per cent of English spellings conform to a general pattern (e.g. *purse/nurse/curse*, *patch/catch/latch*) while only 3 per cent of our words are spelled in a really unpredictable way.

A mere 3 per cent of our words may be orthographically troublesome, but they include some doozies, as one might say. Almost any argument in defence of English spelling begins to look a trifle flimsy when you consider such anomalies as *colonel*, a word that clearly contains no *r* and yet proceeds as if it did, or *ache*, *bury*, and *pretty*, all of which are pronounced in ways that pay the scantest regard to their spellings, or *four* and *forty*, one of which clearly has a *u* and the other of which just as clearly doesn't. In fact, all the 'four' words – *four*, *fourth*, *fourteen*, *twenty-four*, and so on – are spelled with a *u* until we get to *forty* when suddenly the *u* disappears. Why?

As with most things in life, there are any number of reasons for all of these. Sometimes our curious spellings are simply a matter of carelessness. That is why, for instance, *abdomen* has an *e* but *abdominal* doesn't, why *hearken* has an *e* but *hark* doesn't. *Colonel* is perhaps the classic example of this orthographic waywardness. The word comes from the old French *coronelle*, which the French adapted from the Italian *colonello* (from which we get *colonnade*). When the word first came into English in the mid-sixteenth century, it was spelled with an *r*, but gradually the Italian spelling and pronunciation began to challenge it. For a century or more both spellings and pronunciations were commonly used, until finally with inimitable illogic we settled on the French pronunciation and Italian spelling.

The matter of the vanishing *u* from *forty* is more problematic. Chaucer spelled it with a *u*, as indeed did most people until the end of the seventeenth century, and some for half a century or so after that. But then, as if by universal decree, it just quietly vanished. No one seems to have remarked on it at the time. Bernstein suggests that it may have reflected a slight change in pronunciation[2] – to this day many people aspirate *four* and *forty* in slightly different ways – but this begs the question of why the pronunciation changed for the first word and not for the second. In any case, it would be most unusual for the spelling of a word to change to reflect such a minor adjustment of pronunciation.

Usually in English we strive to preserve the old spelling at almost any cost to logicality. Take *ache*. The spelling seems desperately inconsistent today, as indeed it is. Up until Shakespeare's day, *ache* was pronounced *aitch* when it was a noun. As a verb, it was pronounced *ake* – but also, rather sensibly, was spelled *ake*. This tendency to fluctuate between 'ch' and 'k' sounds was once fairly common. It accounts for such pairs as *speech/speak*, *stench/stink*, and *stitch/stick*. But *ache*, for reasons that defy logic, adopted the verb pronunciation and the noun spelling.

English spelling has caused problems for about as long as there have been English words to spell. When the Anglo-Saxons became literate in the sixth century, they took their alphabet from the Romans, but quickly realized that they had three sounds for which the Romans had no letters. These they supplied by taking three symbols from their old runic alphabet: w, þ, and ð. The first, literally double *u*, represented the sound 'w' as it is pronounced today. The other two represented the 'th' sound: þ (called thorn) and ð (called eth and still used in Ireland).

The first Norman scribes came to England and began grappling with what to them was a wholly foreign tongue – a fact clearly evident in many of the spellings from Domesday Book.

In just one small parish in Yorkshire, Hanlith was recorded as Hagenlith, Malham as Malgham, and Calton as Colton – all spellings that were probably never used locally. Many such errors can be attributed to carelessness and unfamiliarity, but others clearly reflect Norman orthographic preferences. The Normans certainly did not hesitate to introduce changes they felt more comfortable with, such as substituting *qu* for *cw*. Had William the Conqueror been turned back at Hastings, we would spell *queen* as *cwene*. The letters *z* and *g* were introduced and the Old English þ and ð were phased out. The Normans also helped to regularize such sounds as *ch* and *sh*, which in Anglo-Saxon could be rendered in a variety of ways. They substituted *o* for *u* in certain words such as *come* and *one*, and they introduced the *ou* spelling as in *house* and *mouse*. These changes made things more orderly and logical for Norman scribes, but not necessarily for later native speakers of English.

As we have seen elsewhere, the absence of a central authority for the English language for three centuries meant that dialects prospered and multiplied. When at last Anglo-Norman died out and English words rushed in to take their place in official and literary use, it sometimes happened that people adopted the spelling used in one part of the country and the pronunciation used in another. That is why we use the western England spellings for *busy* and *bury*, but give the first the London pronunciation 'bizzy' and the second the Kentish pronunciation 'berry'. Similarly, if you've ever wondered how on earth a word spelled *one* could be pronounced 'wun' and *once* could be 'wunce', the answer in both cases is that Southern pronunciations attached themselves to East Midland spellings. Once they were pronounced more or less as spelled – i.e. 'oon' and 'oons'.

Even without the intervention of the Normans, there is every reason to suppose that English spelling would have been a trifle erratic. Largely this is because for a very long time people seemed emphatically indifferent to matters of consistency in spelling. There were exceptions. As long ago as the early thirteenth century a monk named Orm was calling for a more logical and phonetic system for English spelling. (His proposals, predictably, were entirely disregarded, but they tell scholars more about the pronunciation of the period than any other surviving document.) Even so, it is true to say that most people throughout much of the history of the English language have seemed remarkably unconcerned about niceties of spelling – even to the point of spelling one word two ways in the same sentence, as in this description of James I by one of his courtiers, in which just eight words come between two spellings of *clothes*: 'He was of a middle stature, more corpulent though in his clothes than in his body, yet fat enough, his cloathes being ever made large and easie . . .' Even more remarkably perhaps, *A Table Alphabeticall of Hard Words* by Robert Cawdrey, published in 1604 and often called the first English dictionary, spelled *words* two ways on the title page.[3]

Throughout this period you can find names and words spelled in many ways – *where*, for instance, has been variously recorded as *wher*, *whair*, *wair*, *wheare*, *were*, *whear*, and so on. People were even casual about their names. More than eighty spellings of Shakespeare's name have been found, among them Shagspeare, Shakspere, and even Shakestaffe. Shakspere is the spelling insisted on by the *Oxford English Dictionary*. Shakespeare himself did not spell the name the same way twice in any of his six known signatures and even spelled it two ways on one document, his will, which he signed Shakspere in one place and Shakspeare in another. Curiously, the one spelling he never seemed to use himself was Shakespeare. Much is often made of all this, but a moment's reflection should persuade us that a person's signature, whether he be an Elizabethan playwright or a modern orthodontist, is about the least reliable way of determining how he spells his name. Many people scrawl their signatures, and Shakespeare was certainly one of history's scrawlers. In any case, whether he used the spelling himself or not, Shakespeare is how his name appears on most of the surviving legal documents concerning him, as well as on the title pages of his sonnets and on twenty-two of the twenty-four original quarto editions of his plays.

Still, there is no gainsaying that people's names in former times were rendered in a bewildering variety of ways – some of which bore scant resemblance to the owner's preferred name. Christopher Marlowe was sometimes referred to by his contemporaries as Marley. The foremost printer of the Elizabethan age variously signed himself in print John Day or Daye or Daie. Charlton Laird in *The Word* cites a man of the period whose name is variously recorded as Waddington, Wadigton, Wuldingdoune, Windidune, Waddingdon, and many others.

An odd fact of spelling from earlier times is that although writing must have been a laborious affair there was little inclination to compress words or simplify spellings – indeed, by all evidence, the opposite was the case. Cromwell habitually spelled *it* as *itt*, *not* as *nott*, *be* as *bee*, and *at* as *atte*, and such cumbersome spellings can be found in manuscripts right up until the modern period. It seems curious indeed that people were not driven to more compact spellings by writer's cramp if not by urgency.

Before 1400, it was possible to tell with some precision where in Britain a letter or manuscript was written just from the spellings. By 1500, this had become all but impossible. The development that changed everything was the invention of the printing press. This brought a much-needed measure of uniformity to English spelling – but at the same time guaranteed that we would inherit one of the most bewilderingly inconsistent spelling systems in the world.

The printing press, as every schoolchild knows, was invented by Johann Gutenberg. In fact, history may have given Gutenberg more credit than he deserves. There is reason to believe that movable type was actually invented by a Dutchman named Laurens Janszoon Koster (or Coster) and that Gutenberg – about whom we know precious little – learned of the process only when one of Koster's apprentices ran off to Mainz in Germany with some of Koster's blocks and the two struck up a friendship. Certainly it seems odd that a man who had for the first forty years of his life been an obscure stonemason and mirror polisher should suddenly have taken some blocks of wood and a wine press and made them into an invention that would transform the world. What is certain is that the process took off with astonishing speed. Between 1455, when Gutenberg's first Bible was published, and 1500, more than 35,000 books were published in Europe. None of this benefited Gutenberg a great deal – he had to sell his presses to one Johann Fust to pay his debts and died in straitened circumstances in 1468 – but it did attract the attention of an expatriate Englishman living in northern Belgium.

William Caxton (1422–91) was a rich and erudite English businessman based in Bruges, then one of the great trading cities of Europe. In the late fifteenth century, intrigued by the recent development of printing in Germany and sensing that there might be money in it, Caxton set up his own publishing house in his adopted city and there in 1475 he published *Recuyell of the Historyes of Troy*. So, a little ironically, the oldest publication in English was not printed in England, but in Flanders.

Returning to England and setting himself up in the precincts of Westminster Abbey in London (which explains, incidentally, why printing unions to this day use such quaint terms as *chapel* for union branch and *father* for the head of the chapel), Caxton began to issue a torrent of books of all types – histories, philosophies, the works of Chaucer and Malory, and much else – and became richer still. The possibilities for quick and easy wealth led others to set up presses in competition.

By 1640, according to Baugh and Cable, more than 20,000 titles were available in Britain – that's not simply books, but titles. With the rise of printing, there was suddenly a huge push towards regularized spelling. London spellings became increasingly fixed, though differences in regional vocabulary remained for some time – indeed exist to this day to quite a large extent. But just as a Yorkshireman or Scottish Highlander of today must use London English when he reads, so in the sixteenth century the English of the capital became increasingly dominant in printed material of all types. Although many irregularities persisted for some time, and Caxton himself could observe in his famous aforenoted anecdote that a Londoner seeking eggs in nearby Kent could scarcely make himself understood, the trend was clearly towards standardization, which was effectively achieved by about 1650.

Unluckily for us, English spellings were becoming fixed just at the time when the language was undergoing one of those great phonetic seizures that periodically unsettle any tongue. The result is that we have today in English a body of spellings that, for the most part, faithfully reflect the pronunciations of people living 400 years ago. In Chaucer's day, the *k* was still pronounced in words like *knee* and *know*. *Knight* would have sounded (more or less) like 'kuh-nee-guh-tuh', with every letter enunciated. The *g* was pronounced in *gnaw* and *gnat*, as was the *l* in words like *folk*, *would*, and *alms*. In short, the silent letters of most words today are shadows of a former pronunciation. Had Caxton come along just a generation or so later English would very probably have had fewer illogical spellings like *aisle*, *bread*, *eight*, and *enough*.

But it didn't end there. When in the seventeenth century the English developed a passion for the classical languages, certain well-meaning meddlers began fiddling with the spellings of many other words in an effort to make them conform to a Latin ideal. Thus *b*'s were inserted into *debt* and *doubt*, which had previously been spelled *dette* and *doute*, out of deference to the Latin originals, *debitum* and *dubitare*. *Receipt* picked up a *p* by the same method. *Island* gained its *s*, *scissors* its *c*, *anchor* its *h*. *Tight* and *delight* became consistent with *night* and *right*, though without any etymological basis. *Rime* became *rhyme*. In several instances our spelling became more irregular rather than less. Sometimes these changes affected the pronunciation of words, as when *descrive* (or *descryve*) became *describe*, *perfet* (or *parfet*) became *perfect*, *verdit* became *verdict*, and *aventure* had a *d* hammered into its first syllable. At first all these inserted letters were as silent as the *b* in *debt*, but eventually they became voiced.

A final factor in the seeming randomness of English spelling is that we not only freely adopt words from other cultures, but also tend to preserve their spellings. Unlike other borrowing tongues, we are generally content to leave foreign words as they are. So when, say, we need a word to describe a long counter from which food is served, we absorb *buffet*, pronounced 'buffay', unconcerned that it jars with the same word meaning to hit but pronounced 'buffit'. In the same way it seldom bothers us that words like *brusque*, *garage*, and *chutzpah* all flout the usual English pattern. Speakers of many other languages would not abide such acoustic inconsistency.

As time went on, many English speakers grew to feel the same way. By the end of the eighteenth century people were beginning to call for a more orderly and reliable system of spelling. Benjamin Franklin spoke for many when he complained that if spelling were not reformed 'our words will gradually cease to express Sounds, they will only stand for things, as the written words do in the Chinese Language'.[4] In 1768, he published *A Scheme for a New Alphabet and a Reformed Mode of Spelling*, but since this required the creation of six additional letters, it can hardly be called a simplification.

People began to feel passionate about it. Noah Webster not only pushed for simplified spelling, but lobbied Congress to make it a legal requirement – turning America into the only country in history where deviant spelling would be a punishable offence.

Another enthusiast for simplified spelling was Mark Twain, who was troubled not so much by the irregularity of our words as by the labour involved in scribbling them. He became enamoured of a 'phonographic alphabet' devised by Isaac Pitman, the inventor of shorthand (which Pitman called Stenographic Soundhand, thus proving once again that inventors are generally hopeless at naming their inventions).*

'To write the word "laugh",' Twain noted in *A Simplified*

---

*Further, and possibly conclusive, evidence of this was shown in 1874 when Major Walter Clopton Wingfield, an Englishman, invented an outdoor game that he called *sphairixtike*. It only caught on when his friend Arthur Balfour, the future prime minister, suggested he call it *lawn tennis*.

Alphabet, 'the pen has to make fourteen strokes. To write "laff", the pen has to make the same number of strokes – no labour is saved to the penman.' But to write the same word with the phonographic alphabet, Twain went on, the pen had to make just three strokes. To the untrained eye Pitman's phonographic alphabet looks rather like a cross between Arabic and the trail of a sidewinder snake, and of course it never caught on.

But that isn't to say that the movement flagged. Indeed, it gathered pace until by late in the century it seemed as if every eminent person on both sides of the Atlantic – including Darwin, Tennyson, Arthur Conan Doyle, James A. H. Murray (the first editor of the *Oxford English Dictionary*), and of course Twain – was pushing for spelling reform. It is hard to say which is the more remarkable, the number of influential people who became interested in spelling reform or the little effect they had on it.

Spelling reform associations began to pop up all over. In 1876, the newly formed American Philological Association called for the 'urgent' adoption of eleven new spellings – *liv, tho, thru, wisht, catalog, definit, gard, giv, hav, infinit,* and *ar* – though how they arrived at those particular eleven, and what cataclysm they feared would arise if they weren't adopted, is unknown. In this same year, doubtless inspired by America's centennial celebrations, the Spelling Reform Association was formed, and three years later a British version followed.

In 1906, the philanthropist Andrew Carnegie gave $250,000, a whopping sum, to help establish the Simplified Spelling Board. One of the board's first acts was to issue a list of 300 words commonly spelled in two ways – *ax* and *axe*, *judgement* and *judgment*, and so on – and to give endorsement to the simpler of the two. By this means, and with the support of other influential bodies such as the National Education Association, it helped to gain acceptance for the American spellings of *catalog*, *demagog*, and *program* and very nearly, according to H. L. Mencken,[5] succeeded in getting *tho* established. President Theodore Roosevelt was so taken with these easier spellings that he ordered their adoption by the Government Printing Office in all federal documents. For a time simplified spelling seemed to be on its way.

But then, as so often happens, the Simplified Spelling Board became altogether carried away with its success and began to press for more ambitious – some would say more ridiculous – changes. It called for such spellings as *tuf*, *def*, *troble* (for *trouble*), *yu* (for *you*), *filosofy*, and several dozen others just as eye-rattling. It encountered a wall of resistance. Suddenly simplified spelling went out of fashion, a process facilitated by the eruption of World War I and the death of its wealthiest benefactor, Andrew Carnegie. Its friends abandoned it, and the Simplified Spelling Board began a long slide into obscurity and eventual death.

Yet the movement lived fitfully on, most notably in the hands of George Bernard Shaw who wrote archly: 'An intelligent child who is bidden to spell *debt*, and very properly spells it *d-e-t*, is caned for not spelling it with a *b* because Julius Caesar spelled it with a *b*.' Shaw used a private shorthand in his own writing and insisted upon certain mostly small simplifications in the published texts of his own plays – turning *can't*, *won't*, and *haven't* into *cant*, *wont*, and *havnt*, for example. At his death in 1950, he left the bulk of his estate to promote spelling reform. As it happened, death duties ate up almost everything, and the whole business would likely have been forgotten except that his play *Pygmalion* was transformed into the smash hit *My Fair Lady* and suddenly royalties poured in. But, as you won't have failed to notice, this did not lead to any lasting change in the way the world spells English.

One of the last-gasp holdouts against old-fashioned spellings was Colonel Robert R. McCormick (1880–1955), editor and publisher of the *Chicago Tribune*, who for two generations insisted on such spellings as *nite* for *night*, *frate* for *freight*, *iland* for *island*, *cigaret* for *cigarette*, and some 300 others – though never all at once. After his death most of the more jarring spellings were quietly dropped. Oddly, McCormick never called for two of the most common shortenings, *tho* and *thru*.

He just didn't like them, which of course is all the reason that is necessary when it's your newspaper.

So while spelling reform has exercised some of our finest minds for nearly two centuries, the changes attributable to these efforts have generally been few and frequently short-lived. The one notable exception is Noah Webster (about whom more in a later chapter), though even his changes were not nearly as far-ranging as he dreamed.

What is less often noticed is that spelling reform has been quietly going on for centuries, in a small but not insignificant way, and without the benefit of any outside agencies. In that splendidly random way that characterizes most facets of English development, it just happened. Many words have shed a pointless final *e* – *deposite*, *fossile*, and *secretariate*, for instance. *Musick* and *physick* similarly gave up their needless *k*'s. The tendency continues today with simplified spellings like *catalog*, *dialog*, and *omelet* gradually easing out the old spellings of *catalogue*, *dialogue*, and *omelette*, at least in America. Two hundred years ago there were scores of words that could be spelled in two or more ways, but today the list has shrunk to a handful – *ax/axe*, *gray/grey*, *inquire/enquire*, and (outside North America) *jail/gaol* – but even here there is a clear tendency in every English-speaking country to favour one form or the other, to move towards regularity.

Even so, there is still, on the face of it, a strong case for spelling reform. Anyone who has tried to explain to an eight-year-old, or even a teenager, the difference between *wring* and *ring* or between *meet*, *meat*, and *mete*, or why we spell *hinder* with an *e* but *hindrance* without, or why *proceed* has a double *e* but *procedure* doesn't, or why we spell *enough*, *biscuit*, and *pneumonia* in the very peculiar ways that we do will very probably appreciate that. But calls for spelling reform inevitably overlook certain intractable problems. One is that the old spellings are well established – so well established that most of us don't notice that words like *bread*, *thought*, and *once* are decidedly unphonetic. Attempts to simplify and regularize English spelling almost always hav a sumwut strānj and uneskapubly arbitrary lūk abowt them, and ov cors they kawz most reederz to stumbl. There is a great deal to be said for the familiarity of our spellings, even if they are not always sensible. What simplified spelling systems gain in terms of consistency they often throw away in terms of clarity. *Eight* may be a peculiar way of spelling the number that follows seven, but it certainly helps to distinguish it from the past tense of *eat*. Similarly, the syllable *seed* can be spelled a variety of ways in English – *seed, secede, proceed, supersede* – but if in our quest for consistency we were to fix on the single spelling of, say, *seed*, we wouldn't be able to distinguish between *reseed* and *recede*. *Fissure* would become *fisher*; *sew* and *sow* would be *so*. There would be no way to distinguish between *seas* and *seize*, *flees* and *fleas*, *aloud* and *allowed*, *chance* and *chants*, *air* and *heir*, *wrest* and *rest*, *flu*, *flue*, and *flew*, *weather*, *whether*, and *wether*, and countless others. Perplexity and ambiguity would reign (or rain or rein).

And who would decide which pronunciations would be supreme? Would we write *eether* or *eyther*? As we have already seen, pronunciations often bear even less relation to spellings than we appreciate. In spoken American English, many millions of people – perhaps the majority – say *medal* for *metal*, *hambag* for *handbag*, *frunnal* for *frontal*, *tolly* for *totally*, *forn* for *foreign*, and *nookular* for *nuclear*. Shall our spellings reflect these? The fact is, especially when looked at globally, most of our spellings cater to a wide variation of pronunciations. If we insisted on strictly phonetic renderings, *girl* would be *gurl* in most of America (though perhaps *goil* in New York), *gel* in London and Sydney, *gull* in Ireland, *gill* in South Africa, *gairull* in Scotland. Written communications between nations, and even parts of nations, would become practically impossible. And that, as we shall see in the next chapter, is a problem enough already.

9

GOOD ENGLISH AND BAD

Consider the parts of speech. In Latin, the verb has up to 120 inflections. In English it never has more than five (e.g. *see, sees, saw, seeing, seen*) and often it gets by with just three (*hit, hits, hitting*). Instead of using loads of different verb forms, we use just a few forms but employ them in loads of ways. We need just five inflections to deal with the act of propelling a car – *drive, drives, drove, driving*, and *driven* – yet with these we can express quite complex and subtle variations of tense: 'I drive to work every day', 'I have been driving since I was sixteen', 'I will have driven 20,000 miles by the end of this year'. This system, for all its ease of use, makes labelling difficult. According to any textbook, the present tense of the verb *drive* is *drive*. Every secondary school pupil knows that. Yet if we say, 'I used to drive to work but now I don't', we are clearly using the present tense *drive* in a past tense sense. Equally if we say, 'I will drive you to work tomorrow', we are using it in a future sense. And if we say, 'I would drive if I could afford to', we are using it in a conditional sense. In fact, almost the only form of sentence in which we cannot use the present tense form of *drive* is, yes, the present tense. When we need to indicate an action going on right now, we must use the participial form *driving*. We don't say, 'I drive the car now', but rather 'I'm driving the car now'. Not to put too fine a point on it, the labels are largely meaningless.

We seldom stop to think about it, but some of the most basic concepts in English are naggingly difficult to define. What, for instance, is a sentence? Most dictionaries define it broadly as a group of words constituting a full thought and containing, at a minimum, a subject (basically a noun) and predicate (basically a verb). Yet if I inform you that I have just crashed your car and you reply, 'What!' or 'Where?' or 'How?' you have clearly expressed a complete thought, uttered a sentence. But where are the subject and predicate? Where are the noun and verb, not to mention the prepositions, conjunctions, articles, and other components that we normally expect to find in a sentence? To get around this problem, grammarians pretend that such sentences contain words that aren't there. 'What!' they would say, really means 'What are you telling me – you crashed my car?' while 'Where?' is a shorthand rendering of 'Where did you crash it?' and 'How?' translates as 'How on earth did you manage to do that, you old devil you?' or words to that effect. The process is called *ellipsis* and is certainly very nifty. Would that I could do the same with my bank account. Yet the inescapable fact is that it is possible to make such sentences conform to grammatical precepts only by bending the rules. When I was growing up we called that cheating.

In English, in short, we possess a language in which the parts of speech are almost entirely notional. A noun is a noun and a verb is a verb largely because the grammarians say they are. In the sentence 'I am suffering terribly' *suffering* is a verb, but in 'My suffering is terrible', it is a noun. Yet both sentences use precisely the same word to express precisely the same idea. *Quickly* and *sleepily* are adverbs but *sickly* and *deadly* are adjectives. *Breaking* is a present tense participle, but as often as not it is used in a past tense sense ('He was breaking the window when I saw him'). *Broken*, on the other hand, is a past tense participle but as often as not it is employed in a present tense sense ('I think I've just broken my toe') or even future tense sense ('If he wins the next race, he'll have broken the school record'). To deal with all the anomalies, the parts of speech must be so broadly defined as to be almost meaningless. A noun, for example, is generally said to be a word that denotes a person, place, thing, action, or quality. That would seem to

[handwritten marginalia: This is the past tense: I have broken. The present tense would be 'I am breaking my toe.']

126

cover almost everything, yet clearly most actions are verbs and many words that denote qualities – *brave*, *foolish*, *good* – are adjectives.

The complexities of English are such that the authorities themselves often stumble. Each of the following statements by an expert contains a usage that many of his fellow experts would consider quite wrong:

'Prestige is one of the few words that has had an experience opposite to that described in "Worsened Words"' (H. W. Fowler, *A Dictionary of Modern English Usage*, second edition). It should be 'one of the few words that *have* had'.

'The total vocabulary of English is immense and runs to about half a million items. None of us as individuals, of course, knows more than a fairly limited number of these, and uses even less ...' (Randolph Quirk, *The Use of English*). 'None of us ... uses even less'? The sentence appears to be telling us that nobody uses fewer words than he knows – an obvious impossibility. Grammatically, it would be better as 'and we use even less' – and better still as 'and we use even fewer'.

'Each of the variants indicated in boldface type count as an entry' (William and Mary Morris, *The Harper Dictionary of Contemporary Usage*) It should be 'each ... *counts*'.

'It is of interest to speculate about the amount of dislocation to the spelling system that would occur if English dictionaries were either proscribed or (as when Malory or Sir Philip Sidney were writing) did not exist' (Robert Burchfield, *The English Language*). It should be '*was* writing'.

'The prevalence of incorrect instances of the use of the apostrophe ... together with the abandonment of it by many business firms ... suggest that the time is close at hand when this moderately useful device should be abandoned' (Robert Burchfield, *The English Language*). *Together with* functions as a preposition and not as a conjunction and therefore does not govern the verb. The verb should be *suggests*.

'His system of citing examples of the best authorities, of indicating etymology, and pronunciation, are still followed by lexicographers' (Philip Howard, *The State of the Language*). His system are?

'When his fellowship expired he was offered a rectorship at Boxworth ... on condition that he married the deceased rector's daughter' (Robert McCrum *et al.*, *The Story of English*). A misuse of the subjunctive: it should be 'on condition that he marry'.

English grammar is so complex and confusing for the one very simple reason that its rules and terminology are based on Latin – a language with which it has precious little in common. In Latin, to take one example, it is not possible to split an infinitive. So in English, the early authorities decided, it should not be possible to split an infinitive either. But there is no reason why we shouldn't, any more than we should forsake instant coffee and air travel because they weren't available to the Romans. Making English grammar conform to Latin rules is like asking people to play baseball using the rules of football. It is a patent absurdity. But once this insane notion became established grammarians found themselves having to draw up ever more complicated and circular arguments to accommodate the inconsistencies. As Burchfield notes in *The English Language*, one authority, F. Th. Visser, found it necessary to devote 200 pages to discussing just one aspect of the present participle. That is as crazy as it is amazing.

The early authorities not only used Latin grammar as their model, but actually went to the almost farcical length of writing English grammars in that language, as with Sir Thomas Smith's *De Recta et Emendata Linguae Anglicae Scriptione Dialogus* (1568), Alexander Gil's *Logonomia Anglica* (1619), and

John Wallis's *Grammatica Linguae Anglicanae* of 1653 (though even he accepted that the grammar of Latin was ill-suited to English). For a very long time it was taken entirely for granted that the classical languages *must* serve as models. Dryden spoke for an age when he boasted that he often translated his sentences into Latin to help him decide how best to express them in English.

In 1660, Dryden complained that English had 'not so much as a tolerable dictionary or a grammar; so our language is in a manner barbarous'. He believed there should be an academy to regulate English usage, and for the next two centuries many others would echo his view. In 1664, the Royal Society for the Advancement of Experimental Philosophy formed a committee 'to improve the English tongue', though nothing lasting seems to have come of it. Thirty-three years later in his *Essay Upon Projects*, Daniel Defoe was calling for an academy to oversee the language. In 1712, Jonathan Swift joined the chorus with a *Proposal for Correcting, Improving and Ascertaining the English Tongue*. Some indication of the strength of feeling attached to these matters is given by the fact that in 1780, in the midst of the American Revolution, John Adams wrote to the president of Congress appealing to him to set up an academy for the purpose of 'refining, correcting, improving and ascertaining the English language' (a title that closely echoes, not to say plagiarizes, Swift's pamphlet of sixty-eight years before). In 1806, the American Congress considered a bill to institute a national academy and in 1820 an American Academy of Language and Belles Lettres, presided over by John Quincy Adams, was formed, though again without any resounding perpetual benefits to users of the language. And there were many other such proposals and assemblies.

The model for all these was the Académie Française, founded by Cardinal Richelieu in 1635. In its youth, the academy was an ambitious motivator of change. In 1762, after many years of work, it published a dictionary that regularized the spellings of some 5,000 words – almost a quarter of the words then in common use. It took the *s* out of words like *estre* and *fenestre*, making them *être* and *fenêtre*, and it turned *roy* and *loy* into *roi* and *loi*. In recent decades, however, the academy has been associated with an almost ayatollah-like conservatism. When in December 1988 over 90 per cent of French school-teachers voted in favour of a proposal to introduce the sort of spelling reforms the academy itself had introduced 200 years earlier, the forty venerable members of the academy were, to quote the *Sunday Times*, 'up in apoplectic arms' at the thought of tampering with something as sacred as French spelling. Such is the way of the world. Among the changes the teachers wanted and the academicians did not were the removal of the circumflex on *être*, *fenêtre*, and other such words, and taking the *-x* off plurals such as *bureaux*, *chevaux*, and *châteaux* and replacing it with an *-s*. Silent and redundant letters would largely disappear: President Mitterrand would become President Mitéran.

Such actions underline the one almost inevitable short-coming of national academies. However progressive and far-seeing they may be to begin with, they almost always exert over time a depressive effect on change. So it is probably fortunate that the English-speaking world never saddled itself with such a body, largely because as many influential users of English were opposed to academies as favoured them. Samuel Johnson doubted the prospects of arresting change and Thomas Jefferson thought it in any case undesirable. In declining an offer to be the first honorary president of the Academy of Language and Belles Lettres, he noted that had such a body been formed in the days of the Anglo-Saxons English would now be unable to describe the modern world. Joseph Priestley, the English scientist, grammarian, and theologian, spoke perhaps most eloquently against the formation of an academy when he said in 1761 that it was 'unsuitable to the genius of a free nation ... We need make no doubt but that the best forms of speech will, in time, establish themselves by their own superior excellence: and in all controversies, it is better to wait the decisions of time, which are slow and sure, than to take those of synods, which are often hasty and injudicious.'[1]

English is often commended by outsiders for its lack of a stultifying authority. Otto Jespersen as long ago as 1905 was praising English for its lack of rigidity, its happy air of casualness. Likening French to the severe and formal gardens of Louis XIV, he contrasted it with English, which he said was 'laid out seemingly without any definite plan, and in which you are allowed to walk everywhere according to your own fancy without having to fear a stern keeper enforcing rigorous regulations.'[2]

Without an official academy to guide us, the English-speaking world has long relied on self-appointed authorities such as the brothers H. W. and F. G. Fowler and Sir Ernest Gowers in Britain and Theodore Bernstein and William Safire in America, and of course countless others. These figures write books, give lectures, and otherwise do what they can (i.e. next to nothing) to try to stanch (not staunch) the perceived decline of the language. They point out that there is a useful distinction to be observed between *uninterested* and *disinterested*, between *imply* and *infer*, *flaunt* and *flout*, *fortunate* and *fortuitous*, *forgo* and *forego*, and *discomfort* and *discomfit* (not forgetting *stanch* and *staunch*). They point out that *fulsome*, properly used, is a term of abuse, not praise, that *peruse* actually means to read thoroughly, not glance through, that *data* and *media* are plurals. And from the highest offices in the land they are ignored.

In the late 1970s, President Jimmy Carter betrayed a flaw in his linguistic armoury when he said: 'The government of Iran must realize that it cannot flaunt, with impunity, the expressed will and law of the world community.' *Flaunt* means to show off; he meant *flout*. The day after he was elected president in 1988, George Bush told a television reporter he couldn't believe the enormity of what had happened. Had President-elect Bush known that the primary meaning of *enormity* is wickedness or evil, he would doubtless have selected a more flattering term.

When this process of change can be seen happening in our lifetimes, it is almost always greeted with cries of despair and alarm. Yet such change is both continuous and inevitable. Few acts are more salutary than looking at the writings of language authorities from recent decades and seeing the usages that raised their hackles. In 1931, H. W. Fowler was tutting over *racial*, which he called 'an ugly word, the strangeness of which is due to our instinctive feeling that the termination -al has no business at the end of a word that is not obviously Latin'. (For similar reasons he disliked *television* and *speedometer*.) Other authorities have variously – and sometimes hotly – attacked *enthuse, commentate, emote, prestigious, contact* as a verb, *chair* as a verb, and scores of others. But of course these are nothing more than opinions, and, as is the way with other people's opinions, they are generally ignored.

So if there are no officially appointed guardians for the English language, who sets down all those rules that we all know about from childhood – the idea that we must never end a sentence with a preposition or begin one with a conjunction, that we must use *each other* for two things and *one another* for more than two, and that we must never use *hopefully* in an absolute sense, such as 'Hopefully it will not rain tomorrow'? The answer, surprisingly often, is that no one does, that when you look into the background of these 'rules' there is often little basis for them.

Consider the curiously persistent notion that sentences should not end with a preposition. The source of this stricture, and several other equally dubious ones, was one Robert Lowth, an eighteenth-century clergyman and amateur grammarian whose *A Short Introduction to English Grammar*, published in 1762, enjoyed a long and distressingly influential life both in his native England and abroad. It is to Lowth we can trace many a pedant's most treasured notions: the belief that you must say *different from* rather than *different to* or *different than*, the idea that two negatives make a positive, the rule that you must not say 'the heaviest of the two objects', but rather 'the heavier', the distinction between *shall* and *will*, and the clearly nonsensical belief that *between* can apply only to two things and *among* to more than two. (By this reasoning, it would not be possible to say that Paris is between London, Berlin, and Madrid, but rather that it is among them, which would impart a quite different sense.) Perhaps the most remarkable and curiously enduring of Lowth's many beliefs was the conviction that sentences ought not to end with a preposition. But even he was not didactic about it. He recognized that ending a sentence with a preposition was idiomatic and common in both speech and informal writing. He suggested only that he thought it generally better and more graceful, not crucial, to place the preposition before its relative 'in solemn and elevated' writing. Within a hundred years this had been converted from a piece of questionable advice into an immutable rule. In a remarkable outburst of literal-mindedness, nineteenth-century academics took it as read that the very name pre-position meant it must come before something – anything.

But then this was a period of the most resplendent silliness, when grammarians and scholars seemed to be climbing over one another (or each other; it doesn't really matter) in a mad scramble to come up with fresh absurdities. This was the age when, it was gravely insisted, Shakespeare's *laughable* ought to be changed to *laugh-at-able* and *reliable* should be made into *relionable*. Dozens of seemingly unexceptionable words – *lengthy*, *standpoint*, *international*, *colonial*, *brash* – were attacked with venom because of some supposed etymological deficiency or other. Thomas de Quincey, in between bouts of opium taking, found time to attack the expression *what on earth*. Some people wrote *mooned* for *lunatic* and *foresayer* for *prophet* on the grounds that the new words were Anglo-Saxon and thus somehow more pure. They roundly castigated those ignoramuses who impurely combined Greek and Latin roots into new words like *petroleum* (Latin *petra* + Greek *oleum*). In doing so, they failed to note that the very word with which they described themselves, *grammarians*, is itself a hybrid made of Greek and Latin roots, as are many other words that have lived harmlessly in English for centuries. They even attacked *handbook* as an ugly Germanic compound when it dared to show its face in the nineteenth century, failing to notice that it was a good Old English word that had simply fallen out of use. It is one of the felicities of English that we can take pieces of words from all over and fuse them into new constructions – like *trusteeship*, which consists of a Nordic stem (*trust*), combined with a French affix (*ee*), married to an Old English root (*ship*). Other languages cannot do this. We should be proud of ourselves for our ingenuity and yet even now authorities commonly attack almost any new construction as ugly or barbaric.

Today in England you can still find authorities attacking the construction *different than* as a regrettable Americanism, insisting that a sentence such as 'How different things appear in Washington than in London' is ungrammatical and should be changed to 'How different things appear in Washington from how they appear in London'. Yet *different than* has been common in England for centuries and used by such exalted writers as Defoe, Addison, Steele, Dickens, Coleridge, and Thackeray, among others. Other authorities, in both Britain and America, continue to deride the absolute use of *hopefully*. *The New York Times Manual of Style and Usage* flatly forbids it. Its writers must not say, 'Hopefully the sun will come out soon', but rather are instructed to resort to a clumsily passive and periphrastic construction such as 'It is to be hoped that the sun will come out soon.' The reason? The authorities maintain that *hopefully* in the first sentence is a misplaced modal auxiliary – that it doesn't belong to any other part of the sentence. Yet they raise no objection to dozens of other words being used in precisely the same unattached way – *admittedly*, *mercifully*, *happily*, *curiously*, and so on. *Hopefully* is not allowed because, well, because somebody at *The New York Times* once had a boss who wouldn't allow it because his professor had forbidden it, because *his* father thought it was ugly and inelegant, because *he* had been told so by his uncle who was a man of great learning . . . and so on.

Considerations of what makes for good English or bad English are to an uncomfortably large extent matters of prejudice and conditioning. Until the eighteenth century it was correct to say 'you was' if you were referring to one person. It sounds odd today, but the logic is impeccable. *Was* is a singular verb and *were* a plural one. Why should *you* take a plural verb when the sense is clearly singular? The answer – surprise, surprise – is that Robert Lowth didn't like it. 'I'm hurrying, are I not?' is hopelessly ungrammatical, but 'I'm hurrying, aren't I?' – merely a contraction of the same words – is perfect English. *Many* is almost always a plural (as in 'Many people were there'), but not when it is followed by *a*, as in 'Many a man was there'. There's no inherent reason why these things should be so. They are not defensible in terms of grammar. They are because they are.

Nothing illustrates the scope for prejudice in English better than the issue of a split infinitive. Some people feel ridiculously strongly about it. When the British Conservative politician Jock Bruce-Gardyne was economic secretary to the Treasury in the early 1980s, he returned unread any departmental correspondence containing a split infinitive. (It should perhaps be pointed out that a split infinitive is one in which an adverb comes between *to* and a verb, as in *to quickly look*.) I can think of two very good reasons for not splitting an infinitive.

1. Because you feel that the rules of English ought to conform to the grammatical precepts of a language that died a thousand years ago.
2. Because you wish to cling to a pointless affectation of usage that is without the support of any recognized authority of the last 200 years, even at the cost of composing sentences that are ambiguous, inelegant, and patently contorted. To BOLDLY GO..

It is exceedingly difficult to find any authority who condemns the split infinitive – Theodore Bernstein, H. W. Fowler, Ernest Gowers, Eric Partridge, Rudolph Flesch, Wilson Follett, Roy H. Copperud, and others too tedious to enumerate here all agree that there is no logical reason not to split an infinitive.

Otto Jespersen even suggests that, strictly speaking, it isn't actually possible to split an infinitive. As he puts it: ' "To" . . . is no more an essential part of an infinitive than the definite article is an essential part of a nominative, and no one would think of calling "the good man" a split nominative.'[3]

Lacking an academy as we do, we might expect dictionaries to take up the banner of defenders of the language, but in recent years they have increasingly shied away from the role. A perennial argument with dictionary makers is whether they should be *prescriptive* (that is, whether they should prescribe how language should be used) or *descriptive* (that is, merely describe how it is used without taking a position). The most notorious example of the descriptive school was the 1961 *Webster's Third New International Dictionary* (popularly called *Webster's Unabridged*), whose editor, Philip Gove, believed that distinctions of usage were elitist and artificial. As a result, usages such as *imply* as a synonym for *infer* and *flout* being used in the sense of *flaunt* were included without comment. The dictionary provoked further antagonism, particularly among members of the U.S. Trademark Association, by refusing to capitalize trademarked words. But what really excited outrage was its remarkable contention that *ain't* was 'used orally in most parts of the U.S. by many cultivated speakers'.

So disgusted was *The New York Times* with the new dictionary that it announced it would not use it but would continue with the 1934 edition, prompting the language authority Bergen Evans to write: 'Anyone who solemnly announces in the year 1962 that he will be guided in matters of English usage by a dictionary published in 1934 is talking ignorant and pretentious nonsense,' and he pointed out that the issue of the *Times* announcing the decision contained nineteen words condemned by the *Second International*.

Since then, other dictionaries have been divided on the matter. *The American Heritage Dictionary*, first published in 1969, instituted a usage panel of distinguished commentators to rule on contentious points of usage, which are discussed, often at some length, in the text. But others have been more equivocal (or prudent or spineless depending on how you view it). The revised *Random House Dictionary of the English Language*, published in 1987, accepts the looser meaning for most words, though often noting that the newer usage is frowned on 'by many' – a curiously timid approach that at once acknowledges the existence of expert opinion and yet constantly places it at a distance. Among the looser meanings it accepts are *disinterested* to mean uninterested and *infer* to mean imply. It even accepts the existence of *kudo* as a singular – prompting a reviewer from *Time* magazine to ask if one instance of pathos should now be a patho.

It's a fine issue. One of the undoubted virtues of English is that it is a fluid and democratic language in which meanings shift and change in response to the pressures of common usage rather than the dictates of committees. It is a natural process that has been going on for centuries. To interfere with that process is arguably both arrogant and futile, since clearly the weight of usage will push new meanings into currency no matter how many authorities hurl themselves into the path of change.

But at the same time, it seems to me, there is a case for resisting change – at least slapdash change. Even the most liberal descriptivist would accept that there must be *some* conventions of usage. We must agree to spell *cat* c-a-t and not e-l-e-p-h-a-n-t, and we must agree that by that word we mean a small furry quadruped that goes *miaow* and sits comfortably on one's lap and not a large lumbering beast that grows tusks and is exceedingly difficult to house-train. In precisely the same way, clarity is generally better served if we agree to observe a distinction between *imply* and *infer*, *forego* and *forgo*, *fortuitous* and *fortunate*, *uninterested* and *disinterested*, and many others. As John Ciardi observed, resistance may in the end prove futile, but at least it tests the changes and makes them prove their worth.

Perhaps for our last words on the subject of usage we should turn to the last words of the venerable French grammarian Dominique Bonhours, who proved on his deathbed that a grammarian's work is never done when he gazed at those gathered loyally around him and whispered: 'I am about to – or I am going to – die; either expression is used.'

10

ORDER OUT OF CHAOS

How big is the English language? That's not an easy question. Samuel Johnson's dictionary contained 43,000 words. The unabridged *Random House* of 1987 has 315,000. *Webster's Third New International* of 1961 contains 450,000. And the revised *Oxford English Dictionary* of 1989 has 615,000 entries. But in fact this only begins to hint at the total.

For one thing, meanings in English are much more various that a bald count of entry words would indicate. The mouse that scurries across your kitchen floor and the mouse that activates your personal computer clearly are two quite separate entities. Shouldn't they then be counted as two words? And then what about related forms like *mousy, mouselike,* and *mice*? Shouldn't they also count as separate words? Surely there is a large difference between something that is a mouse and something that is merely mousy?

And then of course there are all the names of flora and fauna, medical conditions, chemical substances,* laws of physics, and all the other scientific and technical terms that don't make it into ordinary dictionaries. Of plants and animals alone, there are some 1.4 million named species, but that is only part of the total. One survey of beetles in just nineteen trees in Panama in 1989 found more than 700 species that had

*One of which, incidentally, is said to be the longest word in the English language. It begins *methianylglutaminyl* and finishes 1,913 letters later as *alynalalanylthreonilarginylserase*. I don't know what it is used for, though I daresay it would take some rubbing to get it out of the carpet.

not

been recorded before.[1] So it is clear that there are hundreds of thousands, if not millions, of living things out there waiting to be discovered and named. Total all these things together and you have – well, no one knows. But certainly not less than two or three million words.

So how many of these words do we know? Again, there is no simple answer. Many scholars have taken the trouble (or more probably compelled their graduate students to take the trouble) to count the number of words used by various authors, on the assumption, one supposes, that that tells us something about human vocabulary. Mostly what it tells us is that academics aren't very good at counting. Shakespeare, according to Pei and McCrum, had a vocabulary of 30,000 words, though Pei acknowledges seeing estimates putting the figure as low as 16,000. Lincoln Barnett puts it at 20,000 to 25,000. But most other authorities – Shipley, Baugh and Cable, Howard – put the number at a reassuringly precise 17,677. The King James Bible, according to Laird, contains 8,000 words, but Shipley puts the number at 7,000, while Barnett confidently zeroes in on a figure of 10,442. Who knows who's right?

One glaring problem with even the most scrupulous tabulation is that the total number of words used by an author doesn't begin to tell us the true size of his vocabulary. I know the meanings of *frangible*, *spiffing*, and *cutesy-poo*, but have never had occasion to write them before now. A man of Shakespeare's linguistic versatility must have possessed thousands of words that he never used because he didn't like or require them. Not once in his plays can you find the words *Bible*, *Trinity*, or *Holy Ghost*, and yet that is not to suggest that he was not familiar with them.

Estimates of the size of the average person's vocabulary are even more contentious. Max Müller, a leading German philologist at the turn of the century, thought the average farm labourer had an everyday vocabulary of no more than 300 words. Pei cites an English study of fruit pickers, which put the number at no more than 500, though he himself thought that the figure was probably closer to 30,000. Stuart Berg Flexner, the noted American lexicographer, suggests that the average well-read person has a vocabulary of about 20,000 words and probably uses about 1,500 to 2,000 in a normal week's conversation. McCrum puts an educated person's vocabulary at about 15,000.

There are endless difficulties attached to adjudging how many words a person knows. Consider just one. If I ask you what *incongruent* means and you say, 'It means not congruent', you are correct. That is the first definition given in most dictionaries, but that isn't to say that you have the faintest idea what the word means. Every page of the dictionary contains words we may not have encountered before – *inflationist, forbiddance, moosewood, pulsative* – and yet those meanings we could very probably guess.

At the same time there are many words that we use every day and clearly know and yet might have difficulty proving. How would you define *the* or *what* or *am* or *very*? Imagine trying to explain to a Martian in a concise way just what *is* is. And then what about all those words with a variety of meanings? Take *step*. *The American Heritage Dictionary* lists a dozen common meanings for the word, ranging from the act of putting one foot in front of the other to the name for part of a staircase. We all know all these meanings, yet if I gave you a pencil and a blank sheet of paper could you list them? Almost certainly not. The simple fact is that it is hard to remember what we remember, so to speak. Put another way, our memory is a highly fickle thing. Dr Alan Baddeley, a British authority on memory, cites a study in which people were asked to name the capital cities of several countries. Most had trouble with the capitals of countries like Uruguay and Bulgaria, but when they were told the initial letter of the capital city, they often suddenly remembered and their success rate soared. In another study people were shown long lists of random words and then asked to write down as many of them as they could remember. A few hours later, without being shown the list again, they were asked to write down as many of the words as they could remember then. Almost always the number of words would be nearly identical, but the actual words recalled from one test to another would vary by 50 per cent or more. In other words, there is vastly more verbal information locked away in our craniums than we can get out at any one time. So the problem of trying to assess accurately just how much verbal material we possess in total is fraught with difficulties.

For this reason educational psychologists have tended to shy away from such studies, and such information as exists is often decades old. One of the most famous studies was conducted in 1940. In it, two American researchers, R. H. Seashore and L. D. Eckerson, selected a random word from each left-hand page of a Funk & Wagnalls standard desktop dictionary and asked a sampling of college students to define those words or use them in a sentence. By extrapolating those results on to the number of entries in the dictionary, they concluded that the average student had a vocabulary of about 150,000 words – obviously very much larger than previously supposed. A similar study carried out by K. C. Diller in 1978, cited by Aitchison in *Words in the Mind*, put the vocabulary level even higher – at about 250,000 words. On the other hand, Jespersen cites the case of a certain Professor E. S. Holden who early in the century laboriously tested himself on every single word in *Webster's Dictionary* and arrived at a total of just 33,456 known words. It is clearly unlikely that a university professor's vocabulary would be four to six times smaller than that of the average student. So such studies would seem to tell us more about the difficulties of framing tests than about the size of our vocabularies.

What is certain is that the number of words we use is very much smaller than the number of words we know. In 1923 a lexicographer named G. H. McKnight did a comprehensive study of how words are used and found that just forty-three words account for fully half of all the words in common use, and that just nine account for fully one quarter of all the words in almost any sample of written English. Those nine are: *and*, *be*, *have*, *it*, *of*, *the*, *to*, *will*, and *you*.

By virtue of their brevity, dictionary definitions often fail to convey the nuances of English. *Rank* and *rancid* mean roughly the same thing, but, as Aitchison notes, we would never talk about eating rank butter or wearing rancid socks. A dictionary will tell you that *tall* and *high* mean much the same thing, but it won't explain to you that while you can apply either term to a building you can apply only tall to a person. On the strength of dictionary definitions alone a foreign visitor to your home could be excused for telling you that you have an abnormal child, that your wife's cooking is exceedingly odorous, and that your speech at a recent sales conference was laughable, and intend nothing but the warmest praise.

The fact is that the real meanings are often far more complex than the simple dictionary definitions would lead us to suppose. In 1985, the department of English at the University of Birmingham ran a computer analysis of words as they are actually used in English and came up with some surprising results. The primary dictionary meaning of words was often far adrift from the sense in which they were actually used. *Keep*, for instance, is usually defined as to retain, but in fact the word is much more often employed in the sense of continuing, as in 'keep cool' and 'keep smiling'. *See* is only rarely required in the sense of utilizing one's eyes, but much more often used to express the idea of knowing, as in 'I see what you mean'. *Give*, even more interestingly, is most often used, to quote the researchers, as 'mere verbal padding', as in 'give it a look' or 'give a report'.[2]

In short, dictionaries may be said to contain a certain number of definitions, but the true number of meanings contained in those definitions will always be much higher. As the lexicographer J. Ayton put it: 'The world's largest data bank of examples in context is dwarfed by the collection we all carry around subconsciously in our heads.'

English is changing all the time and at an increasingly dizzy pace. At the turn of the century words were being added at the rate of about 1,000 a year. Now, according to a report in *The New York Times*,[3] the increase is closer to 15,000 to 20,000 a year. In 1987, when Random House produced the second edition of its masterly twelve-pound unabridged dictionary, it included over 50,000 words that had not existed twenty-one years earlier and 75,000 new definitions of old words. Of its 315,000 entries, 210,000 had to be revised. That is a phenomenal amount of change in just two decades. The new entries included *preppy*, *quark*, *flexitime*, *chairperson*, *sunblocker*, and the names of 800 foods that had not existed or been generally heard of in 1966 – *tofu*, *piña colada*, *chapati*, *sushi*, and even *crêpes*.

Unabridged dictionaries have about them a stern, immutable air, as if here the language has been captured once and for all, and yet from the day of publication they are inescapably out of date. Samuel Johnson recognized this when he wrote: 'No dictionary of a living tongue can ever be perfect, since while it is hastening to publication, some words are budding, and some are fading away.' That, however, has never stopped anyone from trying, not least Johnson himself.

The English-speaking world has the finest dictionaries, a somewhat curious fact when you consider that we have never formalized the business of compiling them. From the seventeenth century when Cardinal Richelieu founded the Académie Française, dictionary making has been earnest work indeed. In the English-speaking world, the early dictionaries were almost always the work of one man rather than a ponderous committee of academics, as was the pattern on the Continent. In a kind of instinctive recognition of the mongrel, independent, idiosyncratic genius of the English tongue, these dictionaries were often entrusted to people bearing those very characteristics themselves. Nowhere was this more gloriously true than in the person of the greatest lexicographer of them all, Samuel Johnson.

Johnson, who lived from 1709 to 1784, was an odd candidate for genius. Blind in one eye, corpulent, incompletely educated, by all accounts coarse in manner, he was an obscure scribbler from an impoverished provincial background when he was given a contract by the London publisher Robert Dodsley to compile a dictionary of English.

Johnson's was by no means the first dictionary in English. From *Cawdrey's Table Alphabeticall* in 1604 to his opus a century and a half later there were at least a dozen popular dictionaries, though many of these were either highly specialized or slight (*Cawdrey's Table Alphabeticall* contained just 3,000 words and ran to barely a hundred pages). Many also had little claim to scholarship. *Cawdrey's*, for all the credit it gets as the first dictionary, was a fairly sloppy enterprise. It gave the definition of *aberration* twice and failed to alphabetize correctly on other words.

The first dictionary to aim for anything like comprehensiveness was the *Universal Etymological Dictionary* by Nathaniel Bailey, published in 1721, which anticipated Johnson's classic volume by thirty-four years and actually defined more words. So why is it that Johnson's dictionary is the one we remember? That's harder to answer than you might think.

His dictionary was full of shortcomings. He allowed many spelling inconsistencies to be perpetuated – *deceit* but *receipt*, *deign* but *disdain*, *hark* but *hearken*, *convey* but *inveigh*, *moveable* but *immovable*. He wrote *downhil* with one *l*, but *uphill* with two; *install* with two *l*'s, but *reinstal* with one; *fancy* with an *f*, but *phantom* with a *ph*. Generally he was aware of these inconsistencies, but felt that in many cases the irregular spellings were already too well established to tamper with. He did try to make spelling somewhat more sensible, institutionalizing the differences between *flower* and *flour* and between *metal* and *mettle*, but essentially he saw his job as recording English spelling as it stood in his day, not changing it. This was in sharp contrast to the attitude taken by the revisers of the Académie Française dictionary a decade or so later, who would revise almost a quarter of French spellings.

There were holes in Johnson's erudition. He professed a preference for what he conceived to be Saxon spellings for words like *music*, *critic*, and *prosaic*, and thus spelled them with a final *k*, when in fact they were all borrowed from Latin. He was given to flights of editorializing, as when he defined a *patron* as 'one who supports with insolence, and is paid with flattery' or *oats* as a grain that sustained horses in England and people in Scotland. His etymologies, according to Baugh and Cable, were 'often ludicrous' and his proofreading sometimes strikingly careless. He defined a *garret* as a 'room on the highest floor in the house' and a *cockloft* as 'the room over the garret'. Elsewhere, he gave identical definitions to *leeward* and *windward*, even though they are quite obviously opposites.

Even allowing for the inflated prose of his day, he had a tendency to write passages of remarkable denseness, as here: 'The proverbial oracles of our parsimonious ancestors have informed us, that the fatal waste of our fortune is by small expenses, by the profusion of sums too little singly to alarm our caution, and which we never suffer ourselves to consider together.' *Too little singly?* I would wager good money that that sentence was as puzzling to his contemporaries as it is to us. And yet at least it has the virtue of relative brevity. Often Johnson constructed sentences that ran to 250 words or more, which sound today uncomfortably like the ramblings of a man who has sat up far too late and drunk rather too much port.

Yet for all that, his *Dictionary of the English Language*, published in two volumes in June 1755, is a masterpiece, one of the landmarks of English literature. Its definitions are supremely concise, its erudition magnificent, if not entirely flawless. Without a nearby library to draw on, and with appallingly little financial backing (his publisher paid him a grand total of just £1,575, less than £200 a year, from which he had to pay his assistants), Johnson worked from a garret room off Fleet Street, where he defined some 43,000 words, illustrated with more than 114,000 supporting quotations drawn from every area of literature. It is little wonder that he made some errors and occasionally indulged himself with barbed definitions.

He had achieved in under nine years what the forty members of the Académie Française could not do in less than forty. He captured the majesty of the English language and gave it a dignity that was long overdue. It was a monumental accomplishment and he well deserved his fame.

But its ambitious sweep was soon to be exceeded by a

pernickety schoolteacher/lawyer half a world away in Connecticut. Noah Webster (1758–1843) was by all accounts a severe, correct, humourless, religious, temperate man who was not easily liked, even by other severe, religious, temperate, humourless people. A provincial schoolteacher and not-very-successful lawyer from Hartford, he was short, pale, smug, and boastful. (He held himself superior to Benjamin Franklin because he was a Yale man while Franklin was self-educated.) Where Samuel Johnson spent his free hours drinking and discoursing in the company of other great men, Webster was a charmless loner who criticized almost everyone but was himself not above stealing material from others, most notably from a spelling book called *Aby-sel-pha* by an Englishman named Thomas Dilworth. In the marvellously deadpan phrase of H. L. Mencken, Webster was 'sufficiently convinced of its merits to imitate it, even to the extent of lifting whole passages'. He credited himself with coining many words, among them *demoralize, appreciation, accompaniment, ascertainable,* and *expenditure,* which in fact had been in the language for centuries. He was also inclined to boast of learning that he simply did not possess. He claimed to have mastered twenty-three languages, including Latin, Greek, all the Romance languages, Anglo-Saxon, Persian, Hebrew, Arabic, Syriac, and a dozen more. Yet, as Thomas Pyles witheringly puts it, he showed 'an ignorance of German which would disgrace a freshman', and his grasp of other languages was equally tenuous. According to Charlton Laird, he knew far less Anglo-Saxon than Thomas Jefferson, who never pretended to be an expert at it. Pyles calls his *Dissertations on the English Language* 'a fascinating farrago of the soundest linguistic common sense and the most egregious poppycock'. It is hard to find anyone saying a good word about him.

Webster's first work, *A Grammatical Institute of the English Language* – consisting of three books: a grammar, a reader, and a speller – appeared between 1783 and 1785, but he didn't capture the public's attention until the publication in 1788 of *The American Spelling Book*. This volume (later called the

Elementary Spelling Book) went through so many editions and sold so many copies that historians appear to have lost track. But it seems safe to say that there were at least 300 editions between 1788 and 1829 and that by the end of the nineteenth century it had sold more than sixty million copies – though some sources put the figure as high as a hundred million. In either case, with the possible exception of the Bible, it is probably the best-selling book in American history.

Webster is commonly credited with changing American spelling, but what is seldom realized is how wildly variable his own views on the matter were. Sometimes he was in favour of radical and far-reaching changes – insisting on such spellings as *soop*, *bred*, *wimmen*, *groop*, *definit*, *fether*, *fugitiv*, *tuf*, *thum*, *hed*, *bilt*, and *tung* – but at other times he acted the very soul of orthographic conservatism, going so far as to attack the useful American tendency to drop the *u* from *colour*, *humour*, and the like. The main book with which he is associated in the popular mind, his massive *American Dictionary of the English Language* of 1828, actually said in the preface that it was 'desirable to perpetuate the sameness' of American and British spellings and usages.

Many of the spellings that he insisted on in his *Compendious Dictionary of the English Language* (1806) and its later variants were simply ignored by his loyal readers. They overlooked them, as one might a tic or stammer, and continued to write *group* rather than *groop*, *crowd* rather than *croud*, *medicine* rather than *medicin*, *phantom* for *fantom*, and many hundreds of others. Such changes as Webster did manage to establish were relatively straightforward and often already well underway – for instance, the American tendency to transpose the British *re* in *theatre*, *centre*, and other such words. Yet even here Webster was by no means consistent. His dictionaries retained many irregular spellings, some of which have stuck in English to this day (*acre*, *glamour*) and some of which were corrected by the readers themselves (*frolick*, *wimmen*). Other of his ideas are of questionable benefit. His insistence on dropping one of the *l*'s in words such as *traveller* and *jeweller* (which way they are still spelled in

England) was a useful shortcut, but it has left many Americans unsure whether to write *excelling* or *exceling*, or *fulfilled*, *fullfilled*, or *fulfiled*.

Webster was responsible also for the American *aluminum* in preference to the British *aluminium*. His choice has the fractional advantage of brevity, but defaults in terms of consistency. *Aluminium* at least follows the pattern set by other chemical elements – *potassium*, *radium*, and the like.

But for the most part the differences that distinguish American spelling from British spelling became common either late in his life or after his death, and would probably have happened anyway.

In terms of pronunciation he appears to have been responsible for the American pronunciation of *schedule* rather than the English 'shedjulle' and for the standard pronunciation of *lieutenant* which was then widely pronounced 'lefftenant' in America, as it still is in England today. But just as he sometimes pressed for odd spellings, so he called for many irregular pronunciations: 'deef' for *deaf*, 'nater' for *nature*, 'heerd' for *heard*, 'booty' for *beauty*, 'voloom' for *volume*, and others too numerous (and, I am tempted to add, too laughable) to dwell on. He insisted that *Greenwich* and *Thames* be pronounced as spelled and favoured giving *quality* and *quantity* the short 'à' of *hat*, while giving *advance*, *clasp*, and *grant* the broad 'ah' sound of southern England. No less remarkably, Webster accepted a number of clearly ungrammatical usages, among them 'it is me', 'we was', and 'them horses'. It is a wonder that anyone paid any attention to him at all. Often they didn't.

Nonetheless his dictionary was the most complete of its age, with 70,000 words – far more than Johnson had covered – and its definitions were models of clarity and conciseness. It was an enormous achievement.

All Webster's work was informed by a passionate patriotism and the belief that American English was at least as good as British English. He worked tirelessly, churning out endless hectoring books and tracts, as well as working on the more or less constant revisions of his spellers and dictionaries. In between time he wrote impassioned letters to congressmen, dabbled in politics, proffered unwanted advice to presidents, led his church choir, lectured to large audiences, helped found Amherst College, and produced a sanitized version of the Bible, in which Onan doesn't spill his seed but simply 'frustrates his purpose', in which men don't have testicles but rather 'peculiar members', and in which women don't have wombs (or evidently anything else with which to contribute to the reproductive process).

Like Samuel Johnson, he was a better lexicographer than a businessman. Instead of insisting on royalties he sold the rights outright and never gained the sort of wealth that his tireless labours merited. After Webster's death in 1843, two business-men from Springfield, Massachusetts, Charles and George Merriam, bought the rights to his dictionaries and employed his son-in-law, the rather jauntily named Chauncey A. Good-rich, to prepare a new volume (and, not incidentally, expunge many of the more ridiculous spellings and far-fetched ety-mologies). This volume, the first Merriam-Webster dictionary, appeared in 1847 and was an instant success. Soon almost every home had one. There is a certain neat irony in the thought that the book with which Noah Webster is now most closely associated wasn't really his work at all and certainly didn't adhere to many of his most cherished precepts.

In early February 1884, a slim paperback book bearing the title *The New English Dictionary on Historical Principles*, contain-ing all the words in the language (obscenities apart) between *A* and *ant* was published in Britain at the steepish price of twelve shillings and six pence. This was the first of twelve volumes of the most masterly and ambitious philological exer-cise ever undertaken, eventually redubbed the *Oxford English Dictionary*. The intention was to record every word used in English since 1150 and to trace it back through all its shifting meanings, spelling, and uses to its earliest recorded appear-ance. There was to be at least one citation for each century of its existence and at least one for each slight change of meaning.

To achieve this, almost every significant piece of English literature from the last seven and a half centuries would have to be
not so much read as scoured.

The man chosen to guide this enterprise was James Augustus
Henry Murray (1837–1915), a Scottish-born bank clerk,
schoolteacher, and self-taught philologist. He was an unlikely,
and apparently somewhat reluctant, choice to take on such a
daunting task. Murray, in the best tradition of British ec-
centrics, had a flowing white beard and liked to be photo-
graphed in a long black housecoat with a mortarboard on his
head. He had eleven children, all of whom were, almost from
the moment they learned the alphabet, roped into the endless
business of helping to sift through and alphabetize the several
million slips of paper on which were recorded every twitch and
burble of the language over seven centuries.

The ambition of the project was so staggering that one can't
help wondering if Murray really knew what he was taking on.
In point of fact, it appears he didn't. He thought the whole
business would take a dozen years at most and that it would
fill half a dozen volumes covering some 6,400 pages. In the
event, the project took more than four decades and sprawled
across 15,000 densely printed pages.

Hundreds of volunteers helped with the research, sending in
citations from all over the world. Many of them were, like
Murray, amateur philologists and often they were as eccentric
as he. One of the most prolific contributors was James Platt,
who specialized in obscure words. He was said to speak a
hundred languages and certainly knew as much about com-
parative linguistics as any man of his age, and yet he owned no
books of his own. He worked for his father in the City of
London and each lunchtime collected one book – never more
– from the Reading Room of the British Museum, which he
would take home, devour, and replace with another volume
the next day. At weekends he haunted the opium dens
and dockyards of Wapping and Whitechapel looking for
native speakers of obscure tongues whom he would query on
small points of semantics. He provided the histories of many

thousands of words. But an even more prolific contributor was an American expatriate named Dr W. C. Minor, a man of immense erudition who provided from his private library the etymologies of tens of thousands of words. When Murray invited him to a gathering of the dictionary's contributors, he learned, to his considerable surprise, that Dr Minor could not attend for the unfortunate reason that he was an inmate at Broadmoor, a hospital for the criminally insane, and not sufficiently in possession of his faculties to be allowed out. It appears that during the U.S. Civil War, having suffered an attack of sunstroke, Dr Minor developed a persecution mania, believing he was being pursued by Irishmen. After a stay in an asylum he was considered cured and undertook, in 1871, a visit to England. But one night while walking in London his mania returned and he shot dead an innocent stranger whose misfortune it was to have been walking behind the crazed American. Clearly Dr Minor's madness was not incompatible with scholarship. In one year alone, he made 12,000 contributions to the *OED* from the private library he built up at Broadmoor.

Murray worked ceaselessly on his dictionary for thirty-six years, from his appointment to the editorship in 1879 to his death at the age of seventy-eight in 1915. (He was knighted in 1908.) He was working on the letter U when he died, but his assistants carried on for another thirteen years until in 1928 the final volume, Wise to Wyzen, was issued. (For some reason, volume 12, XYZ, had appeared earlier.) Five years later, a corrected and slightly updated version of the entire set was reissued, under the name by which it has since been known: the *Oxford English Dictionary*. The completed dictionary contained 414,825 entries supported by 1,827,306 citations (out of 6 million collected) described in 44 million words of text spread over 15,487 pages. It is perhaps the greatest work of scholarship ever produced.

The *OED* confirmed a paradox that Webster had brought to light decades earlier – namely, that although readers will appear to treat a dictionary with the utmost respect, they will generally ignore anything in it that doesn't suit their tastes. The *OED*, for instance, has always insisted on *-ize* spellings for words such as *characterize*, *itemize*, and the like, and yet in few places in England, apart from the pages of *The Times* (and not always there), are they observed. The British on the whole still spell almost all such words with *-ise* endings and thus enjoy a consistency with words such as *advertise*, *merchandise*, and *surprise* that Americans fail to achieve. But perhaps the most notable of all the *OED*'s minor quirks is its insistence that Shakespeare should be spelled Shakspere. After explaining at some length why this is the only correct spelling, it grudgingly acknowledges that the commonest spelling 'is perh. Shakespeare'. (To which we might add, it cert. is.)

In the spring of 1989, a second edition of the dictionary was issued, containing certain modifications, such as the use of the International Phonetic Alphabet instead of Murray's own quirky system. It comprised the original twelve volumes, plus four vast supplements issued between 1972 and 1989. Now sprawling over twenty volumes, the updated dictionary is a third bigger than its predecessor, with 615,000 entries, 2,412,000 supporting quotations, almost 60 million words of exposition, and about 350 million keystrokes of text (or one for each native speaker of English in the world). No other language has anything even remotely approaching it in scope. Because of its existence, more is known about the history of English than any other language in the world.

11

OLD WORLD, NEW WORLD

The first American pilgrims happened to live in the midst of perhaps the most exciting period in the history of the English language – a time when 12,000 words were being added to the language and revolutionary activities were taking place in almost every realm of human endeavour. It was also a time of considerable change in the structure of the language. The 104 pilgrims who sailed from Plymouth in 1620 were among the first generation of people to use the *s* form on verbs, saying *has* rather than *hath*, *runs* rather than *runneth*. Similarly, *thee* and *thou* pronoun forms were dying out. Had the pilgrims come a quarter of a century earlier, America might well have preserved those forms, as it preserved other archaisms such as *gotten*.

The new settlers in America obviously had to come up with new words to describe their New World, and this necessity naturally increased as they moved inland. Partly this was achieved by borrowing from others who inhabited or explored the untamed continent. From the Dutch they took *landscape*, *cookie*, and *caboose*. They may also have taken *Yankee*, as a corruption of the Dutch Jan Kees ('John Cheese'). The suggestion is that Jan Kees was a nonce name for a Dutchman in America, rather like John Bull for an Englishman, but the historical evidence is slight. Often the new immigrants borrowed Indian terms, though these could take some swallowing since the Indian languages, particularly those of the eastern part of the continent, were inordinately agglomerative. As Mary Helen Dohan notes in her book on the rise of American

English, *Our Own Words*, an early translator of the Bible into Iroquoian had to devise the word *kummogkodonattootummooetitea-onganunnonash* for the phrase 'our question'. In Massachusetts there was a lake that the Indians called Chargoggagomancha-ugagochaubunagungamaug, which is said to translate as 'You fish on that side, we'll fish on this side, and nobody will fish in the middle.' Not surprisingly, such words were usually shortened and modified. The English-sounding *hickory* was whittled out of the Indian *pawcohiccora*. *Raugraoughcun* was hacked into *raccoon* and *isquonterquashes* into *squash*. *Hoochinoo*, the name of an Indian tribe noted for its homemade liquor, produced *hooch*. Some idea of the bewilderments of Indian orthography are indicated by the fact that Chippewa and Ojibway are different names for the same tribe as interpreted by different people at different times. Sometimes words went through many transformations before they sat comfortably on the English-speaking tongue. *Manhattan* has been variously recorded as *Manhates, Manthanes, Manhatones, Manhatesen, Manhattae*, and at least half a dozen others. Even the simple word *Iowa*, according to Dohan, has been recorded with sixty-four spellings. Despite the difficulties of rendering them into English, Indian names were borrowed for the names of more than half the American states and for countless thousands of rivers, lakes, and towns. Yet Americans borrowed no more than three or four dozen Indian words for everyday objects – among them *canoe, raccoon, hammock*, and *tobacco*.

From the early Spanish settlers, by contrast, the new inhabitants took more than 500 words – though many of these, it must be said, were Indian terms adopted by the Spaniards: among them *rodeo, bronco, buffalo, avocado, mustang, burro, fiesta, coyote, mesquite, canyon*, and *buckaroo*. *Buckaroo* was directly adapted from the Spanish *vaquero* (a cowboy) and thus must originally have been pronounced with the accent on the second syllable. Many borrowings are more accurately described as Mexican than Spanish since they did not exist in Spain, among them *stampede, hoosegow*, and *cafeteria*. *Hoosegow* and *jug* (for jail) were both taken from the Mexican-Spanish *juzgado*, which, despite the spelling, was pronounced more or less as 'hoosegow'. Sometimes it took a while for the pronunciation to catch up with the spelling. *Rancher*, a term borrowed from the Spanish *rancho*, was originally pronounced in the Mexican fashion, which made it something much closer to 'ranker'.

From the French, too, the colonists borrowed liberally, taking the names for Indian tribes, territories, rivers, and other geographical features, sometimes preserving the pronunciation (Sioux, Mackinac) and sometimes not (Illinois, Detroit, Des Plaines, Beloit). They took other words from the French, but often knocked them about in a way that made them look distinctively American, as when they turned *gaufre* into *gopher* and *chaudière* into *chowder*. Other New World words borrowed from the French were *prairie* and *dime*.

Often words arrived by the most improbable and circuitous routes. The word for the American currency, *dollar*, is a corruption of Joachimsthaler, named for a sixteenth-century silver mine in Joachimsthal, Germany. The first recorded use of the word in English was in 1553, spelled *daler*, and for the next two centuries it was applied by the English to various continental currencies. Its first use in America was not recorded until 1782, when Thomas Jefferson, in *Notes on a Money Unit for the United States*, plumped for *dollar* as the name of the national currency on the ground that 'the [Spanish] dollar is a known coin and the most familiar of all to the mind of the people'. That may be its first recorded appearance, but clearly if it was known to the people the term had already been in use for some time. At all events, Jefferson had his way: in 1785 the dollar was adopted as America's currency, though it was not until 1794 that the first dollars rolled off the presses. That much we know, but what we don't know is where the dollar sign ($) comes from. 'The most plausible account,' according to Mario Pei, 'is that it represents the first and last letters of the Spanish pesos, written one over the other.' It is an attractive theory but for the one obvious deficiency that the dollar sign doesn't look anything like a *p* superimposed on an *s*.

Perhaps even more improbable is how America came to be

named in the first place. The name is taken from Americus Vespucius, a Latinized form of Amerigo Vespucci. A semi-obscure Italian navigator who lived from 1454 to 1512, Vespucci made four voyages to the New World though without ever once seeing North America. A contemporary mapmaker wrongly thought Vespucci discovered the whole of the continent and, in the most literal way, put his name on the map. When he learned of his error, the mapmaker, one Martin Waldesmüller, took the name off, but by then it had stuck. Vespucci himself preferred the name Mundus Novus, 'New World'.

In addition to borrowing hundreds of words, the Mundus Novians (far better word!) devised many hundreds of their own. The pattern was to take two already existing English words and combine them in new ways: *bullfrog, eggplant, grasshopper, rattlesnake, mockingbird, catfish*. Sometimes, however, words from the Old World were employed to describe different but similar articles in the New. So *beech, walnut, laurel, partridge, robin, oriole, hemlock*, and even *pond* all describe different things in the two continents.

Settlers moving west not only had to find new expressions to describe features of their new outsized continent – *mesa, butte, bluff*, and so on – but also outsized words that reflected their zestful, virile, wildcat-wrassling, hell-for-leather approach to life. These expressions were, to put it mildly, often colourful, and a surprising number of them have survived: *hornswoggle, cattywampus, rambunctious, absquatulate, to move like greased lightning, to kick the bucket, to be in cahoots with, to root hog or die*. Others have faded away: *monstracious, teetotaciously, helliferocious, conbobberation, obflisticate*, and many others of equal exuberance.

Of all the new words to issue from the New World, the quintessential Americanism without any doubt was *O.K.* Arguably America's single greatest gift to international discourse, *O.K.* is the most grammatically versatile of words, able to serve as an adjective ('Lunch was O.K.'), verb ('Can you O.K. this for me?'), noun ('I need your O.K. on this'), interjection ('O.K., I hear you'), and adverb ('We did O.K.').

It can carry shades of meaning that range from casual assent ('Shall we go?' 'O.K.'), to great enthusiasm ('O.K.!'), to lukewarm endorsement ('The party was O.K.'), to a more or less meaningless filler of space ('O.K., can I have your attention please?').

It is a curious fact that the most successful and widespread of all English words, naturalized as an affirmation into almost every language in the world, from Serbo-Croatian to Tagalog, is one that has no correct agreed spelling (it can be O.K., OK, or okay) and one whose origins are so obscure that it has been a matter of heated dispute almost since it first appeared. The many theories break down into three main camps:

1. It comes from someone's or something's initials – a Sac Indian chief called Old Keokuk, or a shipping agent named Obadiah Kelly, or from President Martin Van Buren's nickname, Old Kinderhook, or from Orrins-Kendall crackers, which were popular in the nineteenth century. In each of these theories the initials were stamped or scribbled on documents or crates and gradually came to be synonymous with quality or reliability.
2. It is adapted from some foreign or English dialect word or place name, such as the Finnish *oikea*, the Haitian Aux Cayes (the source of a particularly prized brand of rum), or the Choctaw *okeh*. President Woodrow Wilson apparently so liked the Choctaw theory that he insisted on spelling the word *okeh*.
3. It is a contraction of the expression Oll Korrect, often said to be the spelling used by the semi-literate seventh President, Andrew Jackson.

This third theory, seemingly the most implausible, is in fact very possibly the correct one – though without involving Andrew Jackson and with a bit of theory one thrown in for good measure. According to Allen Walker Read of Columbia University, who spent years tracking down the derivation of O.K., a fashion developed among young wits of Boston and New York in 1838 of writing abbreviations based on intentional illiteracies. They thought it highly comical to write O.W. for 'oll wright', O.K. for 'oll korrect', K.Y. for 'know yuse', and so on. O.K. first appeared in print on March 23, 1839, in the *Boston Morning Post*. Had that been it, the expression would no doubt have died an early death, but coincidentally in 1840 Martin Van Buren, known as Old Kinderhook from his hometown in upstate New York, was running for reelection as president, and an organization founded to help his campaign was given the name the Democratic O.K. Club. O.K. became a rallying cry throughout the campaign and with great haste established itself as a word throughout the country. This may have been small comfort to Van Buren, who lost the election to William Henry Harrison, who had the no-less-snappy slogan 'Tippecanoe and Tyler Too'.

Although the residents of the New World began perforce to use new words almost from the first day they stepped ashore, it isn't at all clear when they began pronouncing them in a distinctively American way. No one can say when the American accent first arose – or why it evolved quite as it did. As early as 1791, Dr David Ramsay, one of the first American historians, noted in his *History of the American Revolution* that Americans had a particular purity of speech, which he attributed to the fact that people from all over Britain were thrown together in America where they 'dropped the peculiarities of their several provincial idioms, retaining only what was fundamental and common to them all'.

But that is not to suggest that they sounded very much like Americans of today. According to Robert Burchfield, George Washington probably sounded as British as Lord North. On the other hand, Lord North probably sounded more American than would any British minister today. North would, for instance, have given *necessary* its full value. He would have pronounced *path* and *bath* in the American way. He would have given *r*'s their full value in words like *cart* and *horse*. And he would have used many words that later fell out of use in England but were preserved in the New World.

The same would be true of the soldiers on the battlefield,

who would, according to Burchfield, have spoken identically 'except in minor particularities'.[1] Soldiers from both sides would have tended not to say *join* and *poison* as we do today, but something closer to 'jine' and 'pison'. *Speak* and *tea* would have sounded to modern ears more like 'spake' and 'tay', *certain* and *merchant* more like 'sartin' and 'marchant'.

It has been said many times that hostility towards Britain at the end of the Revolutionary War was such that America seriously considered adopting another language. The story has been repeated many times, even by as eminent an authority as Randolph Quirk.* But it appears to be without foundation. Someone *may* have made such a proposal. At this remove we cannot be certain. But what we can say with confidence is that if such a proposal was made it appears not to have stimulated any widespread public debate, which would seem distinctly odd in a matter of such moment. We also know that the Founding Fathers were so little exercised by the question of an official language for the United States that they made not one mention of it in the Constitution. So it seems evident that such a proposal was not treated seriously, if indeed it ever existed.

What is certain is that many people, including both Thomas Jefferson and Noah Webster, expected American English to evolve into a separate language over time. Benjamin Franklin, casting an uneasy eye at the Germans in his native Pennsylvania, feared that America would fragment into a variety of speech communities. But neither of these things happened. It is worth looking at why they did not.

Until about 1840 America received no more than about 20,000 immigrants a year, mostly from two places: Africa in the form of slaves and the British Isles. Total immigration between 1607 and 1840 was no more than one million. Then suddenly, as a consequence of a famine in Ireland in 1845 and

---

*'At the time when the United States split off from Britain, for example, there were proposals that independence should be linguistically acknowledged by the use of a different language from that of Britain' (*The Use of English*, page 3).

immense political upheaval elsewhere, America's immigration became a flood. In the second half of the nineteenth century, thirty million people poured into the country, and the pace quickened further in the early years of the twentieth century. In just four years at its peak, between 1901 and 1905, America absorbed a million Italians, a million Austro-Hungarians, and half a million Russians, plus tens of thousands of other people from scores of other places.

At the turn of the century, New York had more speakers of German than anywhere in the world except Vienna and Berlin, more Irish than anywhere but Dublin, more Russians than in Kiev, more Italians than in Milan or Naples. In 1890 the United States had 800 German newspapers and as late as the outbreak of World War I Baltimore alone had four elementary schools teaching in German only.

Often, naturally, these people settled in enclaves. John Russell Bartlett noted that it was possible to cross Oneida County, New York, and hear nothing but Welsh. Probably the most famous of these enclaves – certainly the most enduring – was that of the Amish who settled primarily in and around Lancaster County in southern Pennsylvania and spoke a dialect that came to be known, misleadingly, as Pennsylvania Dutch. (The name is a corruption of Deutsch, or German.) Some 300,000 people in America still use Pennsylvania Dutch as their first language, and perhaps twice as many more can speak it. The large number is accounted for no doubt by the extraordinary insularity of most Amish, many of whom even now shun cars, tractors, electricity, and the other refinements of modern life. Pennsylvania Dutch is a kind of institution-alized broken English, arising from adapting English words to German syntax and idiom. Perhaps the best known of their expressions is 'Outen the light' for put out the light. Among others:

Nice day, say not?	– Nice day, isn't it?
What's the matter of him?	– What's the matter with him?
It's going to give rain.	– It's going to rain.

Come in and eat yourself.	– Come and have something to eat.
It wonders me where it could be.	– I wonder where it could be.

Pennsylvania Dutch speakers also have a tendency to speak with semi-Germanic accents – saying 'chorge' for *George*, 'britches' for *bridges*, and 'tolt' for *told*. Remarkably, many of them still have trouble, despite more than two centuries in America, with 'v' and 'th' sounds, saying 'wisit' for *visit* and 'ziss' for *this*. But two things should be borne in mind. First, Pennsylvania Dutch is an anomaly, nurtured by the extreme isolation from modern life of its speakers. And second, it is an *English* dialect. That is significant.

Throughout the last century, and often into this one, it was easy to find isolated speech communities throughout much of America: Norwegians in Minnesota and the Dakotas, Swedes in Nebraska, Germans in Wisconsin and Indiana, and many others. It was natural to suppose that the existence of these linguistic pockets would lead the United States to deteriorate into a variety of regional tongues, rather as in Europe, or at the very least result in widely divergent dialects of English, each heavily influenced by its prevailing immigrant group. But of course nothing of the sort happened. In fact, the very opposite was the case. Instead of becoming more divergent, people over the bulk of the American mainland continued to evince a more or less uniform speech. Why should that be?

There were three main reasons. First, the continuous movement of people back and forth across the continent militated against the formation of permanent regionalisms. Americans enjoyed social mobility long before sociologists thought up the term. Second, the intermingling of people from diverse backgrounds worked in favour of homogeneity. Third, and above all, social pressures and the desire for a common national identity encouraged people to settle on a single way of speaking.

People who didn't blend in risked being made to feel like outsiders. They were given names that denigrated their backgrounds: *wop* from the Italian *guappo* (a strutting fellow), *kraut* (from the supposed German fondness for sauerkraut), *yid* (for Yiddish speakers), *dago* from the Spanish Diego, *kike* (from the -*ki* and -*ky* endings on many Jewish names), *bohunk* from Bohemian-Hungarian, *micks* and *paddies* for the Irish. As we saw in the chapter on dialects, the usual pattern was for the offspring of immigrants to become completely assimilated – to the point of being unable to speak their parents' language.

Occasionally physical isolation, as with the Cajuns in Louisiana or the Gullah speakers on the Sea Islands off the East Coast, enabled people to be more resistant to change. It has often been said that if you want to hear what the speech of Elizabethan England sounded like, you should go to the hills of Appalachia or the Ozarks, where you can find isolated communities of people still speaking the English of Shakespeare. To be sure, many of the words and expressions that we think of today as 'hillbilly' words – *afeared, tetchy, consarn it, yourn* (for *yours*), *hisn* (for *his*), *et* (for *ate*), *sassy* (for *saucy*), *jined* (for *joined*), and scores of others – do indeed reflect the speech of Elizabethan London. But much the same claim could be made for the modern-day speech of Boston or Charleston or indeed almost anywhere else. After all, every person in America uses a great many expressions and pronunciations familiar to Shakespeare but which have since died out in England – *gotten, fall* (for the season), the short *a* of *bath* and *path*, and so on. The mountain regions may possess a somewhat greater abundance of archaic expressions and pronunciations because of their relative isolation, but to imply that the speech there is a near replica of the speech of Elizabethan England is taking it too far. Apart from anything else, most of the mountain areas weren't settled for a century or more after Elizabeth's death. H. L. Mencken traced this belief to an early authority, one A. J. Ellis, and then plunged the dagger in with the conclusion that 'Ellis was densely ignorant of the history of the English settlements in America, and ascribed to them a cultural isolation that never existed.' Still, it is easy to find the belief, or something very like it, repeated in many books.

It is certainly true to say that America in general preserved many dozens of words that would otherwise almost certainly have been lost to English. The best noted, perhaps, is *gotten*, which to most Britons is the quaintest of Americanisms. It is now so unused in Britain that many Britons have to have the distinction between *got* and *gotten* explained to them even though they make exactly the same distinction with *forgot* and *forgotten*. *Gotten* also survives in England in one or two phrases, notably 'ill-gotten gains'. *Sick* likewise underwent a profound change of sense in Britain that was not carried over to America. Shakespeare uses it in the modern American sense in *Henry V* ('He is very sick, and would to bed'). Even so, the broader original sense survives in a large number of expressions in Britain, such as *sick bay, sick note, in sickness and in health, to be off sick, sickbed, homesick*, and *lovesick*. Conversely, the British often use *ill* where Americans would only use *injured*, as in newspaper accounts describing the victim of a train crash as being 'seriously ill in hospital'.

Other words and expressions that were common in Elizabethan England that died in England were *fall* as a synonym for autumn, *mad* for angry, *progress* as a verb, *platter* for a large dish, *assignment* in the sense of a job or task (it survived in England only as a legal expression), *deck of cards* (the English now say pack), *slim* in the sense of small (as in slim chance), *mean* in the sense of unpleasant instead of stingy, *trash* for rubbish (used by Shakespeare), *hog* as a synonym for pig, *mayhem, magnetic, chore, skillet, ragamuffin, homespun*, and the expression *I guess*. Many of these words have re-established themselves in England, so much so that most Britons would be astonished to learn that they had ever fallen out of use there. *Maybe* was described in the original *Oxford English Dictionary* in this century as 'archaic and dialectal'. *Quit* in the sense of resigning had similarly died out in Britain. To *leaf through* a book was first recorded in Britain in 1613, but then fell out of use and was reintroduced from America, as was *frame-up*, which the *Oxford English Dictionary* in 1901 termed obsolete, little realizing that it would soon be reintroduced to its native land in a thousand gangster movies.

America also introduced many words and expressions that never existed in Britain, but which have for the most part settled comfortably into domestic life there. Among these words and phrases are – and this really is a bare sampling – *commuter, bedrock, snag, striptease, cold spell, gimmick, baby-sitter, lengthy, sag, soggy, teenager, telephone, typewriter, radio, to cut no ice, to butt in, to sidetrack, hangover, to make good* (to be successful), *fudge, publicity, joyride, bucket shop, blizzard, stunt, law-abiding, department store, notify, advocate* (as a verb), *currency* (for money), *to park, to rattle* (in the sense of to unnerve or unsettle), *hindsight, beeline, raincoat, scrawny, take a backseat, cloudburst, graveyard, know-how, to register* (as in a hotel), *to shut down, to fill the bill, to hold down* (as in keep), *to hold up* (as in rob), *to bank on, to stay put, to be stung* (cheated), and even *stiff upper lip*. In a rather more roundabout way, so to speak, the word *roundabout*, the British term for traffic circles, is of American origin. More precisely, it was a term invented by Logan Pearsall Smith, an American living in England, who was one of the members in the 1920s of the BBC Advisory Committee on Spoken English. This lofty panel had the job of deciding questions of pronunciation, usage, and even vocabulary for the BBC. Before Smith came along, traffic circles in Britain were called gyratory circuses.*

Of course, the traffic has not been entirely one way. Apart from the several thousand words that the British endowed Americans with in the first place, they have since the colonial exodus also given the world *smog, weekend, gadget, miniskirt, radar, brain drain,* and *gay* in the sense of homosexual. Even so, there is no denying that the great bulk of words introduced into the English language over the last two centuries have travelled from west to east.

Almost from the beginning of the colonial experience it has been a common assumption in Britain that a word or turn of

*Smith also wanted traffic lights to be called stop-and-goes and brainwave to be replaced by mindfall, among many other equally fanciful neologisms, but these never caught on.

phrase is inferior simply by dint of its being American-bred. In dismissing the 'vile and barbarous word *talented*', Samuel Taylor Coleridge observed that 'most of these pieces of slang come from America'. That clearly was ground enough to detest them. In point of fact, I am very pleased to tell you, *talented* was a British coinage, first used in 1422. Something of the spirit of the age was captured in Samuel Johnson's observation in 1769 that Americans were 'a race of convicts and ought to be thankful for any thing we allow them short of hanging'.[2] A reviewer of Thomas Jefferson's *Notes on the State of Virginia* (1787) entreated Jefferson to say what he would about the British character, but 'O spare, we beseech you, our mother-tongue.' Another, noting his use of the word *belittle*, remarked: 'It may be an elegant [word] in Virginia, and even perfectly intelligible, but for our part all we can do is to guess at its meaning. For shame, Mr Jefferson!'[3] Jefferson also coined the word *Anglophobia*; little wonder.

As often as not, these sneerers showed themselves to be not only gratuitously offensive but also etymologically under-informed because the objects of their animus were invariably British in origin. Johnson disparaged *glee*, *jeopardy*, and *smoulder*, little realizing that they had existed in England for centuries. *To antagonize*, coined by John Quincy Adams, was strenuously attacked. So was *progress* as a verb, even though it had been used by both Bacon and Shakespeare. *Scientist* was called 'an ignoble Americanism' and 'a cheap and vulgar product of trans-Atlantic slang'.

Americans, alas, were often somewhat snivelling cohorts in this cavilling – perhaps most surprisingly Benjamin Franklin. When the Scottish philosopher David Hume criticized some of his Americanisms, Franklin meekly replied: 'I thank you for your friendly admonition relating to some unusual words in the pamphlet. It will be of service to me. The *pejorate* and the *colonize* . . . I give up as bad; for certainly in writings intended for persuasion and for general information, one cannot be too clear; and every expression in the least obscure is a fault; The *unshakable* too, tho clear, I give up as rather low. The introducing new words, where we are already possessed of old ones sufficiently expressive, I confess must be generally wrong . . . I hope with you, that we shall always in America make the best English of this island our standard, and I believe it will be so.' And yet he went right on introducing words: *eventuate, demoralize, constitutionality*. This servility persisted for a long time among some people. William Cullen Bryant, the editor of the *New York Evening Post* and one of the leading journalists of the nineteenth century in America, refused to allow such useful words as *lengthy* and *presidential* into his paper simply because they had been dismissed as Americanisms a century earlier. Jefferson, more heroically, lamented the British tendency to raise 'a hue and cry at every word he [Samuel Johnson] has not licensed'.

The position has little improved with time. As Baugh and Cable put it, 'The English attitude toward Americanisms is still quite frankly hostile.' To this day you can find authorities in Britain attacking such 'Americanisms' as *maximize, minimize*, and *input*, quite unaware that the first two were coined by Jeremy Bentham more than a century ago and the last appeared more than 600 years ago in Wycliffe's translation of the Bible. *Loan* as a verb (rather than *lend*) is often criticized as an Americanism, when in fact it was first used in England a full eight centuries ago. The stylebook of *The Times* sniffily instructs its staff members that 'normalcy should be left to the Americans who coined it. *The English* [italics mine] is normality.' In point of fact *normalcy* is a British coinage.

Indeed, this xenophobia occasionally touches new peaks of smugness. In 1930, a Conservative Member of Parliament, calling for a quota on the number of American films allowed into Britain, said: 'The words and accent are perfectly disgusting, and there can be no doubt that such films are an evil influence on our language.'[4] More recently, during a debate in the House of Lords in 1978 one of the members said: 'If there is a more hideous language on the face of the earth than the American form of English, I should like to know what it is.' (We should perhaps bear in mind that the House of Lords is a largely powerless, nonelective institution. It is an arresting fact of British political life that a Briton can enjoy a national platform and exalted status simply because he is the residue of an illicit coupling 300 years before between a monarch and an orange seller.)

Even when they have not been actively hostile, the British have often struck an aloof, not to say fantastical, attitude to the adoption of American words. In *The King's English*, the Fowler brothers, usually paragons of common sense in matters linguistic, take the curious and decidedly patronizing view that although there is nothing wrong with American English, and that it is even capable of evincing occasional flashes of genius, it is nonetheless a foreign tongue and should be treated as such. 'The English and the American language and literature are both good things; but they are better apart than mixed.' They particularly cautioned against using three vulgar Americanisms: *placate*, *transpire*, and *antagonize*.

Putting aside the consideration that without America's contribution English today would enjoy a global importance about on a par with Portuguese, it is not too much to say that this attitude is unworthy of the British. It is at any rate an arresting irony that the more dismissive they grow of American usages, the more lavishly they borrow them – to the extent of taking phrases that have no literal meaning in British English. People in Britain talk about doing something on a shoestring even though the word there is *shoelace*. They talk about the 64,000-dollar question, looking like a million bucks, having a mega-bucks salary, stepping on the gas (when they fuel their cars with petrol), and taking a raincheck even though probably not one Briton in a hundred knows what a raincheck is. They have even quietly modified their grammar and idiom to fit the American model. Ernest Gowers, in the revised edition of *A Dictionary of Modern English Usage*, noted that under the influence of American usage the British had begun to change *aim at doing* into *aim to do*, haven't got to *don't have*, begun using *in* instead of *for* in phrases like 'the first time in years', and started for the first time using *begin to* with a negative, as in 'This doesn't begin to make sense'. And these changes go on. Just in the last decade or so, *truck* has begun driving out *lorry*. *Airplane* is more and more replacing *aeroplane*. The American sense of billion (1,000,000,000) has almost completely routed the British sense (1,000,000,000,000).

American spelling, too, has had more influence on the British than they might think. *Jail* rather than *gaol*, *burden* rather than *burthen*, *clue* rather than *clew*, *wagon* rather than *waggon*, *today* and *tomorrow* rather than *to-day* and *to-morrow*, *mask* rather than *masque*, *reflection* rather than *reflexion*, and *forever* and *onto* as single words rather than two have all been nudged on their way towards acceptance by American influence. For most senses of the word *program*, the British still use *programme*, but when the context is of computers they write *program*. A similar distinction is increasingly made with *disc* (the usual British spelling) and *disk* for the thing you slot into your home computer.

Although the English kept the *u* in many words like *humour*, *honour*, and *colour*, they gave it up in several, such as *terrour*, *horrour*, and *governour*, helped at least in part by the influence of American books and journals. Confusingly, they retained it in some forms but abandoned it in others, so that in England we find *honour* and *honourable* but *honorary* and *honorarium*; *colour* and *colouring* but *coloration*; *humour* but *humorist*; *labour* and *labourer* but *laborious*. There is no logic to it, and no telling why some words gave up the *u* and others didn't. For a time it was fashionable to drop the *u* from *honour* and *humour* – Coleridge for one did it – but it didn't catch on.

People don't often appreciate just how much movies and television have smoothed the differences between British and American English, but half a century ago the gap was very much wider. In 1922, when Sinclair Lewis's novel *Babbitt* was published in Britain it contained a glossary. Words that are commonplace in Britain now were quite unknown until the advent of talking pictures – among them *grapevine*, *fan* (in the sense of a sports enthusiast), *gimmick*, and *phoney*. As late as 1955, a writer in the *Spectator* could misapprehend the expression *turn of the century*, and take it to mean midcentury, when the first half turns into the second. In 1939, the preface to *An Anglo-American Interpreter* suggested that 'an American, if taken suddenly ill while on a visit to London, might die in the street through being unable to make himself understood.'[5] That may be arrant hyperbole – there has never been a period, after all, when an American couldn't say, 'Help me, I'm dying in the street' – but it is probably true that the period up to the Second World War marked the age of the greatest divergence between the two main branches of English.

Even now, there remains great scope for confusion, as evidenced by the true story of an American lady, newly arrived in London, who opened her front door to find three burly men on the steps informing her that they were her dustmen. 'Oh,' she blurted, 'but I do my own dusting.' It can take years for an American to master the intricacies of British idiom, and vice versa. In Britain *homely* is a flattering expression; in America it means 'ugly'. In Britain *upstairs* is the first floor; in America it is the second. In Britain *to table a motion* means to put it aside; in America it means to give it priority. *Presently* means 'now' in America; in Britain it means 'in a little while'. Sometimes these can cause considerable embarrassment, most famously with the British expression 'I'll knock you up in the morning', which means to an American 'I'll make you pregnant in the morning.' *To keep your pecker up* is an indecent proposition in America, whereas a reference to a woman's fanny – which to an American is an innocent synonym for the buttocks – would at a British dinner party provoke an embarrassed silence. (You may recognize the voice of experience in this.)

Sometimes these differences in meaning take on a kind of bewildering circularity. A tramp in Britain is a bum in America, while a bum in Britain is a fanny in America, while a fanny in Britain is – well, we've covered that. To a foreigner it must seem sometimes as if we are being intentionally contrary. Consider that in Britain the Royal Mail delivers the post, not the mail, while in America the Postal Service delivers the mail, not the post. These ambiguities can affect scientists as much as tourists. The British billion, as we have already seen, has surrendered to the American billion, but for other numbers agreement has yet to be reached. A decillion in America is a one plus thirty-three zeros. In Britain it is a one plus sixty zeros. Needless to say, that can make a difference.

In common speech, some 4,000 words are used differently in one country from the other. That's a very large number indeed. Some are well known on both sides of the Atlantic – *lift/elevator*, *dustbin/garbage can*, *biscuit/cookie* – but many hundreds of others are still liable to befuddle the hapless traveller. Try covering up the right-hand column below and seeing how many of the American terms in the left-hand column you can identify. If you get more than half you either know the country well or have been watching too many episodes of *Dynasty*.

American	**British**
antsy	fidgety
barf	vomit
boxscore	baseball game summary
cabana	beach hut
cheesecloth	muslin
cotton candy	candy floss
crosswalk	pedestrian crossing
downspout	drainpipe
duplex	semi-detached house
goldbricker	skiver
ground round	best mince
moxie	spunk
hush puppy	cornmeal fritter
lightning bug	glow-worm
overpass	flyover
pacifier	baby's dummy
parking (property)	grassy strip between pavement and street
realtor	estate agent
station wagon	estate car
teeter-totter	see-saw

American	British
trunk (of car)	boot
VCR	video recorder
yard	garden
zucchini	courgette

ENGLISH AS A WORLD LANGUAGE

In Hong Kong you can find a place called the Plastic Bacon Factory. In Naples, according to the *Observer*, there is a sports shop called Snoopy's Dribbling, while in Brussels there is a men's clothing store called Big Nuts, where on my last visit to the city it had a sign saying: SWEAT – 690 FRANCS. (Closer inspection revealed this to be a sweat-shirt.) In Japan you can drink Homo Milk or Poccari Sweat (a popular soft drink), eat some chocolate called Hand-Maid Queer-Aid, or go out and buy some Arm Free Grand Slam Muns ingwear.

In Sarajevo, Yugoslavia, a largely Muslim city seemingly as remote from English-speaking culture as any place in Europe, you can find graffiti saying HEAVY METAL IS LAW! and HOOLI-GAN KINGS OF THE NORTH! In the Europa Hotel in the same city, you will find this message on every door: 'Guests should announce the abandonment of theirs rooms before 12 o'clock, emptying the room at the latest until 14 o'clock, for the use of the room before 5 at the arrival or after the 16 o'clock at the departure, will be billed as one night more.' Is that clear? In Yugoslavia they speak five languages. In not one of them does the word *stop* exist, yet every stop sign in the country says just that.

I bring this up here to make the somewhat obvious observa-tion that English is the most global of languages. Products are deemed to be more exciting if they carry English messages even when, as often happens, the messages don't make a lot of sense. I have before me a Japanese eraser which says: 'Mr

Friendly Quality Eraser. Mr Friendly Arrived!! He always stay near you, and steals in your mind to lead you a good situation.' On the bottom of the eraser is a further message: 'We are ecologically minded. This package will self-destruct in Mother Earth.' It is a product that was made in Japan solely for Japanese consumers, yet there is not a word of Japanese on it. Coke cans in Japan come with the slogan I FEEL COKE & SOUND SPECIAL. A correspondent of the *Economist* spotted a T-shirt in Tokyo that said: O.D. ON BOURGEOISIE MILK BOY MILK. A shopping bag carried a picture of dancing elephants above the legend: ELEPHANT FAMILY ARE HAPPY WITH US. THEIR HUMMING MAKES US FEEL HAPPY. Some of these items betray a distinct, and yet somehow comforting, lack of geographical precision. A shopping bag showing yachts on a blue sea had the message SWITZERLAND: SEASIDE CITY. A range of products manufactured by a company called Cream Soda all used to bear the splendidly vacuous message 'Too fast to live, too young to happy'. Then some spoilsport informed the company of its error and the second half of the message was changed to 'too young too die'. What is perhaps most worrying is that these meaningless phrases on clothing are invading the English-speaking world. I recently saw in a London store a jacket with bold lettering that said: RODEO – 100% BOYS FOR ATOMIC ATLAS. The jacket was made in Britain. Who by? Who for?

So how many people in the world speak English? That's hard to say. We're not even sure how many native speakers there are. Different authorities put the number of people who speak English as a first language at anywhere between 300 million and 400 million. That may seem sloppily imprecise, but there are some sound reasons for the vagueness. In the first place, it is not simply a matter of taking all the English-speaking countries in the world and adding up their populations. America alone has forty million people who don't speak English – about the same as the number of people in England who *do* speak English.

Then there is the even thornier problem of deciding whether

a person is speaking English or something that is *like* English but is really a quite separate language. This is especially true of the many English-based creoles in the world, such as Krio, spoken in Sierra Leone, and Neo-Melanesian (sometimes called Tok Pisin), spoken in Papua New Guinea. According to Dr Loreto Todd of Leeds University, the world has sixty-one such creoles spoken by up to 200 million people – enough to make the number of English speakers soar, *if* you consider them English speakers.

A second and rather harsher problem is deciding whether a person speaks English or simply *thinks* he speaks it. I have before me a brochure from the Italian city of Urbino, which contains a dozen pages of the most gloriously baroque and impenetrable English prose, lavishly garnished with misspellings, unexpected hyphenations, and twisted grammar. A brief extract: 'The integrity and thus the vitality of Urbino is no chance, but a conservation due to the factors constituted in all probability by the approximate framework of the unity of the country, the difficulty od [*sic*] communications, the very concentric pattern of hill sistems or the remoteness from hi-ghly developed areas, the force of the original design proposed in its construction, with the means at the disposal of the new sciences of the Renaissance, as an ideal city even.' It goes on like that for a dozen pages. There is scarcely a sentence that makes even momentary sense. I daresay that if all the people in Italy who speak English were asked to put up their hands, this author's would be one of the first to fly up, but whether he can fairly be said to speak English is, to put it charitably, moot.

So there are obvious problems in trying to put a figure to the number of English speakers in the world. Most estimates put the number of native speakers at about 330 million, as compared with 260 million for Spanish, 150 million for Portuguese, and a little over 100 million for French. Of course, sheer numbers mean little. Mandarin Chinese, or Guoyo, spoken by some 750 million people, has twice as many speakers as any other language in the world, but see how far that will get you in Rome or Rochester. No other language than English is spoken as an official language in more countries – forty-four, as against twenty-seven for French and twenty for Spanish – and none is spoken over a wider area of the globe. English is used as an official language in countries with a population of about 1.6 billion, roughly a third of the world total. Of course, nothing like that number of people speak it – in India, for instance, it is spoken by probably no more than 40 or 50 million people out of a total population of 700 million – but it is still used competently as a second language by perhaps as many as 400 million people globally.

Without any doubt, English is the most important language in the world, and it is not hard to find impressive statistics to prove it. 'Two thirds of all scientific papers are published in English,' says the *Economist*. 'Nearly half of all business deals in Europe are conducted in English,' says *The Story of English*. 'More than seventy per cent of the world's mail is written and addressed in English,' says Lincoln Barnett in *The Treasure of Our Tongue*. It is easy to let such impressive figures run away with us. *The Story of English* states that the main television networks of the United States, Britain, and Canada enjoy audiences that 'regularly exceed one hundred million'. Since the population of the United Kingdom is 56 million and that of Canada only a little over 25 million, that claim would seem to be exaggerated. So too almost certainly is the same book's claim that 'in total there are probably more than a billion speakers of English, at least a quarter of the world's population'.

The simple fact is that English is not always spoken as widely or as enthusiastically as we might like to think. According to *U.S. News & World Report*,[1] even in Switzerland, one of the most polyglot of nations, no more than 10 per cent of the people are capable of writing a simple letter in English.

What is certain is that English is the most studied and emulated language in the world, its influence so enormous that it has even affected the syntax of other languages. According to a study by Magnus Ljung of Stockholm University, more than half of all Swedes now make plurals by adding -s, after the English model, rather than by adding -ar, -or, or -er, in the normal Swedish way. The hunger for English is gargantuan. When the BBC English-teaching series *Follow Me* was first broadcast in China, it drew audiences of up to one hundred million people. (This may also tell us a little something about the quality of alternative viewing in China.) The presenter of the programme, Kathy Flower, an unknown in England, is said to be the most familiar British face in China after the Queen. At all events, there are more people learning English in China than there are people in the United States. The teaching of English, according to the *Economist*, is worth £6 billion a year globally. It is estimated to be Britain's sixth largest source of invisible earnings, worth some £500 million a year.

English words are everywhere. Germans speak of *die Teenagers* and *das Walkout* and German politicians snarl 'No comment' at German journalists. Italian women coat their faces with *col-cream*, Romanians ride the *trolleybus*, and Spaniards, when they feel chilly, don a *sueter*. Almost everyone in the world speaks on the telephone or the telefoon or even, in China, the te le fung. And almost everywhere you can find hamburgers, nightclubs, and television. In 1986, the *Economist* assembled a list of English terms that had become more or less universal. They were: *airport, passport, hotel, telephone, bar, soda, cigarette, sport, golf, tennis, stop, O.K., weekend, jeans, know-how, sex appeal*, and *no problem*. As the *Economist* put it: 'The presence of so many words to do with travel, consumables and sport attests to the real source of these exports – America.'

Usually English words are taken just as they are, but sometimes they are adapted to local needs, often in quite striking ways. The Serbo-Croatians, for instance, picked up the English word *nylon* but took it to mean a kind of shabby and disreputable variation, so that a nylon hotel is a brothel while a nylon beach is the place where nudists frolic. Other nations have left the words largely intact but given the spelling a novel twist. Thus the Ukrainian *herkot* might seem wholly foreign to you until you realize that a *herkot* is what a Ukrainian goes to his barber for. Similarly, unless you heard them spoken, you might not instantly recognize *ajskrym*, *muving pikceris*, and *peda* as the Polish for ice cream, the Lithuanian for moving pictures, and the Serbo-Croatian for payday. The champion of this naturalization process must be the Italian *schiacchenze*, which is simply a literal rendering of the English *shake hands*.

The Japanese are particular masters at the art of seizing a foreign word and alternately beating it and aerating it until it sounds something like a native product. Thus the *sumato* (smart) and *nyuu ritchi* (newly rich) Japanese person seasons his or her conversation with *apputodeito* (up to date) expressions like *gurama foto* (glamour photo), *haikurasu* (high class), *kyapitaru gein* (capital gain), and *rushawa* (rush hour). *Sebiro*, for a suit of clothes, looks convincingly native until you realize that it is a corruption of Savile Row, the London street where the finest suits are made. Occasionally the borrowed words grow. *Productivity* was stretched and mauled until it emerged as *purodakuchibichi*, which, despite its greater length, sits more comfortably on the Japanese tongue. But for the most part the Japanese use the same sort of ingenuity miniaturizing English words as they do in miniaturizing televisions and video cameras. So *modern girl* comes out as *moga*, *word processor* becomes *wa-pro*, *mass communications* becomes *masu-komi*, and *commercial* is brusquely truncated into a short, sharp *cm*. *No-pan*, short for *no-panties*, is a description for bottomless waitresses, while the English words *touch* and *game* have been fused to make *tachi geimu*, a euphemism for sexual petting.

This inclination to hack away at English words until they become something like native products is not restricted to the Japanese. In Singapore transvestites are known as *shims*, a contraction of *she-hims*. Italians don't go to a nightclub, but just to a *night* (often spelled *nihgt*), while in France a self-service restaurant is simply *le self*. European languages also show a curious tendency to take English participles and give them entirely new meanings, so that the French don't go running or jogging, they go footing. They don't engage in a spot of sun-bathing, but rather go in for *le bronzing*. A tuxedo or dinner jacket in French becomes *un smoking*, while in Italy cosmetic surgery becomes *il lifting*. The Germans are particularly inventive at taking things a step further than it ever occurred to anyone in English. A young person in Germany goes from being in his teens to being in his *twens*, a book that doesn't quite become a bestseller is instead *ein steadyseller*, and a person who is more relaxed than another is *relaxter*.

Sometimes new words are made up, as with the Japanese *salaryman* for an employee of a corporation. In Germany a snappy dresser is a *dressman*. In France a *recordman* is not a disc jockey, but an athlete who sets a record, while an *alloman* is a switchboard operator (because he says, 'allo? allo?'). And, just to confuse things, sometimes English words are given largely contrary meanings, so that in France an *egghead* is an idiot while a *jerk* is an accomplished dancer.

The most relentless borrowers of English words have been the Japanese. The number of English words current in Japanese has been estimated to be as high as 20,000. It has been said, not altogether wryly, that if the Japanese were required to pay a licence fee for every word they used, their trade surplus would vanish. A count of Western words, mostly English, used in Japanese newspapers in 1964 put the proportion at just under 10 per cent. It would almost certainly be much higher now. Among the Japanese borrowings:

> erebeta – elevator
> nekutai – necktie
> bata – butter
> beikon – bacon
> sarada – salad
> remon – lemon
> chiizu – cheese
> bifuteki – beefsteak
> hamu – ham
> shyanpu setto – shampoo and set

Not all languages have welcomed the invasion of English words. The French have been more resistant than most. President François Mitterrand declared in 1986, perhaps a trifle excessively: 'France is engaged in a war with Anglo-Saxon.' The French have had a law against the encroachment of foreign words since as early as 1911, but this was considerably bolstered by the setting up in 1970 of a Commission on Terminology, which was followed in 1975 by another law, called the Maintenance of the Purity of the French Language, which introduced fines for using illegal anglicisms, which in turn was followed in 1984 by the establishment of *another* panel, the grandly named Commissariat Général de la Langue Française. You may safely conclude from all this that the French take their language very seriously indeed. As a result of these various efforts, the French are forbidden from saying *pipeline* (even though they pronounce it 'peepleen'), but must instead say *oléoduc*. They cannot take a *jet airplane*, but instead must board an *avion à réaction*. A *hamburger* is a *steak haché*. *Chewing gum* has become *pâte à mâcher*. The newspaper *Le Monde* sarcastically suggested that sandwich should be rendered as 'deux morceaux de pain avec quelque chose au milieu' – 'two pieces of bread with something in the middle'.

Estimates of the number of anglicisms in French have been put as high as 5 per cent, though *Le Monde* thinks the true total is nearer 2 per cent or less. (Someone else once calculated that an anglicism appeared in *Le Monde* once every 166 words – or well under 1 per cent of the time.) So it is altogether possible that the French are making a great deal out of very little. Certainly the incursion of English words is not a new phenomenon. *Le snob*, *le biftek*, and even *le self-made man* go back a hundred years or more, while *ouest* (west) has been in French for 700 years and *rosbif* (roast beef) for 350. More than one observer has suggested that what really rankles the French is not that they are borrowing so many words from the rest of the world but that the rest of the world is no longer borrowing so many from them. As the magazine *Le Point* put it: 'Our technical contribution stopped with the word chauffeur.'

The French, it must be said, have not been so rabidly anglophobic as has sometimes been made out. From the outset the government conceded defeat on a number of words that were too well established to drive out: *gadget, holdup, weekend, blue jeans, self-service, manager, marketing,* and many others. Between 1977 and 1987, there were just forty prosecutions for violations of the language laws, almost always involving fairly flagrant abuses. TWA, for instance, was fined for issuing its boarding passes in English only. You can hardly blame the French for taking exception to that. The French also recognize the global importance of English. In 1988, the élite Ecole Centrale de Paris, one of the country's top engineering academies, made it a requirement of graduation that students be able to speak and write fluent English, even if they have no intention of ever leaving France.

It would be a mistake to presume that English is widely spoken in the world because it has some overwhelming intrinsic appeal to foreigners. Most people speak it not because it gives them pleasure to help out American and British monoglots who cannot be troubled to learn a few words of their language, believe it or not, but because they need it to function in the world at large. They may like a few English words splashed across their T-shirts and shopping bags, but that isn't to say that that is what they want to relax with in the evening.

Go to Amsterdam or Antwerp or Oslo and you will find that almost everyone speaks superb English, and yet if you venture into almost any bookshop in those cities you will usually find only a small selection of books in English. For the most part, people want to read works in their own language. Equally they want to watch television in their own language. In the coastal areas of Holland and Belgium, where most people can both speak English and receive British television broadcasts, most still prefer to watch local programmes even when they are palpably inferior to the British product (i.e. almost invariably). Similarly, two English-language satellite networks in Europe, Sky TV and Super Channel, had some initial success in West Germany, but as soon as two competing satellite networks were set up transmitting more or less the same programmes but dubbed into German, the English-language networks' joint share slumped to less than 1 per cent – about as much as could be accounted for by English-speaking natives living in West Germany. The simple fact is that German viewers, even when they speak English well, would rather watch *Dallas* dubbed badly into German than in the original English. And who can blame them?

In many places English is widely resented as a symbol of colonialism. In India, where it is spoken by no more than 5 per cent of the population at the very most, the constitution was written in English and English was adopted as a foreign language not out of admiration for its linguistic virtues but as a necessary expedient. In a country in which there are 1,652 languages and dialects, including 15 official ones, and in which no one language is spoken by more than 16 per cent of the population, a neutral outside language has certain obvious practicalities. Much the same situation prevails in Malaysia, where the native languages include Tamil, Portuguese, Thai, Punjabi, twelve versions of Chinese, and about as many of Malay. Traditionally, Malay is spoken in the civil service, Chinese in business, and English in the professions and in education. Yet these countries are almost always determined to phase English out. India had hoped to eliminate it as an official language by 1980 and both Malaysia and Nigeria have been trying to do likewise since the 1970s.

There is certainly a good case for adopting an international language, whether it be English or Malaysian or Thraco-Phrygian. Translating is an enormously costly and time-consuming business. An internal survey by the European Community in 1987 found that it was costing it $15 a word, $500 a page, to translate its documents. One in every three employees of the European Community is engaged in translating papers and speeches. A third of all administration costs – $700 million in 1987 – was taken up with paying for translators and interpreters. Every time a member is added to the EC, as most recently with Greece, Spain, and Portugal, the translation problems multiply exponentially. Under the Treaty of Rome each member country's language must be treated equally, and it is not easy even in multilingual Brussels to find linguists who can translate from Dutch into Portuguese or from Danish into Greek.

A more compelling reason for an international language is the frequency and gravity of misunderstandings owing to difficulties of translation. The 1905 draft of a treaty between Russia and Japan, written in both French and English, treated the English *control* and French *contrôler* as synonyms when in fact the English form means 'to dominate or hold power' while the French means simply 'to inspect'. The treaty nearly fell apart as a result. The Japanese involvement in World War II may have been inadvertently prolonged when the Domei news agency, the official government information service, rendered the word *mokusatsu* as 'ignore' when the sense intended was that of 'reserving a reply until we have had time to consider the matter more carefully'.

That may seem a remarkably wide chasm between meanings, but Japanese is particularly susceptible to such discrepancy because it is at once so dense and complex and yet so full of subtlety. It has been suggested, in fact, that it is probably not possible to give accurate simultaneous Japanese–English translations because of the yawning disparity between how the two languages function. To take just one instance, in Japanese it is considered impolite to end a sentence with an unexpected flourish; in English it is a sign of oratorical dexterity of the first order. English speakers, particularly in the context of business or political negotiations, favour bluntness. The Japanese, by contrast, have a cultural aversion to directness and are often reluctant to give a simple yes or no answer. When a Japanese says, 'Kangae sasete kudasai' ('Let me think about it') or 'Zensho shimasu' ('I will do my best') he actually means 'no'. This has led many business people, and on at least one occasion the President of the United States, to go away thinking they had an agreement or understanding that did not actually exist.

This problem of nuance and ambiguity can affect the Japanese themselves. According to John David Morley in *Pictures from the Water Trade*, when Emperor Hirohito went on the radio to announce the Japanese surrender at the end of World War II, he used such vague and arcane language that most of his audience, although listening attentively, didn't have the first idea what he was talking about. In 1988, a member of parliament, Kazuhisa Inoue, began pressing the government to form a committee to come up with ways of making parliamentary debate less dense, suggesting that the Japanese habit of hiding behind rhetoric was heightening the reputation of the 'sneaky Japanese'.[2]

Having said all that, we have a well-practised gift for obfuscation in the English-speaking world. According to *U.S. News & World Report*,[3] an unnamed American airline referred in its annual report to an 'involuntary conversion of a 727'. It meant that it had crashed. At least one hospital, according to *The Times*, has taken to describing a death as 'a negative patient-care outcome'. The Pentagon is peerless at this sort of thing. It once described toothpicks as 'wooden interdental stimulators' and tents as 'frame-supported tension structures'. Here is an extract from the Pentagon's Department of Food Procurement specifications for a regulation Type 2 sandwich cookie: 'The cookie shall consist of two round cakes with a layer of filling between them. The weight of the cookie shall be not less than 21.5 grams and filling weight not less than 6.4 grams. The base cakes shall be uniformly baked with a color ranging from not lighter than chip 27885 or darker than chip 13711 ... The color comparisons shall be made under north sky daylight with the objects held in such a way as to avoid specular refractance.' And so it runs on for fifteen densely typed pages. Every single item the Pentagon buys is similarly detailed: plastic whistles (sixteen pages), olives (seventeen pages), hot chocolate (twenty pages).

Although English is capable of waffle and obfuscation, it is nonetheless generally more straightforward than eastern languages and less verbose than other western ones. As Jespersen notes, where we can say 'first come, first served', the Danes must say 'den der kommer først til møllen får først malet'.[4]

Because of the difficulties inherent in translation, people have been trying for over a century to devise a neutral, artificial language. At the end of the nineteenth century there arose a vogue for made-up languages. Between 1880 and 1907, according to Baugh and Cable,[5] fifty-three universal languages were proposed. Most were enthusiastically ignored, but one or two managed to seize the public's attention. One of the more improbable of these successes was Volapük, invented in 1880 by a German priest named Johann Martin Schleyer. For a decade and a half, Volapük enjoyed a large following. More than 280 clubs sprang up all over Europe to promote it. Journals were established and three international congresses were held. At its peak it boasted almost a million followers. And yet the language was both eccentric and abstruse. Schleyer shunned the letter *r* because he thought it was too difficult for children, the elderly, and the Chinese. Above all, Volapük was obscure. Schleyer claimed that the vocabulary was based largely on English roots, which he said made it easy to learn for anyone already familiar with English, but these links were often nearly impossible to deduce. The word *Volapük* itself was supposed to come from two English roots, *vola* for world and *pük* for speak, but I daresay it would take a linguistic scholar of the first mark to see the connection. Schleyer helped to doom the language by refusing to make any modifications to it, and it died with almost as much speed as it had arisen.

Rather more successful, and infinitely more sensible, has been Esperanto, devised in 1887 by a Pole named Ludovic Lazarus Zamenhoff, who lived in an area of Russia where four languages were commonly spoken. Zamenhoff spent years diligently concocting his language. Luckily he was a determined fellow because at an advanced stage in the work his father, fearing his son would be thought a spy working in code, threw all Ludovic's papers on the fire and the young Pole was forced to start again from scratch. Esperanto is considerably more polished and accessible than Volapük. It has just sixteen rules, no definite articles, no irregular endings, and no illogicalities of spelling. Esperantists claim to have eight million adherents in 110 countries and they say that with three hours of study a week it can be mastered in a year. As evidence of its success as a living language, its proponents point out that it has developed its own body of slang (for example, *luton* for hello, a devil-may-care shortening of the formal word *saluton*) and even its own swear words (such as *merdo*, derived from the French *merde*). Esperanto looks faintly like a cross between Spanish and Martian, as this brief extract, the first sentence from the Book of Genesis, shows: 'En la komenco, Dio kreis le cielon kaj la teron.' Esperanto has one inescapable shortcoming. For all its eight million claimed speakers, it is not widely used. In normal circumstances, an Esperanto speaker has about as much chance of encountering another as a Norwegian has of stumbling on a fellow Norwegian in, say, Mexico.

As a result of these inevitable shortcomings, most other linguistics authorities, particularly in this century, have taken the view that the best hope of a world language lies not in devising a synthetic tongue, which would almost certainly be doomed to failure, but in making English less complex and idiosyncratic and more accessible. To that end, in 1930 Professor C. K. Ogden of Cambridge University devised Basic English, which consisted of paring the English language down to just 850 essential words, including a mere eighteen verbs – *be, come, do, get, give, go, have, keep, let, make, may, put, say, see, seem, send, take,* and *will* – which Ogden claimed could describe every possible action. Thus simplified, English could be learned by most foreigners with just thirty hours of tuition, Ogden claimed. It seemed ingenious, but the system had three flaws.

First, those who learned Basic English might be able to write simple messages, but they would scarcely be able to read anything in English – even comic books and greeting cards would contain words and expressions quite unknown to them. Second, in any language vocabulary is not the hardest part of learning. Morphology, syntax, and idiom are far more difficult, but Basic English did almost nothing to simplify these. Third, and most critically, the conciseness of the vocabulary of Basic English meant that it could become absurdly difficult to describe anything not covered by it, as seen in the word *watermelon*, which in Basic English would have to be defined as 'a large green fruit with the form of an egg, which has a sweet red inside and a good taste'. Basic English got nowhere.

At about the same time, a Professor R. E. Zachrisson of the University of Uppsala in Sweden devised a form of English that he called Anglic. Zachrisson believed that the stumbling block of English for most foreigners was its irregular spelling. He came up with a language that was essentially English but with more consistent spellings. Here is the start of the Gettysburg Address in Anglic: 'Forskor and sevn yeerz agoe our faadherz braut forth on this kontinent a nue naeshon . . .' Anglic won some influential endorsements, but it too never caught on.

Perhaps the most promising of all such languages is Seaspeak, devised in Britain for the use of maritime authorities in busy sea lanes such as the English Channel. The idea of Seaspeak is to reduce to a minimum the possibilities of confusion by establishing set phrases for ideas that are normally expressed in English in a variety of ways. For instance, a partly garbled message might prompt any number of responses in English: 'What did you say?', 'I beg your pardon, I didn't catch that. Can you say it again?', 'There's static on this channel. Can you repeat the message?', and so on. In Seaspeak, only one expression is allowed: 'Say again.' Any error, for whatever reason, is announced simply as 'Mistake', and not as 'Hold on a minute, I've given you the wrong bearings', and so on.

Computers, with their lack of passion and admirable ability to process great streams of information, would seem to be ideal for performing translations, but in fact they are pretty hopeless at it, largely on account of their inability to come to terms with idiom, irony, and other quirks of language. An oft-cited example is the computer that was instructed to translate the expression *out of sight, out of mind* out of English and back in again and came up with *blind insanity*. It is curious to reflect that we have computers that can effortlessly compute pi to

5,000 places and yet cannot be made to understand that there is a difference between *time flies like an arrow* and *fruit flies like a banana* or that in the English-speaking world to make up a story, to make up one's face, and to make up after a fight are all quite separate things. Here at last Esperanto may be about to come into its own. A Dutch computer company is using Esperanto as a bridge language in an effort to build a workable translating system. The idea is that rather than, say, translate Danish directly into Dutch, the computer would first translate it into Esperanto, which could be used to smooth out any difficulties of syntax or idiom. Esperanto would in effect act as a kind of air filter, removing linguistic impurities and idiomatic specks that could clog the system.

Of course, if we all spoke a common language things might work more smoothly, but there would be far less scope for amusement. In an article in *Gentleman's Quarterly* in 1987, Kenneth Turan described some of the misunderstandings that have occurred during the dubbing or subtitling of American movies in Europe. In one movie where a policeman tells a motorist to pull over, the Italian translator has him asking for a sweater (i.e. a pullover). In another where a character asks if he can bring a date to the funeral, the Spanish subtitle has him asking if he can bring a fig to the funeral.

In the early 1970s, according to *Time* magazine, Russian diplomats were issued with a Russian/English phrasebook which fell into Western hands and was found to contain such model sentences as this instruction to a waiter: 'Please give me curds, sower cream, fried chicks, pulled bread and one jelly-fish.' When shopping, the well-versed Soviet emissary was told to order 'a ladies' worsted-nylon swimming pants'.

But of course it works the other way. A Braniff Airlines ad that intended to tell Spanish-speaking fliers that they could enjoy sitting in leather (*en cuero*) seats, told them that they could fly *en cueros* – without clothes on.

In 1977, President Carter, on a trip to Poland, wanted to tell the people, 'I wish to learn your opinions and understand your desires for the future,' but his interpreter made it come out as 'I desire the Poles carnally.' The interpreter also had the president telling the Poles that he had 'abandoned' the United States that day, instead of leaving it. After a couple of hours of such gaffes, the president wisely abandoned the interpreter.

All of this seems comical, but in fact it masks a serious deficiency. Because the richest and most powerful nation on earth could not come up with an interpreter who could speak modern Polish, President Carter had to rely on Polish government interpreters, who naturally 'interpreted' his speeches and pronouncements in a way that fitted Polish political sensibilities. When, for instance, President Carter offered his condolences to dissident journalists who 'wanted to attend but were not permitted to come', the interpreter translated it as 'who wanted to come but couldn't' and thus the audience missed the point. In the same way, President Nixon in China had to rely on interpreters supplied by the Chinese government.

We in the English-speaking world have often been highly complacent in expecting others to learn English without our making anything like the same effort in return. As of 1986, the number of American students studying Russian was 25,000. The number of Russian students studying English was four million – giving a ratio of 160 to one in the Soviets' favour. In 1986, the Munich newspaper *Suddeutsche Zeitung* investigated the studying of German as a foreign language around the world. In the United States, the number of college students taking a German course was 120,000, down from 216,000 in 1966. In the Soviet Union, the number was nine million. The problem is unlikely to get better. Between 1966 and 1986, 150 American colleges and universities cancelled their German programmes. In 1989, some 77 per cent of all new college graduates had taken no foreign language courses.

A presidential commission under Ronald Reagan called the situation scandalous. In 1987, in an effort to redress the balance Congress voted into law the Education for Economic Security Act, which provided an extra $2.45 million to promote the study of foreign languages – or a little over one cent per person in the country. That should really turn the tables. There is evidence to suggest that some members of Congress aren't fully sympathetic with the necessity for a commercial nation to be multilingual. As one congressman quite seriously told Dr David Edwards, head of the Joint National Committee on Languages, 'If English was good enough for Jesus Christ, it's good enough for me.'[6]

Not only are we not doing terribly well at foreign languages, we're not even doing terribly well at English. The problem was well voiced by Professor Randolph Quirk, president of the British Academy and a leading linguistic scholar, when he wrote: 'It would be ironic indeed if the millions of children in Germany, Japan and China who are diligently learning the language of Shakespeare and Eliot took more care in their use of English and showed more pride in their achievement than those for whom it is the native tongue.'

We might sometimes wonder if we are the most responsible custodians of our own tongue, especially when we reflect that the Oxford University Press sells as many copies of the *Oxford English Dictionary* in Japan as it does in America, and a third more than in Britain.

13

NAMES

The English, it has always seemed to me, have a certain genius for names. A glance through the British edition of *Who's Who* throws up a roll call that sounds disarmingly like the characters in a P. G. Wodehouse novel: Lord Fraser of Tullybelton, Captain Alwyne Arthur Compton Farquharson of Invercauld, Professor Valentine Mayneord, Sir Helenus Milmo, Lord Keith of Kinkel. Many British appellations are of truly heroic proportions, like that of the World War I admiral named Sir Reginald Aylmer Ranfulry Plunkett-Ernel-Erle-Drax. The best ones go in for a kind of gloriously silly redundancy towards the end, as with Sir Humphrey Dodington Benedict Sherston Sherston-Baker and the truly unbeatable Leone Sextus Denys Oswolf Fraduati Tollemache-Tolle-mache-de Orellana-Plantagenet-Tollemache-Tollemache, a British army major who died in World War I. The leading explorer in Britain today is Sir Ranulph Twisleton-Wykeham-Fiennes. Somewhere in Britain to this day there is an old family rejoicing in the name MacGillesheatheanaich. In the realms of nomenclature clearly we are dealing here with giants.

Often, presumably for reasons of private amusement, the British pronounce their names in ways that bear almost no resemblance to their spelling. Leveson-Gower is 'looson gore', Marjoribanks is 'marchbanks', Hiscox is 'hizzko', Howick is 'hoyk', Ruthven is 'rivven', Zuill is 'yull', Menzies is 'mingiss'. They find particular pleasure in taking old Norman names and mashing them around until they became something

altogether unique, so that Beaulieu becomes 'bewley', Beau-
champ turns into 'beecham', Prideaux into 'pridducks',
Devereux to 'devrooks', Cambois to 'cammiss', Hautbois to
'hobbiss', Belvoir somehow becomes 'beaver', and Beaudesert
turns, unfathomably, into 'belzer'.

They can perform this trick with even the simplest names,
turning Sinclair into 'sinkler', Blackley to 'blakely', Blount
into 'blunt', Bethune into 'beeton', Cockburn into 'coburn',
Coke into 'cook'. Lord Home becomes 'lord hume', the novelist
Anthony Powell becomes 'pole', P. G. Wodehouse becomes
'woodhouse', the poet William Cowper becomes 'cooper'.
Caius College, Cambridge, is 'keys', while Magdalen College,
Oxford, and Magdalene College, Cambridge, are both pronounced 'mawdlin'.

I could go on and on. In fact, I think I will. Viscount
Althorp pronounces his name 'awltrop', while the rather more
sensible people of Althorp, the Northamptonshire village next
to the viscount's ancestral home, say 'all-thorp'. The Scottish
town of Auchinleck is pronounced 'ock-in-leck', but the local
baron, Lord Boswell of Auchinleck, pronounces it 'affleck'.
There are two Barons Dalziel. One pronounces it 'dalzeel', the
other 'dee-ell'. The family name Ridealgh can be pronounced
'ridalj' or 'riddi-alsh'. Some members of the Pepys family
pronounce it 'peeps' as the diarist Samuel Pepys did, but
others say 'peppiss' and still others say 'pips'. The family name
Hesmondhalgh can be 'hezmondhaw', 'hezmondhalsh', or 'hez-
mondhawltch'. The surname generally said to have the
most pronunciations is Featherstonehaugh, which can be
pronounced in any of five ways: 'feather-stun-haw', 'feerston-
shaw', 'feston-haw', 'feeson-hay', or (for those in a hurry)
'fan-shaw'. But in fact there are two other names with five
pronunciations: Coughtrey, which can be 'kōtry', 'kawtry',
'kowtry', 'kootry', and 'kofftry', and Wriotheseley, which can
be 'rottsly', 'rittsly', 'rizzli', 'rithly', or 'wriotheslee'.

The problem is so extensive, and the possibility of gaffes so
omnipresent, that the BBC employs an entire pronunciation
unit, a small group of dedicated orthoepists (professional pro-

nouncers) who spend their working lives getting to grips with these illogical pronunciations so that broadcasters don't have to do it on the air.

In short, there is scarcely an area of name giving in which the British don't show a kind of wayward genius. Take street names. Just in the City of London, an area of one square mile, you can find Pope's Head Alley, Mincing Lane, Garlick Hill, Crutched Friars, Threadneedle Street, Bleeding Heart Yard, Seething Lane. In the same compact area you can find churches named St Giles Cripplegate, St Sepulchre Without Newgate, All Hallows Barking, and the practically unbeatable St Andrews-by-the-Wardrobe. But those are just their everyday names: often the full, official titles are even more breathtaking, as with The Lord Mayor's Parish Church of St Stephen Walbrook and St Swithin Londonstone, St Benet Sheerhogg and St Mary Bothall with St Laurence Pountney, which is, for all that, just one church.

Equally arresting are British pub names. Other people are content to dub their drinking establishments with pedestrian names like Harry's Bar and the Greenwood Lounge. But a Briton, when he wants to sup ale, must find his way to the Dog and Duck, the Goose and Firkin, the Flying Spoon, or the Spotted Dog. The names of Britain's 70,000 or so pubs cover a broad range, running from the inspired to the improbable. Almost any name will do so long as it is at least faintly absurd, unconnected with the name of the owner, and entirely lacking in any suggestion of drinking, conversing, and enjoying oneself. At a minimum the name should puzzle foreigners – this is a basic requirement of most British institutions – and ideally it should excite long and inconclusive debate, defy all logical explanation, and evoke images that border on the surreal. Among the pubs that meet, and indeed exceed, these exacting standards are the Frog and Nightgown, the Bull and Spectacles, the Flying Monk, and the Crab and Gumboil.

However unlikely a pub's name may sound, there is usually some explanation rooted in the depths of history. British inns were first given names in Roman times, 2,000 years ago, but the present quirky system dates mostly from the Middle Ages, when it was deemed necessary to provide travellers, most of them illiterate, with some sort of instantly recognizable symbol.

The simplest approach, and often the most prudent, was to adopt a royal or aristocratic coat of arms. Thus a pub called the White Hart indicates ancient loyalty to Richard II (whose decree it was, incidentally, that all inns should carry signs), while an Eagle and Child denotes allegiance to the Earls of Derby and a Royal Oak commemorates Charles II, who was forced to hide in an oak tree after being defeated by Cromwell during the English Civil War. (If you look carefully at the pub sign, you can usually see the monarch hiding somewhere in the branches.) The one obvious shortcoming of such a system was that names had to be hastily changed every time a monarch was toppled. Occasionally luck would favour the publicans, as when Richard III (symbolized by a white boar) died and the Earl of Oxford (blue boar) rose to favour, and amends could be simply effected with a pot of paint. But pubkeepers quickly realized that a more cost-effective approach was to stick to generic names, which explains why there are so many pubs called the Queen's Head (about 300), King's Head (400), and Crown (the national champion at more than 1,000).

Many pubs owe their names to popular sports (the Cricketers, the Fox and Hounds, the Cockpit), or to the workaday pursuits of the people who once drank in them. Pubs like the Plough, the Fleece, the Woolpack, and the Shepherd's Rest were clearly frequented by farmers and farmworkers. The Boot was for cobblers, the Anchor for sailors, and the Shoulder of Mutton for butchers. Not all references are so immediately evident. The Beetle and Wedge in Berkshire sounds hopelessly obscure until you realize that a beetle and wedge were basic tools of carpenters 200 years ago.

Many of the very oldest pub names represent religious themes – the Crossed Keys, the Seven Stars, the Hope and

Anchor. The Lamb and Flag, a fairly common name still, was the symbol of the Knights Templar, who rode to the Crusades, and the Saracen's Head and Turk's Head commemorate their enemies' fate. Still other pub names are built around catchphrases, homilies, puns, and bits of philosophy, or are simply of unknown provenance. Names such as the Tumbledown Dick, First and Last, Mortal Man, Romping Donkey, Ram Jam Inn, Live and Let Live, and Man with a Load of Mischief (the sign outside depicts a man with a woman slung over his shoulder) all fall resoundingly into this category.

The picture is further clouded by the consideration that many pub names have been corrupted over the centuries. The Pig and Whistle is said to have its roots in peg (a drinking vessel) and wassail (a festive drink). The Goat and Compasses is sometimes said to come from 'God Encompasseth Us'. The Elephant and Castle, originally a pub and now a district of London, may have been the Infanta de Castille. The Old Bull and Bush, a famous pub on Hampstead Heath, is said to come from Boulogne Bouche and to commemorate a battle in France. Some of these derivations may be fanciful, but there is solid evidence to show that the Dog and Bacon was once the Dorking Beacon, that the Cat and Fiddle was once Caterine la Fidèle (at least it is recorded as such in the Domesday Book), and that the Ostrich Inn in Buckinghamshire began life as the Hospice Inn.

All this is by way of introducing, in a decidedly roundabout manner, how we came to acquire our own names. The study of names is *onomastics*. For much of history, surnames, or last names, were not considered necessary. Two people named, say, Peter, living in the same hamlet, might adopt or be given second names to help distinguish them from each other – so that one might be called Peter White-Head and the other Peter Son of John (or Johnson) – but these additional names were seldom passed on. The business of acquiring surnames was a long one that evolved over centuries rather than years. As might be expected it began at the top of the social scale and worked its way down. In England last names did not become usual until after the Norman conquest, and in many other European countries, such as Holland, they evolved much later still. Most surnames come ultimately, if not always obviously, from one of four sources: place names (e.g. Lincoln, Worthington), nicknames (Whitehead, Armstrong), trade names (Smith, Carpenter), and patronymics, that is names indicating a familial relationship (Johnson, Robertson). In his lifetime a person might be known by a variety of names – for instance, as Peter the Butcher Who Lives by the Well at Putney Green or some such. This would eventually transmute into Peter Butcher or Peter Green or Peter Wells. Often in such cases the person would take his name from the figure on a nearby inn sign. In the Middle Ages, when the ability to read could scarcely be assumed, it was common for certain types of businesses to have symbols outside their doors. The striped barber pole is a survival from those days. A wine merchant would always have a bush by his front door. Hence his neighbour might end up being called George Bush.

Two events gave a boost to the adoption of surnames in England. The first was the introduction of a poll tax in 1379, which led the government to collect the name of every person in the country aged sixteen or over, and the second was the enactment of the Statute of Additions in 1413, which required that all legal documents contain not just the person's given name, but also his or her occupation and place of abode. These two pieces of medieval bureaucracy meant that virtually everyone had to settle on a definite and fixed surname.

It's surprising how many medieval occupations are embedded in modern family names. Some are obvious: Bowman, Archer, Carpenter, Shepherd, Forrester. But many others are not, either because the craft has died or become rare, as with Fuller (a cleanser of cloths) and Fletcher (a maker of bows and arrows) or because the spelling has been corrupted in some way, as with Bateman (a corrupted form of boatman) or because the name uses a regionalism, as with

Akerman (a provincial word for a ploughman). It mustn't be forgotten that this was a time of great flux in the English language, when many regional spellings and words were competing for dominance. Thus such names as Hill, Hall, and Hull could all originally have meant Hill but come from different parts of the country. Smith is the most common name in America and Britain, but it is also one of the most common in nearly every other European language. The German Schmidt, the French Ferrier, Italian Ferraro, Spanish Herrero, Hungarian Kovacs, and Russian Kusnetzov are all Smiths.

English names based on places almost always had prepositions to begin with but these gradually disappeared, so that John of Preston became just John Preston, though occasionally they survive in names like Atwater and Underwood or as remnants in names like Noakes (a contraction of atten Oakes, or 'by the oak trees') or Nash (for atten Ash, 'by the ash tree'). A curious fact about names based on places is that they are so often obscure – mostly from places that few people have heard of. Why should there be so many more Middletons than Londons, so many more Worthingtons than Bristols? The main cities of medieval Britain – London, York, Norwich, and Glasgow – are relatively uncommon as surnames even though many thousands of people lived there. To understand this seeming paradox you must remember that the purpose of surnames is to distinguish one person or family from the great mass of people. If a person called himself Peter of London, he would be just one of hundreds of such Peters and anyone searching for him would be at a loss. So as a rule a person would become known as Peter of London only if he moved to a rural location, where London *would* be a clear identifying feature, but that did not happen often. In the same way, those people named Farmer probably owe their name to the fact that an ancestor left the farm, while names like French, Fleming, Welch, or Walsh (both from Welsh) indicate that the originator was not a resident of those places but rather an emigrant.

Another superficially puzzling thing is why many people have ecclesiastical names like Bishop, Monk, Priest, and Prior when such figures were presumably celibate and unable to pass on their names. The reason here is that part of the original name has probably been lost. The full name may once have been the 'Bishop's man' if he was a servant or 'Priest's Hill' if that was where he lived.

The origins of other names are not immediately apparent because they come from non-English sources. Russell was from the medieval French *roussell*, 'red-haired', while Morgan is Welsh for white-haired. Sometimes strange literal meanings are hidden in innocuous-sounding names. Kennedy means 'ugly head' in Gaelic, Boyd means 'yellow-faced or sickly', Campbell means 'crooked mouth'. The same is equally true of other languages. As Mario Pei notes, Gorky means 'bitter', Tolstoy means 'fat', and Machiavelli means 'bad nails'. Cicero is Roman slang for a wart on the nose (it means literally 'chick-pea').

In America, the situation with surnames is obviously complicated by the much greater diversity of backgrounds of the people. Even so, 183 of the 200 most common last names in America are British. However, a few names that are common in America are noticeably less common in Britain. Johnson is the second most common name in the United States (after Smith), but comes much further down the list in Britain. The reason for this is of course the great influx of Swedes to America in the nineteenth century – though in fact Johnson is not a native Swedish name. It is an Americanizing of the Swedish Jonsson or Johansson. Another name much more often encountered in America than Britain is Miller. In Britain, millers were unpopular throughout much of history because of their supposed tendency to cheat the farmers who brought them grain. So it was not a flattering name. A modern equivalent might be the name Landlord. Most Millers in America were in fact originally Muellers or Müllers. The German word had the same meaning but did not carry the same derogatory connotations.

Many, perhaps most, immigrants to America modified their names in some way to accommodate American spellings and phonics. Often, with difficult Polish or Russian names, this was involuntary; immigrants simply had new names given to them at their port of entry. But more often the people willingly made changes to blend into their adopted country more smoothly and to avoid the constant headache of having to spell their name to everyone. Far easier to change Pfoersching to Pershing, Wistinghausen to Westinghouse, Pappadimitracoupolos to Pappas, Niewhuis to Newhouse, Kuiper to Cooper, Schumacher to Shoemaker, Krankheit to Cronkite, Sjögren to Seagren, Lindqvist to Lindquist, and so on. It wasn't just difficult Slavic and Germanic names that this happened with. Scots named McLeod generally changed the spelling of their name to make it conform with its pronunciation, McCloud, and those named McKay usually gave up telling people that it rhymed with *sky*.

Sometimes people took the opportunity to get rid of undesirable surnames which had been imposed on their ancestors during periods of subjugation. Often these were offensive – either because the giver had a wayward sense of humour or because he hoped to be bribed into making it something less embarrassing. For instance, the Greek name Kolokotronis translates as 'bullet in the ass'. But others kept their names – for instance, the Goldwaters, even though that name was long a synonym for urine.

Another change names sometimes underwent in America was to have the stress altered. For some reason, in American speech there is a decided preference to stress the last or next to last syllable in a person's name. Thus Italians coming to America who called themselves 'Es-PO-si-to' had the name changed to 'Es-po-SI-to'. Again, this happened with British names as well. Purcell, Bernard, and Barnett, which are pronounced in Britain as 'persul', 'bernurd', and 'barnutt', became in America 'pur-SELL', 'ber-NARD', and 'bar-NETT'. But this process wasn't extended to all names:

Mitchell and Barnum, for instance, were left with the stress on the first syllable.

Over time most names have been variously battered and knocked about. We have already seen how the name Waddington was variously rendered as Wadigton, Wuldingdoune, Windidune, and so on. Shakespeare's grandfather usually called himself Shakestaff.* Snooks might have started life as Sevenoaks, Backus might have been Bakehouse. James K. Polk, the eleventh U.S. president, was descended from people named Pollock. Few names haven't been changed at some time or other in their history. This is often most vividly demonstrated in place names.

Cambridge, for instance, was called Grantanbrycge in the tenth century. But the conquering Normans found that a mouthful – they particularly had trouble with *gr* combinations – and began to spell it Cantebrigie. Then it became successively Caumbrigge, Cambrugge, and Caunbrige before finally arriving at its modern spelling. Centuries from now it may be something else again. By a similarly convoluted process Eboracum eventually metamorphosed into York.

These verbal transformations can be remarkably complicated. Brightlingsea, according to P. H. Reaney's *The Origin of English Place Names*, has been spelled 404 ways since the first interloper began to tinker with the Celtic Brictrich. Moreover, because of varying influences a single root may have evolved into a variety of words – Brighton, Brixton, Brislington, and Bricklehampton, improbable as it seems, all began life with the same name: Beorhthelmes.

The successive waves of invading Celts, Romans, Danes, Vikings, Angles, Saxons, Jutes, and Normans all endlessly shaped and reshaped British place names. The result is that England possesses some of the most resplendent place names in the world – names that roll around on the tongue and fill the

*Entirely incidentally, a little-known fact about Shakespeare is that his father moved to Stratford-upon-Avon from a nearby village shortly before his son's birth. Had he not done so, the Bard of Avon would instead be known as the rather less ringing Bard of Snitterfield.

mouth like fine claret: Wendens Ambo, Saffron Walden, Gussage All Saints, Stocking Pelham, Farleigh Wallop, Dunton Bassett, Husbands Bosworth. There are 30,000 place names in Britain and at least half of them are arresting and distinctive – far more than can be accounted for by random activity. They are as integral a part of the glory of the British countryside as thatched cottages, wandering hedgerows, and meadows full of waving buttercups and darting butterflies. As with family names, it is difficult to escape the conclusion that the British have such distinctive place names not because they just accidentally evolved, but rather because the British secretly *like* living in places with names like Lower Slaughter and Great Snoring.

Certainly their spellings and pronunciations are often as unfathomable as those of family names. Occasionally the spellings seem to defy pronunciation – as with Meopham, a town in Kent pronounced 'meppam', or Auchtermuchty, a Scottish town pronounced 'awk-ter-muck-tee' – but more often it is the other way round: the spellings look simple and straightforward. The innocent traveller is thus lulled into a sense of security, little realizing what treacheries they hide, so that Postwick is 'pozzick', Puncknowle is 'punnel', Keighley is 'keethley', Holnicote is 'hunneycut', Cholmondeston is 'chumson', Wyardisbury is 'razebry', Wymondham is 'windham', Flawith is 'floyth'. Dent-de-Lion, a town in Kent, is pronounced 'dandelion' – thus combining the old spelling and modern pronunciation of that pernicious weed.

Sometimes letters or whole syllables are blithely dispensed with, so that Browsholme is pronounced 'brewsum', Wavertree becomes 'wawtree', Ludgvan is 'ludge-un', Darlingscott is 'darskut', and Culzean Castle is 'cullayne'. Lots of names have two or more pronunciations. Harewood in West Yorkshire has 'harwood' for the stately home and 'harewood' for the village that surrounds it. Hednesford, Staffordshire, can be pronounced either 'hedjford' or 'hensford'. Shrewsbury can be 'shrooz-bree' or 'shroze-bree'. Athelstaneford in Scotland can be pronounced as spelled or as 'elshanford'. And at least one place has two spellings *and* two pronunciations – Frithsden/ Friesden, Hertfordshire, which can be pronounced 'frizdun' or 'freezdun'.

England has three villages called Houghton and each has a different pronunciation – respectively 'hoton', 'hawton', and 'howton'. Oughtibridge, South Yorkshire, has four: 'owtibrij', 'awtibrij', 'ootibrij', and 'ōtibrij'. Dittisham, Devon, has three pronunciations: 'dittisham', 'dittisum', 'dittsum'. Adwalton, West Yorkshire, is sometimes pronounced 'Atherton' because the town was formerly called Heather Town. But perhaps the strangest of all is Okeford Fitzpaine, Dorset, which many locals pronounce – for reasons no one can begin to guess at – 'fippenny ockford'.

Sadly, it appears that names are more and more being pronounced as spelled – perhaps a consequence of increased mobility among the British. Pontefract, in West Yorkshire, was once pronounced 'pumfrit', but now it is always pronounced as spelled. The same fate has befallen Cirencester, which once was 'sissiter' but now is usually just 'siren-sester'. Grantham and Walthamstow are both pronounced with 'th' sounds even though etymologically they were Grant-ham and Walt-hamstow, in which ways they were once pronounced. Curiously this does not hold true for the obscure town in Nottinghamshire called Gotham, from which New York City takes its nickname; the locals pronounce it 'Gott-hum'.

In America, obviously, there has been less time to knock the names around, but even so it has sometimes happened, usually as a result of making foreign names more palatable – changing the Ojibway Missikamaa into Michigan or the Dakota Indian Šahíyena into Cheyenne. But occasionally it has happened for no real reason, rather in the English manner, as when Ricksburg, Idaho (named for one Thomas Ricks), transmogrified into Rexburg.

Nor has America had the time to come up with unpronounceable names, though there are a few around – notably Schohomogomoc Hill, New Hampshire (Algonquian for 'place with fire markings near'), Natchitoches, Louisiana (pronounced 'nak-uh-tosh'), and Schaghticoke, New York (pronounced 'skat-uh-kohk'). However, there are many names that most Americans *think* they know how to pronounce that are actually pronounced differently by the locals. Among them:

Boise, Idaho	Boyce-ee
Gettysburg, Pennsylvania	Gettizburg
Pierre, South Dakota	Peer
Quincy, Massachusetts	Quinzy
Monticello, Virginia	Montisello
Lancaster, Pennsylvania	Lankus-ter
Biloxi, Mississippi	Buh-lux-ee
Yakima, Washington	Yak-im-uh
St Ignace, Michigan	Saint Ig-nuss
Concord, Massachusetts and New Hampshire	Conk-urd (or Conkit)
Arkansas River	Ar-kan-zus
Milan, Michigan	Mile-un
Lima, Ohio	Lye-muh
Nevada, Iowa	Nuh-vay-da
Versailles, Tennessee	Vur-sales
Vienna, Georgia	Vye-enna
Houston, Ohio	How-stun
Montevideo, Minnesota	Monna-video
Cairo, Illinois	Kay-ro

Often Americans of earlier generations found it easier to change the spellings of names rather than the pronunciation of outsiders. Thus Worcester, Ohio, became Wooster and Hertford, Connecticut, became Hartford. Many French names were quite naturally Americanized – as with Notre Dame, Detroit, Des Plaines, and St Louis. Dutch names were equally problematic. Sometimes they required only a minor spelling adjustment, converting Haarlem to Harlem and Cape Mey to Cape May, but often they had to be pulled about like toffee until they became something altogether more palatable, so that, as we have already noted, De Kromme Zee became Gramercy and Vlacht Bos ('level forest') became Flatbush. In Florida by a similar process the Spanish Cayo Hueso ('bone island') became Key West.

However, what America does possess in abundance is a legacy of colourful names. A mere sampling: Chocolate Bayou, Dime Box, Ding Dong, and Lick Skillet, Texas; Sweet Gum Head, Louisiana; Whynot, Mississippi; Zzyzx Springs, California; Coldass Creek, Stiffknee Knob, and Rabbit Shuffle, North Carolina; Scratch Ankle, Alabama; Fertile, Minnesota; Climax, Michigan; Intercourse, Pennsylvania; Breakabeen, New York; What Cheer, Iowa; Bear Wallow, Mud Lick, Minnie Mousie, Eighty-Eight, and Bug, Kentucky; Dull, Only, Peeled Chestnut, Defeated, and Nameless, Tennessee; Cozy Corners, Wisconsin; Humptulips, Washington; Hog Heaven, Idaho; Ninety-Six, South Carolina; Potato Neck, Maryland; Why, Arizona; Dead Bastard Peak, Crazy Woman Creek, and the unsurpassable Maggie's Nipples, Wyoming.

Many of these names, alas, have been changed, but quite a few still exist, and some places make a living out of their curious cognomens, most notably Intercourse, Pennsylvania, which does a brisk trade in double entendre postcards. Others draw crowds only occasionally, as with Eighty-Eight, Kentucky, on which attention naturally focused during 1988. One couple came all the way from Casper, Wyoming, to be married on the eighth day of the eighth month of 1988 at 8.08 p.m. in Eighty-Eight. The story goes that the town got its unusual name when the founder, one Dabnie Nunnally, reached in his pocket and found he had eighty-eight cents there. In 1948, for what it's worth, eighty-eight people from Eighty-Eight voted for Truman and eighty-eight voted for Dewey.

It doesn't take a whole lot, it would appear, to persuade people in America to change their town names. In 1950, in response to a challenge from a popular radio show, the people of Hot Springs, New Mexico, voted by four to one to rename their town Truth or Consequences. Their prize was that Ralph Edwards, the host, broadcast his tenth anniversary show from there. The thrill of that occasion was presumably short-lived, but the name has stuck. Four years later, the widow of the athlete Jim Thorpe agreed to have her husband buried in the mountain resort of Mauch Chunk, Pennsylvania, if the people there would rename the town after her husband, and they did. Cody, Wyoming, did the same thing for Buffalo Bill Cody.

In addition to giving places colourful names, the early settlers tended to give their states colourful – if not always terribly flattering – nicknames. Nebraska was once called the Bugeating State and Missouri was the Puke State. Sometimes these nicknames have stuck but nobody is quite sure why. Everybody in America knows that Indiana is the Hoosier State, but nobody now seems to know what a Hoosier is or ever was. Similarly nobody seems too sure of why Iowa calls itself the Hawkeye State.

Often the names we know places by is nothing like the names the locals use. In Italian, it's not Florence, but Firenze, not Naples but Napoli, not Padua but Padova, not Venice but Venezia, not Milan but Milano, not Genoa but Genova. To the Danes it's not Copenhagen but København (pronounced 'koopen-howen'). To the Yugoslavians it's not Belgrade but Beograd. To the Russians it's not Moscow but Moskva. And to the Dutch it's not The Hague but Den Haag. The names of countries are even more at variance with their English versions. Try covering up the left-hand column below and seeing how many you can guess.

Greece	Ellinki Dimokratia
Finland	Suomen Tasavalta
Hungary	Magyar Népköztáraság
Albania	Shqipëri
Japan	Nihon
Greenland	Kalâtdlit Nunât
Jordan	Al Mamlaka al Urduniya al Hashemiyah
South Korea	Han Kook
North Korea	Chosun Minchu-chui Immin Kongwha-guk

Morocco	al-Mamlaka al-Maghrebia
China	Zhonghua Renmin Gonghe Guo
Sweden	Konungariket Sverige
Tonga	Friendly Islands

There are a variety of reasons for this. Sometimes the names we use are simply imposed by outsiders with scant regard for local nomenclature. Korea, for instance, is a Japanese name, not a Korean one. Hungary is a Latin name adapted from Old Russian and thus has nothing to do with the name used by the Hungarians themselves. Bosporus, the name for the strait linking Europe to Asia, is simply the Greek translation of *Oxford*. The local Turks call it Karadeniz Bogazi.

Often place names arise from mishearings or misunderstandings – notably the West Indies, which of course have nothing to do with India. They simply reflect Columbus's startling inability to determine which hemisphere he was in. Yucatán in Mexico means 'What?' or 'What are you saying?' – the reply given by the natives to the first Spanish conquistadors to fetch up on their shores. The term *Dutch* is similarly based on a total misapprehension. It comes from Deutsch, or German, and the error has been perpetuated in the expression Pennsylvania Dutch – who are generally not Dutch at all but German.

Names are in the most literal sense big business. With the increasing globalization of commerce, it is becoming harder and harder to find brand names that are both inoffensive and pronounceable throughout the world. Some idea of the scope of the problem can be seen in the experience of a British company when it decided to sell its vintage port, Cockburn's Dry Tang, in Scandinavia. When it didn't sell well in Sweden the company investigated and learned that '*tang*' means 'seaweed' in Swedish, and clearly the name 'dry seaweed' was not conjuring up the requisite image of quality and premium taste that would lead Swedes to buy it by the sackful. So, at the suggestion of the Swedish importers, the company changed the name on the label to Dry Cock, which sounds very silly to English speakers, but which was a big hit with the Swedes.

However, sales immediately plummeted in Denmark. Urgent investigations showed that *cock* there signifies, of all things, the female genitalia. So yet another name had to be devised. Such are the hazards of international marketing.

Standard Oil, when it decided to change its name, considered Enco until it discovered that *enco* in Japanese means 'stalled car'. Gallaher's, another British company, tried to market a cigarette called Park Lane in Spain, but without much success. It wasn't that it meant anything offensive, but Spaniards simply couldn't pronounce it and were embarrassed to order it. On the other hand, companies do sometimes make something of a virtue of having unusual or difficult names, as with Häagen-Dazs ice cream in the United States, a name selected by its inventor simply because he thought it sounded exotic.

Extraordinary amounts of money and effort are sometimes pumped into the naming of products. A typical example, cited by the *Sunday Times*, was of a Swiss confectionery company that commissioned the British trademark specialist John Murphy to come up with an arresting name for a new Swiss chocolate bar. With the aid of a computer spewing out random names and of groups of specialists who do little more than sit around and think up possible names, Murphy's firm came up with 350 suggestions. But of these the company rejected 302 because they weren't considered sufficiently zippy and delectable, and of the forty-eight remaining possibilities only two were not registered somewhere in the world. Murphy himself has had the same problem. His company is called Novamark in Britain but elsewhere trades as Inter Brand because the name was already taken.

Because of the difficulties, brand names are heavily defended. Rolls-Royce, the car group, deals with about 500 trademark infringement cases a year (mostly plumbers advertising themselves as 'the Rolls-Royce of plumbers' and that sort of thing). Other companies have been less vigilant, or at least less successful. Aspirin, cellophane, yo-yo, and escalator were all once brand names that lost their protection. Many words that are still brand names are often used by the public as if they were not – Band-Aid, Frisbee, Jell-O, Coke, Kleenex, Xerox, and, in England, Hoover, which has achieved the unusual distinction there of becoming the common term for both the appliance and the action ('Did you hoover the carpet?'). There are obvious commercial benefits in forcing your competitors to describe their products as 'cola-flavoured soft drinks' or 'gelatine dessert'.

Despite the efforts involved in building up a good name, a little over a thousand companies a year in the United States opt to change their names. Sometimes this is because of mergers or takeovers, and sometimes, as with USX (formerly U.S. Steel) or Tambrands (formerly Tampax), it is because the company no longer wants to be associated with one particular product. And sometimes, frankly, it's because of an ill-judged whim. In 1987, the chairman of United Airlines, Richard Ferris, spent some $87 million changing the company's name from UAL, Inc., to Allegis. It was widely greeted as a disaster. The New York developer Donald Trump said the name sounded like the 'next world class disease'.[1] After just six weeks, Ferris was deposed. One of his successor's first moves was to change the name back to United Airlines.

Other name changes have been less disastrous but still of questionable benefit to the company. Fewer than 60 per cent of people polled in 1987 knew that Esmark was an American conglomerate – about as many as remembered Swift, the name it had changed from twelve years before. Other companies whose former identities have been submerged for better or worse in new names are Unisys (formed from the merger of Burroughs and Sperry), Trinova (formerly Libbey-Owens-Ford), and Citibank (from First National City Bank).

When a company changes name, the procedure is generally much the same as when a name is sought for a new brand of crisps or washing powder. Usually the company appoints a name specialist such as Novamark or Lippincott & Marrgulies. The specialist then comes up with several hundred or even thousand potential names. These may be suggested by employees or by panels of people chosen for the occasion, or simply churned out randomly by computers. Typically three-quarters of the names must be discarded because they are already trademarked or because they mean something offensive or inappropriate somewhere in the world.

If you are thinking of launching a new product yourself, I can tell you that among the names you cannot use are Sic, Pschitt, Plopp, and Super Piss. The first two are the names of soft drinks in France, the third is a chocolate bar in Taiwan, and the fourth is a Finnish de-icer. Sorry.

14

SWEARING

Among the Chinese, to be called a turtle is the worst possible taunt. In Norwegian, *devil* is highly taboo – roughly equivalent to our *fuck*. Among the Xoxa tribe of South Africa the most provocative possible remark is *hlebeshako* – 'your mother's ears'. In French it is a grave insult to call someone a cow or a camel and the effect is considerably intensified if you precede it with *espèce de* ('kind of') so that it is worse in French to be called a kind of a cow than to be called just a cow. The worst insult among Australian aborigines is to suggest that the target have intercourse with his mother. Incest is in fact so serious in many cultures that often it need be implied in only the vaguest terms, as with *tu madre* in Spanish and *your mama* among blacks in America. Often national terms of abuse are nonsensical, as in the German *schweinehund*, which means 'pig-dog'.

Some cultures don't swear at all. The Japanese, Malayans, and most Polynesians and American Indians do not have native swear words. The Finns, lacking the sort of words you need to describe your feelings when you stub your toe getting up to answer a wrong number at 2.00 a.m., rather oddly adopted the word *ravintolassa*. It means 'in the restaurant'.

But most cultures swear and have been doing so for a very long time. Dr J. N. Adams of Manchester University studied swearing by Romans and found that they had 800 'dirty' words (for want of a better expression). We, by contrast, have only about twenty or so, depending on how you define the term. The Rating Code Office of Hollywood has a list of

seventeen seriously objectionable words that will earn a
motion picture a mandatory R rating. If you add in all the
words that are not explicitly taboo but are still socially doubtful – words like *crap* and *boobs* – the number rises to perhaps
fifty or sixty words in common use. Once there were many
more. More than 1,200 words just for *sexual intercourse* have
been counted.

According to Dr Adams's findings, certain things have not
changed in 1,500 years, most notably a preoccupation with
the size of the male member, for which the Romans provided
many names, among them *tool, dagger, sickle, tiller, stake, sword,*
and (a little oddly perhaps) *worm.* Even more oddly, the two
most common Roman slang words for the penis were both
feminine, while the most common word for female genitalia
was masculine.

Swearing seems to have some near universal qualities. In
almost all cultures, swearing involves one or more of the
following: filth, the forbidden (particularly incest), and the
sacred, and usually all three. Most cultures have two levels of
swearing – relatively mild and highly profane. Ashley Montagu, in *The Anatomy of Swearing*, cites a study of swearing
among the Wik Monkan natives of the Cape York Peninsula.
They have many insults which are generally regarded as
harmless teasing – *big head, long nose, skinny arms* – and a whole
body of very much more serious ones, which are uttered only
in circumstances of high emotion. Among the latter are *big
penis, plenty urine,* and *vagina woman mad.*

English is unusual in including the impossible and the
pleasurable in its litany of profanities. It is a strange and little-
noted idiosyncrasy of our tongue that when we wish to express
extreme fury we entreat the object of our rage to undertake an
anatomical impossibility or, stranger still, to engage in the one
activity that is bound to give him more pleasure than almost
anything else. Can there be, when you think about it, a more
improbable sentiment than 'Get fucked!'? We might as well
snarl, 'Make a lot of money!' or 'Have a nice day!'

Most of our swear words have considerable antiquity.

Modern English contains few words that would be unhesitat-
ingly understood by an Anglo-Saxon peasant of, say, the tenth
century A.D., but *tits* is one of them. So is *fart*, believe it or not.
The Anglo-Saxons used the word *scītan*, which became *shite* by
the 1300s and *shit* by the 1500s. *Shite* is used as a variant of *shit*
in England to this day.

Fuck, it has been suggested, may have sprung from the Latin
futuo, the French *foutre*, or the German *ficken*, all of which have
the same meaning. According to Montagu the word first
appears in print in 1503 in a poem by the Scottish poet
William Dunbar. Although *fuck* has been around for centuries,
possibly millennia, for a long period it fell out of general use.
Before 1503, the vulgar word for sex was to *swive*.

Pussy, for the vagina, goes back at least to the 1600s. *Arse* is
Old English. Common names for the penis, such as *dick*, *peter*,
and *percy* (used variously throughout the English-speaking
world), go back at least 150 years, though they may be very
much older. *Jock* was once also common in this respect, but it
died out, though it survives in *jockstrap*.

It is often hard to trace such terms reliably because they
weren't generally recorded and because they have, for obvious
reasons, seldom attracted scholarly investigation. *Buttocks*, for
instance, goes back to at least the thirteenth century, but *butt*,
its slangy diminutive form, is not recorded until 1859 in America. As Stuart Berg Flexner observes, it seems highly unlikely
that it took 600 years for anyone to think of converting the
former into the latter. Similarly, although *shit* has been around
in various forms since before the Norman Conquest, *horseshit*
does not appear before the 1930s. Again, this seems improbable. The lack of authoritative guidance has sometimes encouraged people to come up with fanciful explanations for
profanities. *Fuck*, it was suggested, was originally a police
blotter acronym standing for 'For Unlawful Carnal Knowledge'. It is nothing of the sort.

After *O.K.*, *fuck* must be about the most versatile of all
English words. It can be used to describe a multitude of
conditions and phenomena, from making a mess of something

(*fuck up*) to being casual or provocative (*fuck around*), to inviting or announcing a departure (*fuck off*), to being estimable (*fucking-A*), to being baffled (*I'm fucked if I know*), to being disgusted (*fuck this*), and so on and on and on. *Fuck* probably reached its zenith during the Second World War. Most people are familiar with the army term *snafu* (short for 'situation normal – all fucked up'), but there were many others in common currency then, among them *fubar* ('fucked up beyond all recognition') and *fubb* ('fucked up beyond belief').

Piss goes back at least to the thirteenth century, but may be even older. It has been traced to the Vulgar Latin *pissiare* and thus could conceivably date from the Roman occupation of Britain. As *piss* became considered indecent, the euphemism *pee* evolved, based simply on the pronunciation of the first letter of the word. In America, *piss* has been documented since 1760 and *pee* since 1788.

The emotional charge attached to words can change dramatically over time. *Cunt* was once relatively harmless. Chaucer dropped it casually and severally into *The Canterbury Tales*, spelling it variously *queynte*, *queinte*, and even *Kent*. The City of London once had an alley favoured by prostitutes called Grope-cuntlane. It was not until the early eighteenth century that the word became indecent. *Shit* was considered acceptable until as recently as the early nineteenth century. *Prick* was standard until the eighteenth century. *Piss* was an unexceptionable word from about 1250 to 1750, a fact still reflected in the common French name for urinals: *pissoirs*. On the other hand, words that seem entirely harmless now were once capable of exciting considerable passion. In sixteenth-century England, *zooterkins* was a pretty lively word. In nineteenth-century England *puppy* and *cad* were highly risqué.

Today the worst swear words in English are probably *fuck*, *shit*, and *cunt*. But until about the 1870s it was much more offensive to be profane. *God damn*, *Jesus*, and even *Hell* were worse than *fuck* and *shit* (insofar as these things are quantifiable). In early swearing religion played a much more prominent role – so much so that in the fifteenth century a common tag for Englishmen in France was *goddams*. Swearing by saints was also common./A relic of this is our epithet *by George*, which is a contraction of 'by St George' and has been around for centuries. *Cock* was for a long time not only a slang term for penis but also a euphemism for God. Thus in *Hamlet* Ophelia could pun: 'Young men will do't, if they come to't; By cock, they are to blame.' Some of these were surprisingly explicit – 'by God's bones', 'by God's body' – but as time went on they were increasingly blurred into more harmless forms, such as *zounds* (for 'God's wounds'), *gadzooks* (for 'God's hooks', the significance of which is obscure), and *God's bodkins* or other variants like *odsbodikins* and *gadsbudlikins*, all formed from 'God's body'.

This tendency to transform profanities into harmless expressions is a particular characteristic of English swearing. Most languages employ *euphemism* (from the Greek, meaning 'to speak well of') in some measure. Germans say the meaningless *Potz blitz* rather than *Gottes Blitz* and the French say *par bleu* for *par Dieu* and *Ventre Saint Gris* instead of *Ventre Saint Christ*. But no other language approaches English for the number of delicate expletives of the sort that you could safely say in front of a maiden aunt: *darn, durn, drat, gosh, golly, goodness gracious, gee whiz, jeepers, shucks*, and so on. We have scores, if not hundreds, of these terms. However, sometimes even these words are regarded as exceptionable, particularly when they are new. *Blooming* and *blasted*, originally devised as mild epithets, were in nineteenth-century England considered nearly as offensive as the more venerable expletives they were meant to replace.

But then of course the gravity of swear words in any language has little to do with the words themselves and much more to do with the fact that they are forbidden. It is a circular effect. Forbidden words are emotive because they are forbidden and they are forbidden because they are emotive.

A remarkable example of this is *bloody* in England, which to most Britons is at least as objectionable a word as *shit* and yet it is meaningless. A number of explanations have been suggested, generally involving either a contraction of an oath such as 'by Christ's blood' or 'by our Lady' or else something to do with menstruation. But there is no historical evidence to favour one view over the other. The fact is that sometime around the sixteenth century people began to say *bloody* and to mean a curse by it. It's now often hard to tell when they meant it as a curse and when they meant it to be taken literally, as when in *Richard III* Richmond says, 'The bloody dog is dead.'

Although Shakespeare had a weakness for double entendre puns, on the whole he was a fairly restrained and not terribly inventive swearer. *Damned* appears 105 times in his thirty-seven plays, but for the rest he was content to insert the odd 'For God's sake', 'a pox on't', 'God's bread', and one 'whoreson jackanapes'. *Julius Caesar*, unusually for the period, has not a single instance of swearing. By contrast, in the same year that *Julius Caesar* was first performed, Ben Jonson's *Every Man in His Humour* offered such colourful phrases as 'Whoreson base fellow', 'whoreson coney-catching rascal' (*coney* being a synonym for pudendum), 'by my fackins faith', and 'I am the rankest cow that ever pissed'. Other of his plays contain even richer expressions: 'I fart at thee', 'Shit o' your head', 'Turd i' your teeth'. Another play of approximately the same period, *Gammer Gurton's Needle*, first performed about 1550, contained literally dozens of instances of swearing: 'by Jesus', 'dirty bastard', 'bawdy bitch', 'for God's sake', and many more in the same vein. It even had a parson describing someone as 'that shitten lout'. Other oaths of the period included such memorable expressions as 'kiss my blindcheeks' and 'stap my vitals'.

Soon after Shakespeare's death, Britain went through a period of prudery of the sort with which all countries are periodically seized. In 1623 an Act of Parliament was passed making it illegal to swear. People were fined for such mild oaths as 'upon my life' and 'by my troth' – mild utterances indeed compared with the 'God's poxes' and 'fackins faiths' of a generation before. In 1649 the laws were tightened even further – to the extent that swearing at a parent became punishable by death.

But the greatest outburst of prudery came in the nineteenth century when it swept through the world like a fever. It was an age when sensibilities grew so delicate that one lady was reported to have dressed her goldfish in miniature suits for the sake of propriety and a certain Madame de la Bresse left her fortune to provide clothing for the snowmen of Paris. Prudery, so often associated with the reign of Queen Victoria (1837–1901), actually considerably predated it. One of the great names in the field was that of Thomas Bowdler, an Edinburgh physician who purified the works of writers such as Shakespeare and Gibbon, boasting that it was his practice to add nothing new to the work, but simply to remove those words that 'cannot with propriety be read aloud in a family'. His ten-volume *Family Shakespeare* appeared in 1818, a year before Victoria was born, so it is clear the queen didn't establish the trend, but simply helped to prolong it. In fact, almost a century before she reigned Samuel Johnson was congratulated by a woman for leaving indecent words out of his dictionary. To which he devastatingly replied: 'So you've been looking for them, have you, Madam?'

It has sometimes been said that prudery reached such a height in the nineteenth century that people took to dressing their piano legs in little skirts lest they rouse anyone to untimely passion. Thomas Pyles in his outstanding *Words and Ways of American English* tracked the story to a book called *Diary in America*, written in 1837 by an English traveller, Captain Frederick Marryat, and concluded that the story was told for comic effect and almost certainly was untrue. Rather more plausible was the anecdote recorded in the same book in which Marryat made the serious gaffe of asking a young lady if she had hurt her leg in a fall. The woman blushingly averted her gaze and told him that people did not use *that* word in America. 'I apologized for my want of refinement, which was attributable to having been accustomed only to *English* society,' Marryat drolly remarked, and asked the lady what was the acceptable term for 'such articles'. *Limbs*, he was told.

It was an age in which the most innocuous words became unacceptable at a rate that must have been dizzying. *Stomach* became a euphemism for *belly* and in its turn was considered too graphic and was replaced by *tummy*, *midriff*, and even *breadbasket*. The conventional terms for the parts of a chicken, such as *breast*, *leg*, and *thigh*, caused particular anxiety and had to be replaced with terms like *drumstick*, *first joint*, and *white meat*. The names for male animals, such as *buck* and *stallion*, were never used in mixed company. Bulls were called *sires*, *male animals*, and, in a truly inspired burst of ridiculousness, *gentleman cows*. But it didn't stop there. Euphemisms had to be devised for any word that had *cock* in it – *haycock* became *haystack*, *cockerel* became *rooster* – and for the better part of a century people with *cock* in their names, such as Hitchcock or Peacock, suffered unspeakable embarrassment when they were required to make introductions. Americans were rather more squeamish in these matters than the British, going so far as to change the old English *titbit* to *tidbit*.

Against such a background one can easily imagine the shock that must have gripped readers of *The Times* who turned to their paper one morning in January 1882 and found a lengthy report on a parliamentary speech by the attorney general concluding with the unexpectedly forthright statement: 'The speaker then said he felt inclined for a bit of fucking.' Not surprisingly, it caused a sensation. The executives of *The Times* were so dumbstruck by this outrage against common decency that four full days passed before they could bring themselves to acknowledge the offence. After what was doubtless the most exhaustive internal investigation ever undertaken at the newspaper, it issued an apology: 'No pains have been spared by the management of this journal to discover the author of a gross outrage committed by the interpolation of a line in the speech by Sir William Harcourt reported in our issue of Monday last. This malicious fabrication was surreptitiously introduced before the paper went to press. The matter is now under legal investigation, and it is to be hoped that the perpetrator will be brought to punishment.' But if they hadn't caught him after four days I doubt if they ever did. In any case, he or someone of like sensibilities struck again six months later when an advertisement appeared promoting a book about 'Every-day Life in our Public Schools. Sketched by Head Scholars. With a Glossary of Some Words used by Henry Irving in his disquisition upon fucking.' Whatever soul or souls were responsible for this sequel, they kept their peace thereafter – though I have been told that when Queen Victoria opened the Clifton Suspension Bridge the sentence 'Her Majesty then passed over the bridge' came out in *The Times* as 'Her Majesty then pissed over the bridge.' Whether this embellishment of the facts was intentional or fortuitous (or even possibly apocryphal) I could not say.

The Victorian horror at the thought of swearing in print has lingered up to our own day. According to Ashley Montagu, as recently as 1947 *Technology Review*, a publication of the Massachusetts Institute of Technology read almost exclusively by scientists and technocrats, changed the expression 'doing his damnedest' to 'doing intensely his very best'. Ten years later the same author used the same phrase in a book and again had it cut. Montagu also cites the instance in 1941 of a federal judge threatening a lawyer with contempt for using a base and indecent word in his court. The word was *darn*. In 1948, Burges Johnson actually managed to write a book on swearing, *The Lost Art of Profanity*, without once mentioning any of the four-letter words. He would not have had it published otherwise. And as late as 1949, the Hollywood Production Code banned the word *dames*. In that year, as Mario Pei notes, a movie called *Dames Don't Talk* had its title changed to *Smart Girls Don't Talk*.

The editors of the *Random House Dictionary* of 1966 decided, after considerable agonizing, not to insert any four-letter words. They did not appear until the publication of *RHD-II* in 1987. The original *Oxford English Dictionary*, despite its determination to chart every word in the language, contained none of the four-letter words, though they did appear in the supplements to the *OED*, which began to appear in 1972. They also appeared in the *Concise Oxford Dictionary* from about the same time.

In 1988, William Safire managed to write a column in *The New York Times Magazine* about the expression *the shit hit the fan* without actually mentioning *shit*. The closest he came was to talk about the use of 'a scatological noun just before the familiar *hit the fan*'. During the Watergate hearings, *The Times* did print the term *candyass*, used by Richard Nixon, but did so only reluctantly. The paper's stylebook continues to say that *goddamn* 'should not be used at all unless there is a compelling reason'. And the National Transportation Safety Board displayed extraordinary delicacy when it published a transcript of cockpit voice recordings during the crash of a United Airlines jet in Sioux City, Iowa, in 1989. An example: 'We're not going to make the runway, fellows. We're going to have to ditch this son of a [word deleted] and hope for the best.'[1]

The British are relatively broad-minded about language, even in their advertisements. In 1989 Epson, the printer company, ran a lighthearted ad in British newspapers about the history of printing, which contained the statement that 'a Chinese eunuch called Cai Lun, with no balls but one hell of an imagination, invented paper'. I doubt very much that any American newspaper would accept an ad referring explicitly to the testicular condition of the inventor of paper.

Most of the quality newspapers in Britain have freely admitted expletives to their pages when the circumstances were deemed to warrant it. Their first opportunity to do so was in 1960 when a court decided that *Lady Chatterley's Lover* could be printed in full without risk of doing irreversible damage to society's well-being. Three British publications, the *Observer*, the *Guardian*, and the *Spectator*, took the opportunity to print *fuck* themselves and were promptly censured by the Press Council for doing so. But the word has appeared many times in the British press since then, generally without any murmur of complaint. (Ironically, the tabloid newspapers, though usually specializing in matters of sex and prurience, are far more skittish when it comes to printing swear words.)

In 1988 British papers were given an outstanding opportunity to update their position on obscenities when the captain of the England cricket tream, Mike Gatting, reportedly called the umpire of an important match 'a fucking, cheating cunt'. Only one newspaper, the *Independent*, printed all the words without asterisks. It was the first time that *cunt* had appeared in a British newspaper.

Some words are less innocent than they seem. *Bollix* is commonly used in America to describe a confused situation, as in this quotation from the *Philadelphia Inquirer*:[2] 'It was the winless Giants' third loss of the bollixed strike-torn season.' Or this one from American Airlines' inflight magazine, *American Way*: 'Our faux pas of the month for February was the crossword puzzle titled Heavy Stuff, which was all bollixed up.'[3] It is probably safe to assume that neither writer was aware that *bollix* is a direct adaptation of *bollocks* (or *ballocks*), meaning 'testicles'. It is still used in England to describe the testicles and also as a cry to express disbelief, similar to *bullshit* in American usage. As Pyles notes, Barnacle Bill the Sailor was originally Ballocky Bill and the original words of his ballad were considerably more graphic and sexual than the innocent phrases beloved by generations of children. The American slang word *nuts* also means 'testicles' – though oddly when used as an exclamation it becomes wholly innocent. Other words concealing unsavoury origins include *bumf*, which is short for *bumfodden* or 'toilet paper' in German, and *poppycock*, an adaptation of a Dutch word meaning 'soft dung'. (In answer to the obvious question, yes, they also have a word for firm dung – in fact two: *poep* and *stront*.)

A few swear words have evolved different connotations in Britain and America. In America, a person who is pissed is angry; in Britain he's drunk. *Bugger*, a wholly innocent word in

America, is not at all welcome in polite conversation in Britain. As Pyles notes, until 1934 you could be fined or imprisoned for writing or saying it. A bugger in Britain is a sodomite. Although *bugger* is unacceptable, *buggery* is quite all right: it is the term used by both the legal profession and newspapers when someone is accused of criminal sodomy.

15

WORDPLAY

Six days a week an Englishman named Roy Dean sits down and does in a matter of minutes something that many of us cannot do at all: he completes the crossword puzzle in *The Times*. Dean is the, well, the dean of the British crossword. In 1970, under test conditions, he solved a *Times* crossword in just 3 minutes and 45 seconds, a feat so phenomenal that it has stood unchallenged for twenty years.

Unlike American crosswords, which are generally straightforward affairs, requiring you merely to fit a word to a definition, the British variety are infinitely more fiendish, demanding mastery of the whole armoury of verbal possibilities – puns, anagrams, palindromes, lipograms, and whatever else springs to the deviser's devious mind. British crosswords require you to realize that *carthorse* is an anagram of *orchestra*, that *contaminated* can be made into *no admittance*, that *emigrants* can be transformed into *streaming*, *Cinerama* into *American*, *Old Testament* into *most talented*, and *World Cup team* into (a stroke of genius, this one) *talcum powder*. (How did anyone *ever* think of that?) To a British crossword enthusiast, the clue 'An important city in Czechoslovakia' instantly suggests Oslo. Why? Look at *Czech*(OSLO)*vakia* again. 'A seed you put in the garage' is *caraway*, while 'HIJKLMNO' is *water* because it is H-to-O or H_2O. Some clues are cryptic in the extreme. The answer to 'Sweetheart could take Non-Commissioned Officer to dance' is *flame*. Why? Well, a noncommissioned officer is an NCO. Another word for sweetheart is *flame*. If you add NCO to *flame* you get *flamenco*, a kind of dance. Get it? It is a wonder to me that anyone ever completes them. And yet many Britons take inordinate pride not just in completing them but in completing them quickly. A provost at Eton once boasted that he could do *The Times* crossword in the time it took his morning egg to boil, prompting one wag to suggest that the school may have been Eton but the egg almost certainly wasn't.

According to a Gallup poll, the crossword is the most popular sedentary recreation. The very first crossword, containing just thirty-two clues, appeared in the New York *World* on December 21, 1913. It had been thought up as a space filler by an expatriate Englishman named Arthur Wynne, who called it a word-cross. (Remember what I said about inventors never quite getting the name right?) It became a regular feature in the *World*, but nobody else picked it up until April 1924 when a fledgling publishing company called Simon and Schuster brought out a volume of crossword puzzles, priced at $1.35. It was an immediate hit and two other volumes were quickly produced. By the end of the first year the company had sold half a million copies, and crossword puzzles were a craze across America – so much so that for a time the Baltimore and Ohio Railroad installed dictionaries in each of its cars for the convenience of puzzle-solving travellers who had an acute need to know that Iliamna is the largest lake in Alaska or that oquassa is a kind of freshwater fish.

Despite this huge popularity, the most venerable papers on both sides of the Atlantic refused for years to acknowledge that the crossword was more than a passing fad. *The Times* held out until January 1930, when it finally produced its first crossword (devised by a Norfolk farmer who had never previously solved one, much less constructed one). To salve its conscience at succumbing to a frivolous game, *The Times* printed occasional crosswords in Latin. Its namesake in New York held out for another decade and did not produce its first crossword until 1942.

Only one other word game has ever challenged the crossword puzzle for popularity and respectability and that's

Scrabble. Scrabble was introduced by a games company called
Selchow and Righter in 1953, though it had been invented, by
one Alfred Butts, more than twenty years earlier in 1931. Butts
clearly didn't have too much regard for which letters are used
most often in English. With just ninety-eight tiles, he insisted
on having at least two of each letter, which means that *q*, *j*,
and *z* appear disproportionately often. As a result, success at
Scrabble generally involves being able to come up with obscure
words like *zax* (a hatchetlike tool) and *xi* (the fourteenth letter
of the Greek alphabet). Butts intentionally depressed the
number of *s*'s to discourage the formation of plurals, though he
compensated by increasing the number of *i*'s to encourage the
formation of suffixes and prefixes. The highest score, according
to Alan Richter, a former British champion writing in the
Atlantic in 1987, was 3,881 points. It included the word *psycho-
analyzing*, which alone was worth 1,539 points.

Wordplay is as old as language itself, and about as various.
As Tony Augarde notes in his scholarly and yet endlessly
absorbing *Oxford Guide to Word Games*, many verbal pastimes
go back to the furthest reaches of antiquity. Palindromes, sentences that read the same backwards as forwards, are at least
2,000 years old. The ancient Greeks often put 'Nispon anomi-
mata mi monan opsin' on fountains. It translates as 'Wash the
sin as well as the face.' The Romans admired them, too, as
demonstrated by 'In girum imus nocte et consumimur igni'
('We enter the circle after dark and are consumed by fire'),
which was said to describe the action of moths. The Romans
also liked anagrams – scrambling the letters of a word or phrase
to form new words or phrases – and turned 'Quid est veritas?'
('What is truth?') into 'Est vir qui adest' ('It is this man here').

Among the earliest instances of wordplay, Augarde cites a
Greek anagram dating from the third century B.C. and, earlier
still, a lipogram by the Greek Lasus, from the fifth century
B.C. in which the poet intentionally avoided using the letter *s*.
So it is safe to say that wordplay is very old and effectively
universal. Even Christ reputedly made a pun when He said:
'Thou art Peter: upon this rock I shall build my Church.' It

doesn't make a lot of sense from the wordplay point of view until you realize that in ancient Greek the word for Peter and for rock was the same.

Wordplay in English is as old as our literature. In the eighth century A.D., Cynewulf, one of the first English poets, wrote four otherwise serious religious poems into each of which he artfully wove acrostics of his own name, presumably for no other reason than that it amused him. Verbal japes of one type or another have been a feature of English literature ever since. Shakespeare so loved puns that he put 3,000 of them – that's right, 3,000 – into his plays, even to the extent of inserting them in the most seemingly inappropriate places, as when in *King Henry IV, Part I*, the father of Hotspur learns of his son's tragic death and remarks that Hotspur is now Coldspur. The most enduring names in English, from Lewis Carroll to James Joyce, have almost always been associated with wordplay. Even Samuel Johnson, as we have seen, managed to insert a number of jokes into his great dictionary – an action that would be inconceivable in other languages.

The varieties of wordplay available in English are almost without number – puns, tongue-twisters, anagrams, riddles, cryptograms, palindromes, clerihews, rebuses, crossword puzzles, spelling bees, and so on ad infinitum. Their effect can be addictive. Lewis Carroll, an obsessive deviser and player of wordgames, once sat up all night trying to make an anagram of William Ewart Gladstone before settling on 'Wild agitator, means well'. Some diligent scholar, whose identity appears now to be lost, set his attention on that famous Shakespearean nonce word in *Love's Labour's Lost, honorificabilitudinitatibus,* and concluded that it must contain an anagram proving that Shakespeare didn't write the plays, and came up with 'Hi ludi F. Baconis nati tuiti orbi', which translates as 'These plays, born of F. Bacon, are preserved for the world.' Think of the hours of labour that *that* must have involved. According to the *Guinness Book of Records*, a man in the county of Hereford & Worcester wrote a palindrome of 65,000 words in 1983. Whether or not it makes much sense – and I would almost bet my house that it doesn't – we can but admire the dedication that must have gone into it.

Possibly the most demanding form of wordplay in English – or indeed in any language – is the palindrome. The word was first used in English by Ben Jonson in 1629. A good palindrome is an exceedingly rare thing. Most of them require a generosity of spirit to say that they make much sense, as in 'Mad Zeus, no live devil, lived evil on Suez dam' or Stiff, O dairyman, in a myriad of fits' or 'Straw? No, too stupid a fad. I put soot on warts', all three of which deserve an A+ for length and a D– for sensibility. Or else they involve manipulations of spelling, as the short but notable 'Yreka Bakery' or the rather more venerable 'Lewd I did live, & evil did I dwel.' This last, according to Willard R. Espy in *The Game of Words*, was written by the English poet John Taylor and is the first recorded palindrome in English, though in fact it isn't really a palindrome since it only works if you use an ampersand instead of *and*.

The reason there are so many bad palindromes, of course, is that they are so very difficult to construct. So good ones are all the more cherishable for their rarity. Probably the most famous palindrome is one of the best. It manages in just seven words to tell an entirely sensible story: 'A man, a plan, a canal, Panama!' That is simply inspired. Others that have the virtue of making at least some kind of sense:

Norma is as selfless as I am, Ron.
Was it Eliot's toilet I saw?
Too far, Edna, we wander afoot.
Madam, I'm Adam.
Sex at noon taxes.
Are we not drawn onward, we few, drawn onward to new era?
Able was I ere I saw Elba.
Sums are not set as a test on Erasmus.
Satan, oscillate my metallic sonatas.

This last, I realize, does not even begin to pass the plausibility test, but so what? Anyone ingenious enough to work *oscillate*, *metallic*, and *sonatas* into one palindrome is exempt from all requirements bearing on sense. The Greeks and Romans also had a kind of palindrome in which it is the words rather than the letters that are read in reverse order – rather as if the English sentence 'Jack loves Jill, not Jane' had its word order reversed to read 'Jane, not Jill, loves Jack', giving an entirely new sense. This kind of palindrome has never caught on in the English-speaking world, largely because English doesn't lend itself to it very well. I've been working on it most of the afternoon (I told you wordplay is addictive) and the best I can come up with is 'Am I as stupid as you are?' which reads backwards as well as forwards but, alas, keeps the same sense in both directions.

Not far removed from the palindrome is the anagram, in which the letters of a word or name are jumbled to make a new, and ideally telling, phrase. Thus 'Ronald Wilson Reagan' becomes 'Insane Anglo Warlord', 'Spiro Agnew' becomes 'Grow a Penis'. Again, one can but gasp at the ingenuity and dedication that have gone into some of them. What kind of mind is it that can notice that 'two plus eleven' and 'one plus twelve' not only give the same result but use the same letters? Other famous or notable anagrams:

Western Union = no wire unsent
circumstantial evidence = can ruin a selected victim
a stitch in time saves nine = this is meant as incentive
William Shakespeare = I am a weakish speller (or) I like Mr
    W. H. as a pal, see? (or) we all make his praise
funeral = real fun
The Morse Code = here come dots
Victoria, England's Queen = governs a nice quiet land
parishioners = I hire parsons
intoxicate = excitation
schoolmaster = the classroom
mother-in-law = woman Hitler

Another form of wordplay is the *rebus*, a kind of verbal

riddle in which words and symbols are arranged in a way that gives a clue to the intended meaning. Can you, for example, guess the meaning of this address?

Wood
John
Mass

It is 'John Underwood, Andover, Massachusetts'. Many books and articles on word games say that such an address was once put on an envelope and that the letter actually got there, which suggests either that the postal service was once a lot better or writers more gullible than they are now. These days the rebus is a largely forgotten form, except on American licence plates, where owners sometimes feel compelled to tell you their name or what they do for a living (like the doctor who put SAY AH), pose a metaphysical question (Y ME) or a provocative one (RUNVS), or just offer a friendly farewell (ALLBCNU). My favourite was the licence plate on a truck from a McDonald's Farm that just said EIEIO. If nothing else, these vanity plates tell us something about the spirit of the age. According to a 1984 report in the *Los Angeles Times*,[1] the most frequently requested plate in 1970 was PEACE. By 1984 that had been replaced by GO FOR IT.

The French, in accordance with their high regard for the cerebral, have long cultivated a love of wordplay. In the Middle Ages, they even had a post of Anagrammatist to the King. One of the great French wordplayers was the novelist Georges Perec, who before his early death in 1982 was a guiding force in the group called OuLiPo (for Ouvroir de Littérature Potentielle) whose members delighted in setting themselves complex verbal challenges. Perec once wrote a novel without using the letter *e* (such compositions are called *lipograms*) and also composed a 5,000-letter palindrome on the subject of, you guessed it, palindromes.

An example of a French rebus is 'Ga = I am very hungry'. To understand it you must know that in French capital *G* ('G grand') and small *a* ('a petit') are pronounced the same as 'J'ai grand appétit.' N'est-ce pas? But the French go in for many other games, including some we don't have. One of the more clever French word games is the *holorime*, a two-line poem in which each line is pronounced the same but uses different words. As you will quickly see from the following example, sense often takes a backseat to euphony in these contrivances:

> Par le bois du Djinn, ou s'entasse de l'effroi,
> Parle! Bois du gin, ou cent tasses de lait froid!

It translates roughly as 'When going through the Djinn's woods, surrounded by so much fear, keep talking. Drink gin or a hundred cups of cold milk.' We have the capacity to do this in English – 'I love you' and 'isle of view' are holorimic phrases and there must be an infinity of others. William Safire cites the American grandmother who thought that the line in the Beatles' song about 'the girl with kaleidoscope eyes' was 'the girl with colitis goes by', which would seem to offer rich potential to budding holorimistes. A rare attempt to compose an English holorime was made by the humorist Miles Kington (from whom the previous example is quoted) in 1988 when he offered the world this poem, called *A Lowlands Holiday Ends in Enjoyable Inactivity*:

> In Ayrshire hill areas, a cruise, eh, lass?
> Inertia, hilarious, accrues, hélas.

From this I think we can conclude that the definitive English holorime has yet to be written. However, an old children's riddle does seem to come close. It is the one that poses the question 'How do you prove in three steps that a sheet of paper is a lazy dog?' The answer: (1) a sheet of paper is an ink-lined plane; (2) an inclined plane is a slope up; (3) a slow pup is a lazy dog.

We may not have holorimes in English, but we do have tricks that the French don't have. *Clerihews*, for instance. Named after their deviser, one E. Clerihew Bentley, an English journalist, they are pithy poems that always start with someone's name and purport, in just four lines, to convey the salient facts of the subject's life. To wit:

> Sir Humphrey Davy
> Detested gravy
> He lived in the odium
> Of having invented sodium.

The closest America has come to producing an equivalent to clerihews were the Burma-Shave signs that graced U.S. highways for half a century. Devised in 1926 by Allan Odell, son of the founder of the Burma-Shave company, these consisted of five or six signs spaced one hundred feet apart which gave a witty sales jingle for Burma-Shave shaving cream. Some examples: 'A peach / looks good / with lots of fuzz / but man's no peach / and never was. / BURMA-SHAVE.' Or 'Don't take a curve / at 60 per. / We hate to lose / a customer. / BURMA-SHAVE.' Some of the best ones never made it to the roadside because they were considered too risqué for the time. For instance: 'If wifie shuns / your fond embrace / don't shoot / the iceman / feel your face.' As recently as the 1960s, there were still 7,000 sets of Burma-Shave signs along American roadsides. But the Highway Beautification Act of 1965 put an end to the erection of any new ones, and the old ones were quickly whisked away by souvenir hunters. Now they are so much a thing of the past that a publicity woman at American Safety Razor, the company that now owns the Burma-Shave name, had never even heard of them.

We have a deep-rooted delight in the comic effect of words in English, and not just in advertising jingles but at the highest level of endeavour. As Jespersen notes: 'No literature in the world abounds as English does in characters made ridiculous to the reader by the manner in which they misapply or distort "big" words,'[2] and he cites, among others, Sheridan's Mrs Malaprop, Fielding's Mrs Slipslop, Dickens's Sam Weller, and Shakespeare's Mistress Quickly.

All of these were created for comic effect in plays and novels, but sometimes it comes naturally, as with that most famous of word muddlers, the Reverend William Spooner, warden of New College, Oxford, from 1903 to 1924, whose habitual transposition of sounds – *metaphasis* is the technical term – made him famous in his own lifetime and gave the world a word: *spoonerism*. A little-known fact about Spooner was that he was an albino. He was also famously boring, a shortcoming that he himself acknowledged when he wrote plaintively of his sermons in his diary: 'They are so apt to be dull.' In a profile in the London *Echo* in 1905, the reporter noted that Spooner 'has been singularly unsuccessful in making any decided impression upon his own college'. But his most outstanding characteristic was his facility for turning phrases on their heads. Among the more famous utterances invariably attributed to him are 'Which of us has not felt in his heart a half-warmed fish?' and, to a delinquent undergraduate: 'You have hissed my mystery lectures. You have tasted a whole worm. You will leave Oxford on the next town drain.' At an optician's he is said to have asked, 'Have you a signifying glass?' and when told they did not, replied, 'Oh, well, it doesn't magnify.' But as his biographer William Hayter notes, Spooner became so well known for these transpositions that it is sometimes impossible to know which he really said and which were devised in his name. He *is* known to have said 'in a dark glassly' and to have announced at a wedding ceremony that a couple were now 'loifully jawned', but it is altogether possible that he actually said very few of the spoonerisms attributed to him and that the genuine utterances weren't nearly as comical as those he was credited with, like the almost certainly apocryphal 'Please sew me to another sheet. Someone is occupewing my pie.'

What is certain is that Spooner suffered from a kind of metaphasis of thought, if not always of word. These are generally well attributed. Outside New College chapel he rebuked a student by saying: 'I thought you read the lesson badly today.'

'But, sir, I didn't read the lesson,' protested the student.

'Ah,' said Spooner, 'I thought you didn't,' and walked on.

On another occasion he approached a fellow don and said, 'Do come to dinner tonight to meet our new Fellow, Casson.'

The man answered, 'But, Warden, I *am* Casson.'

To which Spooner replied, 'Never mind, come all the same.'

Another colleague once received a note from Spooner asking him to come to his office the next morning on a matter of urgency. At the bottom there was a P.S. saying that the matter had now been resolved and the colleague needn't bother coming after all.

Spooner well knew his reputation for bungling speech and hated it. Once when a group of drunken students called at his window for him to make a speech, he answered testily, 'You don't want to hear me make a speech. You just hope I'll say one of those . . . *things*.'

In addition to mangling words in amusing ways, something else we can do in English that they cannot always do in other languages is construct intentionally ambiguous sentences that can be taken in either of two ways, as in the famous, if no doubt apocryphal, notice in a restaurant saying: 'Customers who think our waiters are rude should see the manager.' There is a technical term for this (isn't there always?). It's called *amphibology*. An admirable example of this neglected art was Benjamin Disraeli's airy note to an aspiring author: 'Thank you so much for the book. I shall lose no time in reading it.' Samuel Johnson didn't quite utter an amphibology, but he neared it in spirit, when he wrote to another would-be author, 'Your work is both good and original. Unfortunately, the parts that are good aren't original, and the parts that are original aren't good.'

Occasionally people grow so carried away with the possibilities of wordplay that they weave it into their everyday language. The most famous example of this in America is *boontling*, a made-up language once spoken widely in and around Boonville, California. According to one story on how it began (and there are several to choose from) two sets of brothers, the Duffs and the Burgers, were sitting around the Anytime Saloon in Boonville one day in 1892 when they decided for reasons of amusement to devise a private language based partly on their common Scottish-Irish heritage and partly on words from the Pomo Indians living nearby, but mostly on their own gift for coming up with colourful secret words. The idea was that no one would be able to understand what they were talking about, but as far as that went the plan was a failure because soon pretty well everyone in town was talking Boontling, or harpin' boont as they put it locally, and for at least forty years it became the common linguistic currency in the isolated town a hundred miles north of San Francisco. It became so much a part of the local culture that some people sometimes found it took them a minute or two to readjust to the English-speaking world when they ventured out of their valley. With time, the language grew to take in about 1,200 words, a good many of them salacious, as you might expect with a private language.

Many expressions were taken from local characters. Coffee was called *zeese* after the initials of a camp cook named Zachariah Clifton who made coffee you could stand a spoon up in. A hardworking German named Otto inspired the term *otting* for diligent work. A goatee became a *billy ryan*. A kerosene lantern was a *floyd hutsell*. Pie was called *charlie brown* because a local of that name always ate his pie before he ate the rest of his meal. A prostitute was a *madge*. A doctor was a *shoveltooth* on account of the protruding teeth of an early G.P. Other words were based on contractions – *forbs* for four bits, *toobs* for two bits, *hairk* for a haircut, *smalch* for small change. Others contained literary or biblical allusions. Thus an illegitimate child was a *bulrusher*. Still others were metaphorical. A heavy rain was a *trashlifter* and a really heavy rain was a *loglifter*. But many of the most memorable terms were onomatopoeic, notably one of the terms for sexual intercourse, *ricky chow*, said to be the noise bedsprings make when pressed into urgent service. A great many of the words had a sexual provenance, such as *burlapping*, a euphemism for the sexual act, based on a local anecdote involving a young couple found passing an hour in that time-honoured fashion on a stack of old gunny sacks at the back of the general store.

Although some people can still speak Boontling, it is not as widely used as it once was. In much better shape is cockney rhyming slang, as spoken in the East End of London. Rhyming slang isn't a separate language, but simply a liberal peppering of mysterious and often venerable slang words.

Cockneys are among the most artful users of English in the world. A true cockney (the word comes from Middle English *cokeney*, 'cock's egg', slang for a townsperson) is said to have been born within the sound of Bow Bells – these being the famous (and famously noisy) bells of St Mary-le-Bow Church in Cheapside in the City of London. However, for a generation or so no one has been born within their sound for the elemental reason that they were destroyed by German bombs in World War II. In any case, the rise of the City of London as the capital's financial district meant that cockneys had long since been dispersed to more outlying districts of the East End where the bells of Bow rang out exceedingly faintly, if at all.

The East End of London has always been a melting pot, and they've taken terms from every wave of invaders, from French Huguenot weavers in the sixteenth century to Bangladeshis of today. Many others have come from their own eye-opening experiences overseas during the period of empire and two world wars. *Shufti*, for 'have a look at', and *buckshee*, for 'something that is free', both come from India. 'Let's have a parlyvoo' (meaning 'a chat') comes obviously from the French *parlez-vous*. Less obvious is the East End expression *san fairy ann*, meaning 'don't mention it, no problem', which is a corruption of the French 'ça ne fait rien'. The cockneys have also devised hundreds of terms of their own. 'Hang about' means 'wait a minute'. 'Leave it out' means 'stop, don't keep on at me'. 'Straight up' means 'honestly, that's the truth'. Someone who is misbehaving is 'out of order' or 'taking liberties'.

But without a doubt their most singular contribution to English has been rhyming slang. No one knows when cockney rhyming slang began, but it has certainly been popular since the mid-nineteenth century. As with general slang, some of the terms exist only for a short while before dying out, while others

234

live on for scores of years, sometimes moving out into the wider world where their low origins and true meanings are often mercifully unappreciated.

The two most often cited examples of rhyming slang are *apples and pears* = *stairs* and *trouble and strife* = *wife*. In point of fact, you could live a lifetime on the Mile End Road and not once hear those terms. But there are scores of others that are used daily, such as 'use yer loaf' (short for *loaf of bread* = *head*), 'have a butcher's' (short for *butcher's hook* = *look*), or 'how you doin,' my old china?' (short for *china plate* = *mate*). A complicating factor is that the word that rhymes is almost always dropped and thus the etymology is obscure. *Titfer* means 'hat': originally it was *tit-for-tat* = *hat*. *Tom* means 'jewellery'. It's short for *tomfoolery* = *jewellery*. There's a technical term for this process as well: *hemiteleia*.

A further complication is that cockney pronunciation is often considerably at variance with conventional British pronunciation, as evidenced by *rabbit* (to chatter mindlessly) coming from *rabbit and pork* = *talk*. In the East End both *pork* and *talk* rhyme (more or less) with *soak*. (Something of the flavour of cockney pronunciation is found in the old supposed cockney spelling of the London district of Ealing: 'E for 'eaven, A for what 'orses eat, L for where you're going, I for me, N for what lays eggs, and G for God's sake keep yer ears open.')

Sometimes these words spawn further rhymes. *Bottle*, for instance, has long meant 'arse' (from *bottle and glass* = *arse*). But at some point that in turn spawned *Aristotle*, often shortened to Aris' (as in 'Oo, I just fell on my Aris') and that in turn spawned *plaster* (from plaster of Paris). So you have this convoluted genealogy: *plaster* = *plaster of Paris* = *Aris* = *Aristotle* = *bottle* = *bottle and glass* = *arse*.

Several cockney rhyming slang terms have taken residence in America. In nineteenth-century London, *dukes* meant 'hands' (from *Duke of Yorks* = *forks* = *hand*), but in America it came to mean 'fist', and lives on in the expression 'put up your dukes'. *Bread* as a slang synonym for *money* comes from *bread and honey*. To *chew the fat* comes from *have a chat* and *brass tacks* comes from *facts*. And if you've ever wondered why a Bronx cheer is called a *raspberry*, you may wish to bear in mind that a popular dessert in Britain is called a raspberry tart.

16

THE FUTURE OF ENGLISH

In 1787, when representatives of the new United States gathered in Philadelphia to draw up a Constitution that could serve as a permanent blueprint for the American way of life, it apparently did not occur to them to consider the matter of what the national language should be. Then, and for the next two centuries, it was assumed that people would speak English. But in the 1980s a growing sense of disquiet among many Americans over the seepage of Spanish, Vietnamese, and other immigrant languages into American society led some of them to begin pressing for laws making English the official language.

According to the Census Bureau, 11 per cent of people in America speak a language other than English at home. In California alone, nearly one fifth of the people are Hispanic. In Los Angeles, the proportion of Spanish speakers is more than half. New York City has 1.5 million Hispanics and there are a million more in the surrounding area. Bergenline Avenue in New Jersey runs for ninety blocks and throughout most of its length is largely Spanish-speaking. All told in America there are 200 Spanish-language newspapers, 200 radio stations, and 300 television stations. The television stations alone generated nearly $300 million of Spanish-language advertising in 1987.

In many areas, English speakers are fearful of being swamped. Some even see it as a conspiracy, among them the former U.S. Senator S. I. Hayakawa, who wrote in 1987 that he believed that 'a very real move is afoot to split the U.S. into a bilingual and bicultural society'.[1] Hayakawa was instrumental in founding U.S. English, a pressure group designed to promote English as the lone official language of the country. Soon the group had 350,000 members, including such distinguished 'advisory supporters' as Saul Bellow, Alistair Cooke, and Norman Cousins, and was receiving annual donations of $7.5 million. By late 1988, it had managed to have English made the official language of seventeen states – among them Arizona, Colorado, Florida, Nebraska, Illinios, Virginia, Indiana, Kentucky, Georgia, and California.

It is easy to understand the strength of feeling among many Americans on the matter. A California law requiring that bilingual education must be provided at schools where more than twenty pupils speak a language other than English sometimes led to chaos. At one Hollywood high school, on parents' night every speech had to be translated from English into Korean, Spanish, and Armenian. As of December 1986, California was employing 3,364 state workers proficient in Spanish in order to help non-English speakers in matters concerning courts, social services, and the like. All of this, critics maintain, cossets non-English speakers and provides them with little inducement to move into the American mainstream.

U.S. English and other such groups maintain that linguistic divisions have caused unrest in several countries, such as Canada and Belgium – though they generally fail to note that the countries where strife and violence have been most pronounced, such as Spain, are the ones where minority languages have been most strenuously suppressed. It is interesting to speculate also whether the members of U.S. English would be so enthusiastic about language regulations if they were transferred to Quebec and found their own language effectively outlawed.

U.S. English insists that a national English-language law would apply only to government business, and that in unofficial, private, or religious contexts people could use any language they liked. Yet it was U.S. English that tried to take an American phone company to court for inserting Spanish advertisements in the Los Angeles Yellow Pages. That would hardly seem to be government business. And many Hispanics feel that there would be further encroachments on their civil liberties – such as the short-lived 1985 attempt by Dade County in Florida to require that marriage ceremonies be conducted only in English. U.S. English says that it would not ban bilingual education, but would insist that its aim be transitional rather than encouraging entrenchment.

The most unpleasant charge is that all of this is a thinly veiled cover for racism, or at least rampant xenophobia. As an outsider, it is difficult not to conclude sometimes that there is a degree of overreaction involved. What purpose, after all, is served by making Nebraska officially English? Nor is it immediately evident how the public good would be served by overturning a New York law that at present stipulates that the details of consumer credit transactions be printed in Spanish as well as English. If U.S. English had its way, they would be printed only in English. Would such a change really encourage Hispanics to learn English or would it simply lead to their exploitation by unscrupulous lenders?

There is little evidence to suggest that people are refusing to learn English. According to a 1985 study by the Rand Corporation, 95 per cent of the children of Mexican immigrants can speak English. By the second generation more than half can speak *only* English. There is after all a huge inducement in terms of convenience, culture, and income to learn the prevailing language. As the Stanford University linguist Geoffrey D. Nunberg neatly put it: 'The English language needs official protection about as much as the Boston Celtics need elevator shoes.'

Perhaps a more pressing concern ought to be not with the English used by Hispanics and other ethnic groups so much as the quality of English used in America generally. A great deal of newsprint has been consumed in recent years with reports of the decline in American educational attainments, particularly with regard to reading and writing. According to *U.S. News & World Report*,[2] between 1973 and 1983, the proportion of high school students scoring 600 or higher on their Scholastic Aptitude Tests dropped from 10 per cent to 7 per cent. Between 1967 and 1984 verbal scores on the SAT exams slumped from an average of 466 to 424, a decline of nearly 10 per cent. It is perhaps little wonder. Over the same period, the proportion of high school students receiving four years of English instruction more than halved from 85 per cent to 41 per cent. *U.S. News & World Report* put the number of functionally illiterate adults in America at twenty-seven million – that is about one in every six people aged twenty-one or over. These illiterate adults account for an estimated three-quarters of the American unemployed and their numbers are growing by two million a year.

What has been generally overlooked in all the brouhaha about declining educational standards is that there is nothing new in all this. As long ago as 1961, a body called the Council for Basic Education, in a report called *Tomorrow's Illiterates*, estimated that more than a third of all American students were 'seriously retarded in reading'. In his 1964 book *The Treasure of Our Tongue*, Lincoln Barnett noted that a professor at Columbia University tested 170 history graduate students on whether they could correctly identify twenty common abbreviations, such as B.C., A.D., ibid., i.e., and the like, and one large Roman numeral. 'Of the 170,' Barnett wrote, 'only one understood all 20 abbreviations, only 17 understood more than 15, about half the class understood no more than four, and of that half not one could translate MDCLIX into 1659.' These, remember, were graduate students in history at an Ivy League university.

It must be said that it seems a trifle harsh to ask youngsters to master their native language when America fails to demand the same of its national leaders. Consider for a moment President George Bush explaining why he would not support a ban on semi-automatic weapons: 'But I also want to have – be the President that protects the rights of, of people to, to have arms. And that – so you don't go so far that the legitimate rights on some legislation are, are, you know, impinged on.' As Tom

Wicker noted in an article in *The New York Times*[3] critically anatomizing the president's speaking abilities, 'Could he not express himself at least in, like, maybe, you know, sixth- or seventh-grade English, rather than speaking as if he were Dan Quayle trying to explain the Holocaust?' But compared with the vice-president, Mr Bush is an extemporaneous speaker of the first mark. Here is Vice-President Quayle speaking off the cuff to a Thanksgiving festival in Charles City, Virginia: 'I suppose three important things certainly come to my mind that we want to say thank you. The first would be our family. Your family, my family – which is composed of an immediate family of a wife and three children, a larger family with grandparents and aunts and uncles. We all have our family, whichever that may be.'[4] And they said oratory was dead.

But perhaps the most important question facing English as it lumbers toward the twenty-first century is whether it will remain one generally cohesive tongue or whether it will dissolve into a collection of related but mutually incomprehensible sublanguages. In 1978, in a speech to 800 librarians in Chicago, Robert Burchfield, then the chief editor of the *Oxford English Dictionaries*, noted his belief that British English and American English were moving apart so inexorably that within 200 years they could be mutually unintelligible. Or as he rather inelegantly put it: 'The two forms of English are in a state of dissimilarity which should lead to a condition of unintelligibility, given another two hundred years.'(And this from the man chosen to revise Fowler's *Modern English Usage*!) The assertion provoked a storm of articles on both sides of the Atlantic, almost all of them suggesting that Burchfield was, in this instance, out of his mind.

People, it must be said, have been expecting English to fracture for some time. Thomas Jefferson and Noah Webster, as we have seen, both expected American English to evolve into a discrete language. So did H. L. Mencken in the first edition of *The American Language*, though by the 1936 edition he had reversed this opinion, and was suggesting, perhaps only half in jest, that British English was becoming an American dialect. The belief was certainly not uncommon up until the end of the nineteenth century. In the 1880s, Henry Sweet, one of the most eminent linguistic authorities of his day, could confidently predict: 'In another century . . . England, America and Australia will be speaking mutually unintelligible languages.' But of course nothing of the sort happened – and, I would submit, is not likely to now.

Following the controversy aroused by his speech, Burchfield wrote an article in the *Observer* defending his lonesome position. After expressing some surprise at the response to his remarks, which he said had been made 'almost in passing', he explained that he felt that 'the two main forms of English separated geographically from the beginning and severed politically since 1776, are continuing to move apart and that existing elements of linguistic diversity between them will intensify as time goes on'. This is not quite the same thing as saying they are becoming separate languages, but it is still a fairly contentious assertion.*

The main planks of Burchfield's defence rest on two principal beliefs. The first is that the divergence of languages is a reasonable historical presumption. In the past, most languages have split at some point, as when the mutually intelligible North Germanic dialects evolved into the mutually unintelligible languages of German, Dutch, and English. And, second, Burchfield observed that English already has many words that cause confusion. 'It is easy to assemble lists of American expressions that are not (or are barely) intelligible to people in this country,' he wrote in the *Observer*, and cited as examples *barf*,

---

*Burchfield himself insists that he never made any exact forecast of how long it would take the two branches of English to drift apart. He has written: 'At a huge and confusing press conference afterwards, reporters translated this general statement [that American English and British English are continually moving apart] into a precise forecast of 200 years and this was of course the story that was circulated throughout the world. There was nothing I could do to stop it once the press conference cameras and pens had done their work.' (At the risk of sounding cynical, I find it hard to think of a better occasion on which to set the record straight than when one has the world's cameras trained on him.)

boffo, *badmouth*, *schlepp*, and *schlock*. That may be true (though in point of fact, most Britons could gather the meaning of these words from their context) but even so the existence of some confusing terms hardly establishes permanent linguistic divergence. An Iowan travelling through Pennsylvania would very probably be puzzled by many of the items he found on menus throughout the state – *soda*, *scrapple*, *subs*, *snits*, *fat cakes*, *funnel cakes*, and several others all would be known either by other names or not at all to the Iowan. Yet no one would suggest that Iowa and Pennsylvania are evolving separate languages. The same is surely no less true for American and British English.

In the late 1940s, the *Daily Mail* ran an article discussing American expressions that would be 'positively incomprehensible' to the average English person. These included *commuter*, *seafood*, *rare* as applied to meat, *mean* in the sense of nasty, *dumb* in the sense of stupid, *intern*, *dirt road*, and *living room*. Putting aside the consideration that the *Daily Mail* must have had a very low opinion of its readers to conclude that they could not surmise the meaning of *seafood* and *dirt road* even if they hadn't heard them before, the simple fact is that all those terms are now known throughout Britain and several of them – *seafood*, *commuter*, *rare meat* – are now established as the invariable words for those items. There will no doubt always be a substantial pool of words that will be largely unshared by the two countries. But there is absolutely no evidence to suggest that the pool is growing. As the *Daily Mail* example shows, what happens is that the unfamiliar words tend to become familiar over time and then are replaced by other new words.

The suggestion that English will evolve into separate branches in the way that Latin evolved into French, Spanish, and Italian seems to me to ignore the very obvious consideration that communications have advanced a trifle in the intervening period. Movies, television, books, magazines, record albums, business contacts, tourism – all these are powerfully binding influences. At the time of writing, a television viewer in Britain could in a single evening watch *Neighbours*, an Australian soap opera, *Cheers*, an American comedy set in Boston, and *EastEnders*, a British programme set among cockneys in London. All of these bring into people's homes in one evening a variety of vocabulary, accents, and other linguistic influences that they would have been unlikely to experience in a single lifetime just two generations ago. If we should be worrying about anything to do with the future of English, it should be not that the various strands will drift apart but that they will grow indistinguishable. And what a sad, sad loss that would be.

NOTES

Chapter 1: The World's Language
1. *Observer*, 26 October 1980.
2. All cited in *TheNew York Times*, 18 June 1989.
3. Charlton Laird, *The Miracle of Language* (Greenwich, Ct: Fawcett Publications, 1953), p. 54.

Chapter 2: The Dawn of Language
1. *Natural History*, March 1987.
2. Reported in *Scientific American*, January 1984.
3. By Kenneth Wexler and colleagues at the University of California at Irvine, cited by the *Economist*, 28 April 1984.

Chapter 3: Global Language
1. Cited in the *Economist*, 27 February 1988.
2. Peter Trudgill, *Sociolinguistics: An Introduction to Language and Society* (London: Penguin Books, 1983), p. 115 ff.

Chapter 4: The First Thousand Years
1. Quoted in the *Independent*, 6 July 1987.
2. Albert C. Baugh and Thomas Cable, *A History of the English Language* (London: Routledge & Kegan Paul, 1978), p. 80.
3. Simeon Potter, *Our Language* (London: Penguin Books, 1976), p. 25.
4. Kenneth Clark, *Civilisation: A Personal View* (New York: Harper & Row, 1969), p. 18.
5. All of these cited by Baugh and Cable, op. cit., p. 176.

6. C. L. Barber, *The Story of Language* (London: Pan Books, 1972), p. 152.

7. Lincoln Barnett, *The Treasure of Our Tongue* (New York: Alfred A. Knopf, 1964), p. 97.

8. Robert McCrum, William Cran, and Robert MacNeil, *The Story of English* (New York: Penguin Books, 1987), p. 61.

9. David Burnley, *A Guide to Chaucer's Language* (London: Macmillan, 1983), p. 10.

10. Barber, op. cit., p. 183.

11. Mario Pei, *The Story of Language* (Philadelphia: J. B. Lippincott, 1949), p. 128.

12. Otto Jespersen, *The Growth and Structure of the English Language* (New York: Doubleday, 1956), p. 251.

Chapter 5: Where Words Come From
1. Baugh and Cable, op. cit., p. 227.

2. Pei, op. cit., p. 151.

3. Robert Burchfield, *The English Language* (Oxford: Oxford University Press, 1986), p. 46.

4. Taken from 'Red Pants', by Robert K. Sebastian, in the Winter 1989 issue of *Verbatim*.

5. Burchfield, op. cit., p. 112.

6. Cited by Baugh and Cable, op. cit., p. 225.

7. Pei, op. cit., p. 153.

Chapter 6: Pronunciation
1. Cited by Barnett, op. cit., p. 175.

2. Jean Aitchison, *Words in the Mind: An Introduction to the Mental Lexicon* (Oxford: Basil Blackwell, 1987), p. 96.

3. Jespersen, op. cit., p. 213.

4. Burchfield, op. cit., p. 41.

Chapter 7: Varieties of English
1. Potter, op. cit., p. 168.

2. Thomas Pyles, *Words and Ways of American English* (New York: Random House, 1952), p. 270.

3. Trudgill, op. cit., p. 23.

Chapter 8: Spelling
1. Burchfield, op. cit., p. 91.
2. Theodore M. Bernstein, *Dos, Don'ts and Maybes of English Usage* (New York: Times Books, 1977), p. 87.
3. David Crystal, *Who Cares about English Usage?* (London: Penguin Books, 1984), p. 204.
4. Philip Howard, *The State of the Language* (London: Penguin Books, 1986), p. 149.
5. H. L. Mencken, *The American Language: An Inquiry into the Development of English in the United States*, 4th edn, and two supplements, abridged (New York: Alfred A. Knopf, 1963), p. 491.

Chapter 9: Good English and Bad
1. Quoted by Baugh and Cable, op. cit., p. 269.
2. Jespersen, op. cit., p. 16.
3. ibid., p. 222.

Chapter 10: Order out of Chaos
1. Reported in the *Economist*, 6 January 1990.
2. *Sunday Times*, 31 March 1985.
3. *New York Times*, 3 April 1989.

Chapter 11: Old World, New World
1. Burchfield, op. cit., p. 36.
2. Quoted by Pyles, op. cit., p. 106.
3. ibid., p. 17.
4. Quoted by Norman Moss, *What's the Difference?* (London: Arrow Books, 1978), p. 12.
5. Potter, op. cit., p. 169.

Chapter 12: English as a World Language
1. *U.S. News & World Report*, 18 February 1985.
2. *The New York Times*, 27 May 1988.
3. *U.S. News & World Report*, op. cit.
4. Jespersen, op. cit., p. 6.
5. Baugh and Cable, op. cit., p. 7.

6. Quoted in the *Guardian*, 30 April 1988.

Chapter 13: Names
1. Quoted in the *New York Times*, 14 June 1987.

Chapter 14: Swearing
1. Published in the *New York Times*, 19 September 1989.
2. *Philadelphia Inquirer*, 7 October 1987.
3. *American Way*, 1 May 1988.

Chapter 15: Wordplay
1. Quoted in *Verbatim*, Vol. XIV, No. 4.
2. Jespersen, op. cit., p. 150.

Chapter 16: The Future of English
1. *Education Digest*, May 1987.
2. *U.S. News & World Report*, op. cit.
3. *New York Times*, 24 February 1988.
4. Quoted in the *Des Moines Register*, 23 November 1988.

SELECT BIBLIOGRAPHY

Aitchison, Jean. *Words in the Mind: An Introduction to the Mental Lexicon*. Oxford: Basil Blackwell, 1987.

Aitchison, Jean. *Language Change: Progress or Decay*. London: Fontana Paperbacks, 1981.

American Heritage Dictionary, first edition. New York: American Heritage Publishing Company, 1969.

Augarde, Tony. *The Oxford Guide to Word Games*. Oxford: Oxford University Press, 1986.

Baddeley, Alan. *Your Memory: A User's Guide*. London: Penguin Books, 1982.

Barber, C. L. *The Story of Language*. London: Pan Books, 1972.

Barnett, Lincoln. *The Treasure of Our Tongue*. New York: Alfred A. Knopf, 1964.

Baugh, Albert C., and Thomas Cable. *A History of the English Language*. London: Routledge & Kegan Paul, 1978.

Bernstein, Theodore M. *Dos, Don'ts & Maybes of English Usage*. New York: Times Books, 1977.

Bernstein, Theodore M. *The Careful Writer*. New York: Atheneum, 1967.

Blake, Robert (ed.). *The English World*. London: Thames and Hudson, 1982.

Bleiler, Everett F. *Essential Japanese Grammar*. New York: Dover Publications, 1963.

Boorstin, Daniel J. *The Discoverers: A History of Man's Search to Know His World and Himself*. London: Penguin Books, 1986.

Boulton, Marjorie. *The Anatomy of Language*. London: Routledge & Kegan Paul, 1959.

Bryant, Margaret. *Current American Usage*. New York: Funk & Wagnalls, 1962.

Burchfield, Robert. *The English Language*. Oxford: Oxford University Press, 1986.

Burnley, David. *A Guide to Chaucer's Language*. London: Macmillan, 1983.

Cameron, Kenneth. *English Place-Names*. London: B. T. Batsford, 1961.

Cassidy, Frederic G. (chief editor). *Dictionary of American Regional English, Volume 1, A–C*. Cambridge, Ma: Belknap Press of Harvard University Press, 1985.

Claiborne, Robert. *Our Marvelous Native Tongue: The Life and Times of the English Language*. New York: Times Books, 1983.

Clark, Kenneth. *Civilisation: A Personal View*. New York: Harper & Row, 1969.

Concise Oxford Dictionary of Current English Usage. Oxford: Oxford University Press, 1982.

Copperud, Roy H. *American Usage: The Consensus*. New York: Van Nostrand Reinhold Company, 1970.

Cottle, Basil. *Names*. London: Thames and Hudson, 1983.

Cross, Donna Woolfolk. *Word Abuse*. New York: Coward, McCann and Geoghegan, 1979.

Crystal, David. *Who Cares About English Usage?* London: Penguin Books, 1984.

Crystal, David. *The English Language*. London: Penguin Books, 1988.

Dickson, Paul. *Words*. New York: Dell Books, 1982.

Dohan, Mary Helen. *Our Own Words*. Baltimore: Penguin Books, 1975.

Donaldson, Gerald. *Books*. Oxford: Phaidon Press, 1981.

Drabble, Margaret (ed.). *The Oxford Companion to English Literature*. London: Guild Publishing, 1985.

Ehrlich, Eugene and Raymond Hand, Jr. *NBC Handbook of Pronunciation*, 4th edn. New York: Harper & Row, 1984.

Espy, Willard R. *An Almanac of Words at Play*. New York: Clarkson N. Potter, Inc., 1975.

Espy, Willard R. *Another Almanac of Words at Play*. New York: Clarkson N. Potter, Inc., 1980.

Espy, Willard R. *O Thou Improper, Thou Uncommon Noun*. New York: Clarkson N. Potter, Inc., 1978.

Espy, Willard R. *The Game of Words*. New York: Bramhall House, 1972.

Evans, Bergen and Cornelia. *A Dictionary of Contemporary American Usage*. New York: Random House, 1957.

Field, John. *Discovering Place-Names*. Aylesbury, Bucks.: Shire Publications, 1976.

Flexner, Stuart Berg, and others. *I Hear America Talking*. New York: Van Nostrand Reinhold Co., 1976.

Foster, Brian. *The Changing English Language*. London: Macmillan, 1968.

Fowler, H. W. *A Dictionary of Modern English Usage*, 2nd edn, revised by Sir Ernest Gowers. Oxford: Clarendon Press, 1965.

Fowler, H. W. and F. G. *The King's English*. Oxford: Oxford University Press, 1931.

Gowers, Sir Ernest. *The Complete Plain Words*. London: Penguin, 1977.

Gowlett, John. *Ascent to Civilization: The Archaeology of Early Man*. London: Galley Press, 1984.

Harris, Sydney J. *The Best of Sydney J. Harris*. Boston: Houghton Mifflin, 1976.

Hayakawa, S. I. *Language in Action*. New York: Harcourt, Brace and Company, 1941.

Hayter, William. *Spooner*. London: W. H. Allen, 1977.

Hendrickson, Robert. *American Talk: The Words and Ways of American Dialects*. New York: Viking Penguin Inc., 1986.

Holt, Alfred H. *Phrase and Word Origins*. New York: Dover Publications, 1961.

Howard, Philip. *A Word in Your Ear*. London: Penguin Books, 1985.

Howard, Philip. *The State of the Language*. London: Penguin Books, 1986.

Howard, Philip. *New Words for Old*. London: Hamish Hamilton, 1977.

Howard, Philip. *Words Fail Me*. London: Hamish Hamilton, 1980.

Hudson, Kenneth. *The Dictionary of Diseased English*. London: Macmillan Press, 1977.

Jespersen, Otto. *The Growth and Structure of the English Language*. Garden City, NY: Doubleday & Co., 1956.

Jordan, Lewis (ed.). *The New York Times Manual of Style and Usage*. New York: Times Books, 1976.

Knowler, John. *Trust an Englishman*. London: Jonathan Cape, 1972.

Laird, Charlton. *The Miracle of Language*. Greenwich, Ct: Fawcett Publications, 1953.

Laird, Charlton. *The Word*. New York: Simon & Schuster, 1981.

Large, J. A. *The Foreign-Language Barrier: Problems in Scientific Communication*. London: André Deutsch, 1983.

Least Heat Moon, William. *Blue Highways*. Boston/Toronto: Little, Brown and Co., 1982.

McCrum, Robert, William Cran, and Robert MacNeil. *The Story of English*. New York: Penguin Books, 1987.

Marshall, Mary. *Bozzimacoo: Origins and Meanings of Oaths and Swear Words*. Walton-on-Thames: M. & J. Hobbs, 1975.

Mencken, H. L. *The American Language: An Inquiry into the Development of English in the United States*, 4th edn and two supplements, abridged. New York: Alfred A. Knopf, 1963.

Michaels, Leonard, and Christopher Ricks (eds.). *The State of the Language*. Berkeley: University of California Press, 1980.

Millington, Roger. *The Strange World of the Crossword*. Walton-on-Thames: M. & J. Hobbs, 1974.

Montagu, Ashley. *The Anatomy of Swearing*. New York: Collier Books, 1967.

Moorhouse, Alfred C. *The Triumphs of the Alphabet*. New York: Henry Schuman, 1953.

Morley, John David. *Pictures from the Water Trade: An Englishman in Japan*. London: André Deutsch, 1985.

Morris, William and Mary. *Harper Dictionary of Contemporary Usage*. New York: Harper & Row, 1975.

Newman, Edwin. *Strictly Speaking*. New York: Warner Books, 1975.

Newman, Edwin. *A Civil Tongue*. New York: Warner Books, 1977.

Nicolson, Harold. *The English Sense of Humour*. London: Constable, 1956.

Onions, C. T. (ed.). *The Oxford Dictionary of English Etymology*. Oxford: Oxford University Press, 1966.

Onions, C. T. (ed.). *Modern English Syntax*. 7th edn, prepared by B. D. H. Miller). London: Routledge & Kegan Paul, 1971.

Oxford English Dictionary. Compact edition. Oxford: Oxford University Press, 1971.

Oxford Guide to the English Language. London: Guild Publishing, 1986.

Palmer, Frank. *Grammar*. London: Penguin Books, 1982.

Partridge, Eric. *Usage and Abusage*. London: Penguin Books, 1981.

Partridge, Eric. *The Penguin Dictionary of Historical Slang*. London. Penguin Books, 1972.

Pearsall, Ronald. *Collapse of Stout Party: Victorian Wit and Humour*. London: Weidenfeld & Nicolson, 1974.

Pei, Mario. *The Story of Language*. Philadelphia: J. B. Lippincott Company, 1949.

Phythian, B. A. *A Concise Dictionary of Correct English*. London: Hodder and Stoughton, 1979.

Pointon, G. E. (ed.). *BBC Pronouncing Dictionary of British Names*. Oxford: Oxford University Press, 1983.

Potter, Simeon. *Our Language*. London: Penguin Books, 1976.

Price, B. E., and E. Tweed. *Geographical Studies in North America*. Edinburgh: Oliver & Boyd, 1985.

Pyles, Thomas. *Words and Ways of American English*. New York: Random House, 1952.

Quirk, Randolph. *The Use of English*. London: Longmans, 1969.

Reaney, P. H. *The Origin of English Place Names*. London: Routledge & Kegan Paul, 1985.

Renfrew, Colin. *Archaeology and Language: The Puzzle of Indo-European Origins*. London: Jonathan Cape, 1987.

Roback, Abraham. *A Dictionary of International Slurs*. Waukesha, Wis.: Maledicta Press, 1979.

Safire, William. *What's the Good Word?* New York: Times Books, 1982.

Safire, William. *On Language*. New York: Avon Books, 1980.

Scragg, D. G. *A History of English Spelling*. Manchester: Manchester University Press, 1974.

Shaw, George Bernard. *Pygmalion*. Baltimore: D. C. Heath & Co., 1942.

Shaw, Harry. *Dictionary of Problem Words and Expressions*. New York: McGraw-Hill Book Company, 1975.

Sherk, William. *Five Hundred Years of New Words*. Toronto: Doubleday Canada Ltd, 1983.

Shipley, Joseph T. *In Praise of English: The Growth and Use of Language*. New York: Times Books, 1977.

Shorter Oxford English Dictionary. London: Book Club Associates, 1983.

Simon, John. *Paradigms Lost: Reflections on Literacy and Its Decline*. New York: Clarkson N. Potter, Inc., 1980.

Smith, Elsdon C. *The Story of Our Names*. New York: Harper & Brothers, 1950.

Stewart, George R. *American Place-Names: A Concise and Selective Dictionary for the Continental United States of America*. New York: Oxford University Press, 1976.

Strunk Jr, William, and E. B. White. *The Elements of Style*, 3rd edn. New York: Macmillan, 1979.

Trudgill, Peter. *Sociolinguistics: An Introduction to Language and Society*. London: Penguin Books, 1983.

Upton, Clive, Stewart Sanderson, and John Widdowson. *Word Maps: A Dialect Atlas of England*. London: Croom Helm, 1987.

Wakelin, Martyn. *The Archaeology of English*. London: B. T. Batsford, 1988.

Watzlawick, Paul. *How Real Is Real?: Communication, Disinformation, Confusion*. London: Souvenir Press, 1983.

Wilson, P. G. *German Grammar*. London: English Universities Press, 1962.

Wolff, Diane. *Chinese for Beginners*. New York: Barnes and Noble Books, 1974.

Wood, Frederick T. *Current English Usage*, revised by R. H. and L. M. Flavell. London: Macmillan Press, 1981.

Wrenn, C. L. *A Study of Old English Literature*. London: George G. Harrap & Co., 1967.

INDEX